The Politics of Nationalism and Ethnicity

Also by James Kellas

The Scottish Political System
Modern Scotland

The Politics of Nationalism and Ethnicity

Second Edition

James G. Kellas

First edition 1991
Reprinted three times
Second edition 1998

 Published by
MACMILLAN PRESS LTD
Houndmills, Basingstoke, Hampshire RG21 6XS
and London
Companies and representatives throughout the world

ISBN 0–333–73192–1 hardcover
ISBN 0–333–73193–X paperback

A catalogue record for this book is available from the British
Library.

This book is printed on paper suitable for recycling and made
from fully managed and sustained forest sources.

10   9   8   7   6   5   4   3   2   1
07 06 05 04 03 02 01 00 99 98

Printed in Malaysia

Published in the United States of America 1998 by
ST. MARTIN'S PRESS, INC.,
Scholarly and Reference Division,
175 Fifth Avenue, New York, N.Y. 10010

ISBN 0–312–21553–3

Contents

List of Tables

Acknowledgements

I first studied nationalism as an undergraduate student of Joseph Frankel at the University of Aberdeen in 1957–8, and later specialised in the study of Scottish politics as a university lecturer. Once more, the subject of nationalism came to the fore, in the form of Scottish nationalism. As a Visiting Professor of Political Science at the University of Pittsburgh in 1985–6, I taught a course on nationalism generally, and had regular discussions on the subject with Richard Cottam (an expert on Middle East nationalism), Dennison Rusinow (an historian with a particular interest in Balkan nationalism) and Christina Paulston (a linguist specialising in language survival). These sessions broadened my perspective considerably.

At the University of Glasgow, I have kept up a continuous discourse on nationalism with colleagues, many of whom are experts on political theory and the study of particular areas of the world. Most of these will perhaps be surprised at the content of this book, and perhaps alarmed. I hope they do not mind my thanking them here, but they are of course not a party to what I have written.

Special thanks are due to Avril Johnstone, who coped with the frequent revisions during the production of the original typescript.

JAMES G. KELLAS

Preface to the
Second Edition

Since the first edition was published in 1991, much of the material contained in it has had to be changed and updated. The USSR has disintegrated into its 'national' components, as have Yugoslavia and Czechoslovakia. In general, the eastern European communist bloc has been replaced by independent nation-states, each showing its own strong nationalism. Meanwhile, in the rest of Europe, nationalism vied with the supranational European Union for the loyalty of governments and peoples. Again, nationalism showed its continuing strength in the face of integration. The old states, such as Britain, France, Spain, Belgium and Canada, continued to be threatened by nationalisms within them, but none broke up entirely. Nationalist and ethnic conflict continued unabated in Africa and Asia.

Apart from updating, there has been some alteration of emphasis. There is more specifically on politics and less on other aspects of nationalism and ethnicity which do not impinge clearly on politics. A somewhat different approach has been adopted for international relations, to take account of the effect that international society has on nationalism in aspiring nation-states, notably those in the former states of Yugoslavia, Czechoslovakia and the USSR. This 'top–down' view can be contrasted with the 'bottom–up' perspective, which sees international society as the product of nationalism.

The theory presented has not been altered, but account has been taken of criticisms by some reviewers. It is true that the theory is as much a collection of interlocking and interdependent aspects of nationalism as an hypothesis which can be falsified, unless one rejects entirely one or more of its 'building-blocks'. For example, some would remove the block which links nationalism to aspects of human nature. The problem is: what evidence can be found to verify or falsify this (or any other) part of theory? As the study of human genes progresses rapidly, we shall no doubt be able in the future to determine if our genes are in any way related to ethnocentric and nationalist behaviour.

As for politics, the period since the first edition has amply demonstrated that nationalism and ethnicity are as relevant at the end of the twentieth century as at any other time in history.

JAMES G. KELLAS

Introduction

Nationalism and ethnicity are central to the subject of politics, whether in the world of action or in the realm of study. Countless wars, revolts and conflicts have been the result of the passions which nation and 'kith and kin' have aroused in human beings. It has been estimated that more than ten million lives were lost between 1945 and 1975 alone as a result of ethnic violence (Horowitz, 1985, p. xi, quoting Isaacs, 1975, p. 3). That total has probably risen by another two million since 1975, and is almost certainly on the increase. Hundreds of thousands died in Rwanda and Zaire in the mid-1990s. The Government of Croatia reported that the country had suffered 13,583 deaths and nearly 40,000 injured in the 'homeland war' of 1991–5, and neighbouring Bosnia-Hercegovina experienced perhaps 200,000 deaths in the same period. Two thousand died in 1989 alone in ethnic violence in the Punjab, and as many in Sri Lanka. Deaths and injuries because of ethnic violence have also been common in Azerbaijan, Kashmir, Burma in Asia, and in the Basque country and Northern Ireland in Europe, to name only a few examples. Nationalist passions are probably the strongest in the whole political spectrum, and are generally stronger today than those aroused by religion, class, individual or group interest.

These passions are not all negative, however. Nationalism has been considered essential to the establishment of a modern industrial society (Gellner, 1983), and the 'the sole vision and rationale of political solidarity today' (Smith, 1991, p. 176). It gives legitimacy to the state, and inspires its citizens to feel an emotional attachment towards it. It can be a source of creativity in the arts, and enterprise in the economy. Its power to mobilise political activity is unsurpassed, especially in the vital activity of 'nation-building'. It is intimately connected with democracy.

The student of politics is faced with many problems when tackling this subject. Not only are the manifestations of nationalism and ethnicity widespread and complex, but there is also a very large and contradictory literature in this field, with works by sociologists, philosophers and historians as well as by political scientists. This is understandable, given the universal scope and importance of the subject. But the spread across disciplines has tended to produce not so much a synthesis as several partial views. In the case of political science, it is not clear that there is a distinctive view at all. Certainly, there is no integrated theory of the politics of nationalism which, while taking account of the many theories relating to the subject, focuses especially on the political dimension and produces an integrated theoretical analysis. This is especially needed, as it is politics which gives the most powerful expression to nations and ethnic groups.

While this book attempts to develop such a theory, it also aims to provide an introduction to, and explain, all the major approaches to the subject. Some of these approaches are mutually exclusive, but others can complement each other. For example, while it is difficult to reconcile the view that human nature leads to nationalism with the view that nationalism arose in a specific period in history, it is possible to show that nationalist behaviour has both cultural and economic determinants. This reconciles some linguistic studies of nationalism with certain Marxist and other materialist writers. For political scientists, the focus is on the state and political power. Nationalism and ethnic politics are related to the state and the struggle for control of political resources. Thus the agenda stretches to constitutions, parties, groups, leaders and voters. These interact with the cultural and economic forces and may explain when nationalism is successful and when it is not.

Definitions

A serious problem for students of the subject is the ambiguity in the meaning of the words used. At this stage, the reader will find it useful to consider the following basic terms, which will recur throughout this book. As there is no agreed meaning for them, rather an emerging consensus in the literature, it cannot be claimed that a 'correct' meaning is given here. But a working definition of each is essential for further study (a major glossary of concepts and terms in the study of ethnicity has been prepared by Professor F. W. Riggs of the University of Hawaii, under the auspices of the International Social Science Council's Committee on Conceptual and Terminological Analysis (INTER-COCTA)) (Riggs, 1985).

Nation   A nation is a group of people who feel themselves to be a community bound together by ties of history, culture and common ancestry. Nations have 'objective' characteristics which may include a territory, a language, a religion, or common descent (though not all of these are always present), and 'subjective' characteristics, essentially a people's awareness of its nationality and affection for it. In the last resort it is 'the supreme loyalty' for people who are prepared to die for their nation.

The term 'nation' is also commonly applied to states, as in the United Nations, consisting of the 'nations' of the world. While many states share the features of nations, and can be called 'nation-states', there are also nations within states, and such states are correctly called 'multinational states'. For centuries there were multinational empires such as the Austrian, Ottoman and Russian Empires, and today there are states consisting of more than one nation such as the United Kingdom, Switzerland, Belgium and Canada. The Union of Soviet Socialist Republics (USSR) was composed of over one hundred 'nationalities', and this term was officially preferred there to 'nations', for political reasons. 'Nations' in communist ideology are linked to nationalism, with the possible break-up of the state, while 'nationalities' are expected to have predominantly cultural aspirations. Nevertheless, the titular nationalities of the fifteen Soviet republics (those that gave their names to the republics) were able to claim that they ought to be 'nation-states', and broke away from the USSR on that basis.

In this work, 'nation' is used independently of 'state' and 'ethnic group', but these terms overlap in some cases. For example, Denmark, Iceland and Japan are states in which nearly all the citizens belong to one nation, meaning a social community. That nation can also be analysed in terms of ethnicity, but as will shortly be explained, 'ethnic group' has special connotations in contemporary politics. In some works, the terms 'ethnonation' and 'ethnonationalism' are used to distinguish an ethnic nation and ethnic nationalism from 'nation' meaning state, and 'nationalism' meaning patriotism. Here, **'ethnic nation'** is used where a nation consists of one ethnic group, '**social nation**' where several ethnic groups form one nation, and '**official nation**' for the nationalism of the state.

Nationalism   Nationalism is both an ideology and a form of behaviour. The ideology of nationalism builds on people's awareness of a nation (national self-consciousness) to give a set of attitudes and a programme of action. These may be cultural, economic or political. Since 'nation' can be defined in 'ethnic', 'social' or 'official' senses, so nationalism can take these forms also.

In all cases, nationalism seeks to defend and promote the interests of the nation. The political aspect of nationalism is seen most clearly in the demand for national self-determination, or 'home rule'. For states, 'official nationalism' means patriotism and the defence of 'national sovereignty' in international relations. All types of nationalism seek a political expression for the nation, most strongly in independent statehood. Nationalists may settle for less, however. They may be content (at least, for a time) for the nation to be a unit in a federal state (e.g. Quebec in Canada) or to have devolution in a unitary state (e.g. Wales in the United Kingdom (UK) and Catalonia in Spain). It must be said, however, that not all federalists or devolutionists would recognise themselves as nationalists, for many would see nationalism as undesirable since it could lead to the disintegration of the state. Lastly, nationalists, especially ethnic nationalists, may engage only in 'pressure group' politics, with no territorial aim regarding home rule. Their aim is rather the protection and advancement of the ethnic group within the state.

As a form of political behaviour, nationalism is closely linked to ethnocentrism (see below) and patriotism. Nationalist behaviour is based on the feeling of belonging to a community which is the nation. Those who do not belong to the nation are seen as different, foreigners or aliens, with loyalties to their own nations. Nationalist behaviour in its strongest form is seen in the 'supreme sacrifice' of death for one's nation. In milder forms, it shows itself in prejudice relating to foreigners, stereotyping of other nations, and solidarity with co-nationals. 'Official nationalism' or patriotism is sometimes given a more noble status than other forms of nationalism, and may conflict with these.

Patriotism focuses loyalty on the state, while 'social' and 'ethnic' nationalism may seek the disintegration of the state.

Ethnic group 'Ethnic group' and 'ethnocentrism' are comparable with 'nation' and 'nationalism'. The difference between them is that 'ethnic group' is more narrowly defined than 'nation', and 'ethnocentrism' is more rooted in social psychology than is 'nationalism', which has explicitly ideological and political dimensions. Ethnic groups are generally differentiated from nations on several dimensions: they are usually smaller; they are more clearly based on a common ancestry; and they are more pervasive in human history, while nations are perhaps specific to time and place. Ethnic groups are essentially **exclusive** or **ascriptive**, meaning that membership in such groups is confined to those who share certain inborn attributes. Nations on the other hand are more *inclusive* and are culturally or politically defined. However, it is often possible to trace the origins of nations and nationalism to ethnic groups and their ethnocentric behaviour (Kohn, 1944; Smith, 1986).

In contemporary political usage, the term 'ethnic group' is frequently used to describe a quasi-national kind of 'minority group' within the state, which has somehow not achieved the status of a nation. Thus, 'ethnic politics' in Britain means the politics of recent non-white immigrants, while 'nationalism' is applied to the English, Scots, Welsh and Irish. The English are often considered in England to be neither 'ethnic' nor 'nationalist', rather 'patriotic'. Other people may see the English as ethnic and nationalist, and the English themselves show themselves to be such in politics, particularly with regard to the other nations of the United Kingdom, or to the black population in England.

'Race relations' is yet another dimension involved here. **'Race'** is distinguished from 'nation' and 'ethnic group' mainly because races are discussed in predominantly biological terms, with particular emphasis on phenotypical distinctions such as skin colour, stature, etc., and presumed genetic distinctions. (Decisions of the Commission for Racial Equality and of Industrial Tribunals in Scotland in 1997 have, however, included Scots and English as equivalent to 'races' in terms of illegal discrimination

(Glasgow *Herald*, 29 August 1997).) '**Racism**' matches 'nationalism' as an ideology and type of behaviour, and is related to 'race' rather than to 'nation'. It is even more negatively assessed generally than nationalism, and has led to political action to counteract it (e.g. race relations legislation, civil rights movements, anti-apartheid campaigns, etc.).

Ethnocentrism 'Ethnocentrism' is basically a psychological term, although it is also used generally in the study of society and politics. It can be related to 'nationalism' and 'racism', but its focus is strictly on the individual's relationship with an ethnic group rather than with a 'nation' or a 'race'. Ethnocentrism gives a general and perhaps even universal basis for a type of behaviour which also underlies nationalism and racism. It is essentially concerned with an individual's psychological biases towards his/her ethnic group, and against other ethnic groups. Favourable attitudes are held about the 'ingroup' (here the ethnic group, nation or race), and unfavourable ones about the 'outgroup' (other ethnic groups, nations or races). The intensity of ethnocentric attitudes and behaviour varies from the mild and peaceful to the belligerent and megalomaniac (van der Dennen in Reynolds, *et al.*, 1987, p. 1). The causes of ethnocentrism in general and the explanations for its different forms are complex and have been the subject of various sociobiological, psychological and sociological studies (see for example, LeVine and Campbell, 1972; Adorno, 1950; Forbes, 1985; Reynolds *et al.*, 1987).

Ethnicity Ethnicity is the state of being ethnic, or belonging to an ethnic group. It is a more neutral term than ethnocentrism which, as we have seen, denotes prejudicial attitudes favouring one ethnic group and rejecting others. While some nations may be called 'ethnic nations', there are ethnic groups who do not claim to be nations. The difference may be found in the character of ethnic politics compared with nationalist politics. Nationalism focuses on 'national self-determination', or home rule in a national territory. Ethnic politics in contrast are largely concerned with the protection of rights for members of the group within the existing state, with no claim for a territorial 'homeland'. However, these distinctions are not made by all scholars. The field of 'ethnic studies' includes nations and nationalism, and many nations have 'ethnic origins' (Smith, 1986).

Argument

The central aim of this book is to provide an **integrated theory of the politics of nationalism and ethnicity**. The theory is constructed from 'building-blocks' which lead in sequence from one to the other. Within each building-block are posited 'necessary' and 'sufficient' conditions. A full treatment of this theory is given in the concluding chapter, and a synopsis of it in tabular form at the end.

Essentially, the theory starts with the hypothesis of a link between certain traits in human nature and ethnicity and ethnocentrism. Nationalism and ethnic politics display characteristics of emotion and intensity which appear to derive from instinctive behaviour, and from a human predisposition to show loyalty to 'ingroups' and hostility to 'outgroups' (ethnocentrism).

Particular ethnic groups and nations become such groups through informal processes of interaction, and from the more sophisticated influence of nationalist ideology and political structures, especially states. 'Nationalism' is an ideology which claims supreme loyalty from individuals for the nation and asserts the right of 'national self-determination' or self-government for the nation. There are other nationalist ideologies which make claims for the nation, such as its inherent superiority to other nations. Their appeal is based on an analogy between nations and 'kin', and they tap instinctive feelings of ethnocentrism.

The context in which nationalism flourishes is determined by a complex interaction of political, economic and cultural developments in history. While the ideology of nationalism has spread throughout the world, the differing contexts of time and place have given nationalism and ethnicity differing political forms.

Central to all aspects of political nationalism, however, are two related patterns:

1. The importance of **national identity**, whether determined (ascribed, irrespective of personal choice) or through **national self-determination**, that is, the ability to freely determine

one's own national identity, culture (including language, education, religion), and form of government. In either case, political nationalism links nations to political power, through parties, elections and political institutions, with a nation-state its ideal expression.

2. The desire to overcome social and political systems of **domination** and **exclusion** in which nations other than one's own wield predominant power. This power can be just a matter of predominant numbers in a democratic system, or non-democratic rule by one nation. Exclusion operates when citizenship is denied to members of particular nations, and/or access to education or the media in a national language (to give only one example of such exclusions) is restricted or denied. Exclusions also operate at a political level, as when the top positions are reserved (or in effect reserved) for the members of one nation.

   Such systems are typically empires and ·multinational states in which one (or occasionally more than one) nation holds a position of **hegemony**. Only a 'consociational democracy' or 'consociationalism' (see below) can overcome such a system of hegemony in a multinational state.

What accounts for hegemony and its accompanying nationalist reaction in a multinational state has interested many writers. A particularly strong explanation is that which relates to perceptions of 'uneven economic development' affecting different nations and ethnic groups, coupled with a 'cultural division of labour'. In this division of labour, particular nations occupy different occupations and life chances in a hierarchy, with one nation exerting hegemony. This leads to a nationalist reaction in the dominated nations. Such a reaction is linked to the development of general political aspirations for democracy, and to cultural changes (e.g. widespread education and a desire for cultural status).

The democratic alternative to nationalist ideology which demands a nation-state is cultural pluralism and consociationalism, based on a multinational or multiethnic 'consensus' state. For such a state to succeed, certain strategies must be adopted. In international relations, supranationalism and 'integration' face similar obstacles, and consociationalism there is more difficult to achieve. Yet strategies for international integration can also be devised.

Structure of the Book

The chapters of the book are based on the building-blocks of the theory. Chapter 1 discusses **human nature** (biology and psychology) and its connection with ethnicity and ethnocentrism. Chapter 2 describes the emergence of the **idea of the nation and the ideology** of nationalism. Chapters 3, 4 and 5 put these in a **historical context**, with generalisation about **types** of nationalisms and nationalist movements. Chapters 6, 7 and 8 deal with contemporary **case studies** of nationalism and ethnic politics, distinguishing between different parts of the world. Chapter 9 looks at **cultural pluralism, consociational democracy** and other methods of **political accommodation** in a multinational and multiethnic state. Chapter 10 discusses nationalism in **international relations**. Chapter 11 describes the **integrated theory** of the politics of nationalism and ethnicity.

1

Ethnicity and Human Nature

The most difficult and controversial part of the study of nationalism is trying to find a general explanation for its existence. Scholars are divided into those who go back to something called 'human nature', where instinctive behaviour is to be found, and those who look only for historical, cultural and economic explanations ('contexts'). The former have the problem that what is universally true is not much use in explaining particular differences in the world. The latter have great difficulty in explaining why the passions aroused by nationalism are so strong and universal, so that they seem to transcend mere circumstances to tap deep-seated emotions.

In this chapter we look at writings on nationalism and ethnicity which focus on human nature, but we shall also take account of the arguments against such an approach. On balance, this book accepts that human nature (in so far as that can be defined) plays some part in explaining why ethnicity and ethnocentrism (including, at particular times, nationalism) have been so pervasive and powerful in human history. But the evidence is ambiguous, for the balance between 'nature' and 'nurture' in human affairs is not easy to determine. In any case, in the theory presented here, human nature is only a 'necessary condition' for the many manifestations of nationalism and ethnic politics in history. Why particular nations and nationalisms develop is a matter for historical explanation. Thus, for there to be 'sufficient conditions' in any particular case relating to nationalism and ethnicity, explanations which go beyond human nature must be invoked.

Yet the basic question remains: why should people (universally?) distrust and dislike foreigners, and prefer 'their own kind'? Why does ethnocentrism (and its related form, nationalism) lead to wars and legitimise 'the supreme sacrifice', to die for one's ethnic group/ nation? Is Robert Burns to be believed when he wrote:

> 'It's coming yet, for a' that,
> That man to man, the warld o'er,
> Shall brothers be for a' that.'?

This is rhetoric which invokes the extension of family ties to humanity as a whole. 'The Brotherhood of Man' has inspired 'universalists' in politics, and has led to institutions such as the United Nations, with its Universal Declaration of Human Rights (1948). But in the rhetoric of nationalism 'brotherhood' means something different from sympathy and common interest with one's fellow human beings; it implies a closer blood relationship ('brothers-in-law' are of course not usually close blood relations, but 'brothers' of a kind, nevertheless).

Blood relationships are fundamental to life and to reproduction. Politics is concerned intimately with the impact which such relationships have on human beings. We all understand what 'father' and 'mother' means, as well as 'brother', 'sister' and 'cousin'. Even more distant relations can arouse sympathy and lead to nepotism (favouring one's relations). The 'whole family' is a ready-made structure from our basic experience, which can be translated into politics (the 'British family of nations'). The 'Fatherland', the 'Motherland', 'kith and kin', are ideas which are powerful political resources, appealing to human instincts, and they have endured throughout the ages as objects of supreme emotion and loyalty. Wales is 'the Land of our Fathers'; Jews have traditionally defined themselves as descended from a Jewish mother, and the Law of Return of Israel allows Jews the right to live in the 'National Home of the Jewish People'; Germany does the same for certain members of the 'Volk'; some Afrikaner nationalists formed themselves into a 'Brotherhood'; many British people felt sympathy for their 'kith and kin' in Rhodesia, despite their illegal Unilateral Declaration of Independence in 1965, and for the (British) Falkland Islanders when they were invaded by Argentina in 1982. Citizens are expected to be ready to die for their 'Fatherland'/'Motherland', and it may even be natural to want to do so. One would hardly die willingly for one's job, one's social class, or even one's state, if that is not seen as the 'Fatherland'.

Why is this so? We can see that the rhetoric of nationalism draws heavily on the idea of the nation as a family, but is there any scientific reason why people should respond so strongly to such an appeal? We are born with genetic characteristics and instincts, and we cannot escape from them, although they can be cultivated in several directions. They are certainly the most primordial of human attributes, and apparently the most powerful. It is little wonder that such resources are so easily and prominently tapped in politics. If there is a biological basis to nationalism and ethnocentrism it is easier to make sense of the kind of politics which results. Perhaps no other form of political activity is drawn so clearly from what some maintain are the biological 'givens' of human nature.

But how much politics is determined by biology? Our genes have been studied as never before, and human behaviour, as well as our physical make-up and propensity to illness or health is increasingly attributed by geneticists to particular genes. But most biologists look to social factors to explain at least part of these phenomena. In the relatively new field of 'sociobiology', scientists (natural and social) are engaged in fierce arguments, many of which are directly concerned with our subject (see for example, van den Berghe, 1981; Reynolds, Falger and Vine (eds), 1987; Shaw and Wong, 1989; Kecmanovic, 1996). The theories of 'inclusive fitness' and 'kin selection', most obviously appropriate to animal behaviour, can be brought to bear on human behaviour too. Inclusive fitness is a theory in genetics first propounded by W. D. Hamilton in 1964. It has been summarised as follows:

> genes will spread if their carriers act to increase not only their own fitness or reproductive success but also that of other individuals carrying the same genes. A person's inclusive fitness is his or her personal fitness plus the increased fitness of relatives that he or she has in some way caused by his or her actions. (Reynolds *et al.*, 1987, p. xvii)

The way to achieve 'inclusive fitness' is 'kin selection', or mating with relatives, and animal behaviour gives evidence for instinctive propensities to do this. 'Kin selection', however, is not the same as 'group selection', a much-disputed theory in biology.

In 'kin selection' there is no hard-and-fast boundary involved
between groups of mating individuals, as might be found
between ethnic groups or nations. Rather, 'kin selection' is a con-
sequence of 'gene selection' or 'individual selection', which gives
rise to a 'mathematical probability' of mating and 'altruistic
behaviour' among those most closely related to each other
(Dawkins, 1989, pp. 7, 94) . 'Group selection', on the other hand,
would appear to relate more directly to ethnicity and nationalism, if ethnic groups and nations are the groups involved.

How much of this is relevant to politics? Potentially, a great
deal, but at this stage in scientific theorising it is impossible to
know how valid these theories are, even for non-human biology,
since they are relatively new, and controversial. Nevertheless,
these hypotheses are repeated here since they are part of the academic literature on nationalism and ethnicity. For this author, the
balance of evidence seems to support the view that human
nature includes instincts which are related to ethnocentrism and
nationalist behaviour. For most social scientists, however, such
ideas are anathema, since they seem to deny human freedom to
escape from nationalist and racist prejudices and behaviour.

Even if the sociobiological approach is accepted, that does not
imply any consensus regarding the effects of biology on political
behaviour. In the collection of essays entitled *The Sociobiology of
Ethnocentrism* (Reynolds *et al.*, 1987), the editors, after reviewing
the biological explanations for ethnocentrism, reject the idea
that selfishness and racism are 'genetic imperatives' of human
nature (p. xv). Moreover, they state that 'There are no theoretical
grounds for supposing that we cannot identify ourselves with
humanity as a whole' (p. xix). But they also present biological
evidence which points to instinctive behaviour, especially kin
selection among animals. In so far as human beings are subject
to animal behaviour, sociobiology must be taken seriously.
Students of nationalism and ethnicity should be aware of the
claims made by sociobiologists, and should test them against the
evidence. So far, their theories do not amount to conventional
science, especially with reference to human behaviour.

A more orthodox view than that of the sociobiologists is that
human behaviour is the result of culture and learning rather
than biology. If there is a biological component to ethnocentrism
and nationalist behaviour, these writers argue, it is activated by

society and politics, and can be suppressed or sublimated in the same way by these. But the evidence for that is as controversial as for the hypothesis that we are subject to our genes in this regard. Clearly, in human affairs there is an interaction between genes and environment, and neither is independent of the other.

The universal presence of ethnocentrism gives some support to the argument that it is genetically determined, but the form it has taken over the ages has varied considerably. It might even lie dormant politically in certain conditions. For example, the drive to reproduce one's genes through 'kin selection' may have little explanatory power in the conditions of a mobile and ethnically (genetically) mixed modern society. We may have few relations around us to mate with. But 'kin selection' instincts (if they exist) may still provide a necessary condition for nationalist behaviour, xenophobia and ethnic/racial discrimination, even if the sufficient conditions for such behaviour derive from political, social and economic circumstances. The biggest deficiency of sociobiological theories for the study of politics is that they are of little use in explaining why particular ethnic groups exist, and how nations were formed in history. Nor can they explain the *political contexts* in which ethnocentrism and nationalism flourish. So we have to move on to other types of theory if we are to understand fully the *politics* of nationalism and ethnicity.

Language is closely linked to ethnicity and nationalism, and it is also a facet of human nature. One political scientist (Laponce, 1985) has used certain 'neurophysiological and neuropsychological findings' to assert that there are physical reasons why particular languages are spoken by particular nations. He also suggests that unilingualism in a 'mother tongue' is more natural than bilingualism, for neurophysiological and neuropsychological reasons. A dominant language, he says, will drive out a minority language in a bilingual or multilingual state, unless that state is divided into unilingual territories, as in Belgium and Switzerland. His conclusion for Quebec in Canada is that the French language there can only survive in a unilingual Quebec polity, since Canada as a whole is predominantly English-speaking. He thus supports the Quebec Nationalists and Liberals who seek an officially French-only-speaking Quebec.

Laponce is unusual in introducing a neurophysiological element into the discussion of language and nationalism, and as with the sociobiologists we are left wondering what scientific validity there is to his argument. One thing is clear. Whether the result of human nature or not, language divisions are strongly related to ethnicity and nationalism, and we shall see in Chapter 2 that many nineteenth-century nationalists based their ideology of nationalism on the claims of language communities to national independence.

Yet another way to approach human nature and its relationship with nationalism is through social psychology. Social psychologists have conducted experiments which have thrown light on how humans behave as members of groups. These experiments add to our understanding of the politics of nationalism and ethnicity.

In a well-known study of inter-group conflict and cooperation (Sherif, 1961), boys who were divided into two groups called 'the Rattlers' and 'the Eagles' developed hostility towards the opposite group when put into competitive situations. It seems that humans, when combined together in an ingroup, have a propensity for hostility towards members of an outgroup, especially if that group is clearly defined and there is competition between the ingroup and the outgroup. They will also develop a sense of community with the other members of the ingroup, even where no other common attributes exist. Even so, if group goals require cooperation with other groups, such cooperation is forthcoming.

If this propensity for ingroup/outgroup hostility is given some substance or supporting instinctive behaviour because of the ethnic character of the groups, then the conflict may be more serious, if one accepts the special biological nature of ethnicity and ethnocentrism (but even football rivalries can lead to violence and apparent hatred!). Suppose then that two groups are clearly defined as separate nations such as the English and the Scots, and people are firmly allocated to one or other of these nations. Since the idea of a nation is linked to kinship, even if the 'kin' are mainly distant relations or even 'fictive' kin (no real genetic relationship, but one that is believed to exist), we have in nationalism a combination of biological ethnocentrism, psychological ingroup/outgroup hostile propensities, and cultural and political differences. This makes it a special form of political behaviour and one which can be studied along with related forms of behaviour such as xenophobia, discrimination and racism (as in Reynolds *et al.*, 1987).

Dusan Kecmanovic, a clinical psychologist, ventures into the 'mass psychology of ethnonationalism', a neglected if vitally important field. He accepts the sociobiological analysis and adds his own analysis of how social psychology explains nationalist behaviour. Asserting that 'individuals feel at ease, more comfortable amid people like themselves' (p. 4), he shows that in circumstances of insecurity and threats from outsiders, the nation offers a refuge of a peculiarly comprehensive kind with a family-like identity. While the context of the threat to that security has still to be explained, it seems that, once a threat is made, people draw together in mutual defence along with their co-nationals as perhaps the last remaining place to turn to, and which can be relied on. This may mean, as in former Yugoslavia, a redrawing of identities and the splitting of actual families along ethnic lines. So, paradoxically, nationalism, while appealing to family-like sentiments and instincts, may destroy the 'nuclear' families that people belong to (Kecmanovic, 1996, pp. 85–6).

Once again, however, the student of nationalism should be aware that although a human nature or psychological approach looks promising, and may provide the necessary conditions for ethnocentrism and nationalism, as well as an explanation for the kind of behaviour associated with it, the specification of the sufficient conditions in any case requires an analysis of the nature of the groups and their conflicts. The distance (real or perceived) between groups on a genetic and cultural scale is likely to exacerbate mutual ethnocentrism and nationalism. Conversely, similar groups will usually exhibit less hostility towards each other. This may be contradicted by history, however. The Scots and English fought bitter wars, although closely related genetically. So did the British and the Germans in the twentieth century, also ethnic 'cousins'. They were also quite close culturally. So their hostility was essentially *political*. This means the threats to personal and national security are not necessarily explained by genetic differences, but are invariably political disputes and struggles for power which cut across genetic distinctions.

Groups may pursue goals of 'rational self-interest' leading to 'realistic group conflict', or they may display frustration or displacement leading to 'irrational ingroup–outgroup hostility' (LeVine and Campbell, 1972; Reynolds *et al.*, 1987). Depending on circumstances then, nationalism can be called either 'rational' or 'irrational' (Isaiah Berlin called it 'pathological', but that cannot apply to all nationalism!). Either way, it seems that it is firmly related to a human propensity to identify with an ingroup and oppose an outgroup, once these are established and perceived as in a competitive relationship, especially one which is perceived as a threat to the very existence of people's national identity. 'Boundary maintenance' is the aim of groups which feel threatened by other groups, and this applies to ethnic groups and nations too (Barth, 1969). They fight to preserve their territory, their language and their economic interests. So the activity of boundary maintenance in groups is paralleled in the nationalism of nations. However, Barth stresses that such groups are not 'givens', but the product of ever-changing situations.

An important political aspect is the perception of majority and minority status for national groups within the state. This gives a special psychological and political character to the ingroup–outgroup conflict. It is of course the state (or states) which provides the context for such a relationship. Thus, in Nigeria, the rhyme went:

I am a Hausa,	We are majorities,
Thou art an Ibo,	You are minorities,
He/she is a Yoruba.	They are different.

(quoted by Kirk-Greene, 1988, p. 159)

When the Nigerian federal structure made these identities highly political in the 1960s, civil war followed. Similarly, in Northern Ireland, the 'majority community' (Protestants/Unionists) faces the 'minority community' (Catholics/Nationalists) in endemic conflict. But here there is the added complication that in the context of a united Ireland, the Protestants become a minority group. Thus both Catholics and Protestants in Northern Ireland have psychological behaviour characteristic of minority groups.

Psychologists have paid particular attention to group 'stereotyping', and this is also a universal feature of ethnocentric or nationalist behaviour. 'Negative stereotyping' of foreigners gives substance to national identity in people's minds, and justifies national self-determination or sacrifices in wars against other nations. People of other nations are 'different', and usually threatening or inferior. In two world wars, British people called the Germans 'Huns', a barbarian tribe. In a more peaceful context, Scots often see English people as snobbish, and the Irish as lazy or irrational. That this may be the result of contacts in Scotland with particular English and Irish people is likely, and illustrates how stereotypes can be built up from unrepresentative samples.

Of course, all this is vague and general, and not necessarily very useful in explaining particular political situations. The biological and psychological characteristics of human beings have not evolved greatly since the 'hunter-gatherer' society of several thousand years ago. Yet contemporary society is very different from that of prehistoric man. Today it is rare to find kin groups driven by instincts in a struggle for survival against the natural environment. Our society is the product of several thousand years of cultural and technological development, and is now highly mobile, and increasingly mixed genetically. Nevertheless, appeals to kin, and against the threats posed by foreigners, are still powerful.

When we apply sociobiological theories to concrete examples in contemporary politics, their deficiencies become apparent. Let us take nationalism in the United Kingdom. The ethnic (kin) groups which make up the present population of Britain are for the most part not easily defined biologically nor can they be readily recognised in physical appearance. Apart from the recent New Commonwealth immigrants, who are well-defined and recognised because of their colour, the original ethnic groups such as the Picts, Britons, Celts, Angles, Saxons, Danes and Normans, have largely merged in a larger ethnicity. The division between 'Scots', 'Welsh', 'English' and 'Irish' is only partly ethnic, either in biology (relatedness) or in psychology (perceived identity). There is certainly a core of ethnic distinctiveness present in these categories, but over the centuries inter-marriage has occurred quite widely, especially between the English and the Scots and the Welsh. That is not to say, however, that appeals to ethnicity and nationhood fall on deaf ears. In recent years, cases relating to racial discrimination have involved Scots and English as well as 'blacks'.

Identity is only partly a spontaneous feeling that people have. It relates to the position they have in society, especially their membership of groups such as churches, which like nations can inspire emotion and supreme loyalties. When church and nation coincide, as they often do, the effect is to reinforce a sense of national identity. Thus the Scots and English each have their own national Church, presbyterian and episcopal respectively. Wales favours nonconformity, and the Republic of Ireland is almost entirely Roman Catholic. The Armenians' strong nationalism is linked to their identity as Christians in a Moslem environment. This religious difference, in a climate of Moslem fundamentalism, has led to their being the object of violence and even genocide. But their national identity is more than religious, since it is also made up of a language and consciousness of common descent. These indicators of nationality are not so marked in Scotland, England and Wales. Nevertheless, churches, and their related school systems, have been powerful transmitters of nationality from one generation to the next in the nations of the British Isles. If there is a pattern of dominance and exclusion in the state based on which nation you belong to, then nationalism can be mobilised.

This affects national identity. Such identity is partly imposed on people from outside their own group. Politics enters into this, since it is often the state which classifies people according to ethnic group, nationality and race. This may, or may not, be accepted entirely by the people concerned, but it usually leads to dual or multiple identities, especially when a historic national identity is overlaid with a contemporary political status such as citizenship, or with a new 'national' identification derived from the state (the official nation).

An example of this is the dual sense of national identity felt by most Scots and English people. Nearly all Scots feel a Scottish national identity, but most also feel British. This is because Scotland has been part of Great Britain since 1707, and there is a sense of identity with the state as well as with the Scottish nation. It is also true that the British state makes Scots conscious of their Scottish nationality. It does this by preserving a legal, political and administrative distinction between Scotland and England. Scots law, the Scottish Office, and Scottish education are powerful influences which make Scots Scottish and not English. English people, for their part, are made aware of being English by the state for some purposes (as in the Established Church of England), but for other purposes 'England' seems to mean 'Britain' (as in the Bank of England, the British state bank). It is little wonder then that English people are less sure than Scots of the difference between their historic nationality (English) and their modern citizenship (British). They often say 'English' or 'England' to mean 'British' and 'Britain', something that Scots cannot do with the terms 'Scottish' and 'Scotland'. Nevertheless, English people, like Scots, display dual national identity as 'English' and 'British', as for example in their loyalties to England in football and to Britain in international relations.

Similar situations are found in other parts of the world. 'Russians' identified with the USSR, and with their own nationality. 'Yugoslavs' were a national category in the old Yugoslavia, and (*Facts about the Socialist Federal Republic of Yogoslavia*, Belgrade: The Federal Secretariat for Information, 1985, p. 8). 1.2 million (5.4 per cent) identified themselves as such, out of a total population of 22.4 million, in 1981. In practice, most of these were of mixed ethnicity, in particular areas such as Bosnia, Croatia and Vojvodina. But such identity was not sufficient to keep Yugoslavia together, as it succumbed to the stronger Slovene, Croat, Serb and Bosnian identities. Under the Austro-Hungarian Empire (1867–1918), the identity 'Austrian' could cover any of the multitude of ethnicities in that state, but in reality the superior identities were the ethnic ones, and these took over from the Austrian identity.

So 'national identity' is not a straightforward, exclusive concept. There are often dual identities, combining two national identities, or more correctly one 'ethnonational' identity and one 'state' identity. In some places there may be more than two identities of this kind (e.g. Egyptian, Arab, Moslem), which may lead to conflicts of loyalty. In this book, the assumption is that the nation normally commands the supreme loyalty, but that may not be true in all cases.

Empirical evidence on national loyalties has been produced through surveys in several countries. Such a survey of Scottish national identity in 1986 found that 53 per cent expressed a degree of 'dual nationality' (Scottish and British) and 45 per cent 'single nationality' (39 per cent Scottish only, and 6 per cent British only) (see Table 1.1). During the election campaign of 1992, this had changed to 76 per cent dual nationality and 22 per cent single nationality. In the 1997 election campaign,

Table 1.1   *Scottish national identity, 1986*
Q.   'We are interested to know how people living in Scotland
see themselves in terms of nationality. Which of these statements
best describes how you regard yourself?'

.	Total	Party supported			
		Con.	Lab.	All	SNP
	%	%	%	%	%
Scottish, not British	39	27	37	34	58
More Scottish than British	30	29	35	26	29
Equally Scottish and British	19	22	20	28	7
More British than Scottish	4	10	2 ·	3	3
British, not Scottish	6	10	4	7	2
Don't know	2	2	2	1	1

Sources: L. Moreno, 'Scotland and Catalonia: The Path to Home Rule' in
D. McCrone and A. Brown (eds), *The Scottish Government Yearbook 1988*
(Edinburgh: Unit for the Study of Government in Scotland, 1988),
p. 171, quoting in part a *System Three Scotland* survey. Responses by party
are taken from the original survey, not shown by Moreno.

69 per cent in Scotland claimed dual Nationality and 27 per cent
single Nationality. In England the corresponding figures were
77 per cent and 17 per cent, and in Wales 65 per cent and 28 per
cent (Table 1.2).

That these responses are to some extent politically determined
is seen in the considerable variation in the responses according to
the time in which the questions are asked. There is also a
difference according to which political party is supported. Thus
58 per cent of Scottish National Party supporters in 1986 chose an
exclusively Scottish identity, while only 27 per cent of Conservative
Party supporters did so. As nearly all (*c.* 90 per cent) of the
Scottish population is Scots-born, the different identities are not
just a function of whether respondents were Scots-born or not.
Rather they reflect the political connotations of national identity.
Those choosing a dual identity were probably expressing support
for Scotland's membership of the United Kingdom, and those
choosing only a Scottish identity were probably more inclined
towards national self-determination for Scotland outside Britain.

Table 1.2 *Single and multiple national identities in England, Wales and Scotland, 1997*

	Country of residence		
	England %	Wales %	Scotland %
English/Welsh/Scottish not British	8	13	23
More English/Welsh/Scottish than British	16	29	39
Equally English/Welsh/Scottish and British	46	26	26
More British than English/Scottish/Welsh	15	10	4
British not English/Scottish/Welsh	9	15	4
Other description	5	4	3
None of the above	1	2	1
N	*2551*	*182*	*882*

Sources: British and Scottish Election Surveys, 1997: A. Heath and J. Kellas, 'Nationalisms and Constitutional Questions', *Scottish Affairs, Special Issue: Understanding Constitutional Change* (1998), p. 113.

That a sense of dual national identity is widespread is supported by research in other countries. In Catalonia for example, there is an even greater amount of dual Catalan/Spanish nationality (reaching 78 per cent in 1994) than Scottish/British identity, despite (or because of?) the widespread use of the Catalan language and the success of Catalan nationalism in achieving devolution in 1979. 'Only Catalan' identity was 10 per cent in 1995; 'more Catalan than Spanish' was 17 per cent; 'as much Spanish as Catalan' was 44 per cent; 'more Spanish than Catalan' was 16 per cent; and 'only Spanish' was 12 per cent. There is fluctuation here, too, as in Scotland. Dual identity was 77 per cent in 1986, 61 per cent in 1992 and 78 per cent in 1994. Catalan single identity increased from 6 per cent in 1990 to 17 per cent in 1992, then fell to 10 per cent in 1995. (Moreno and Arriba, 1996, pp. 83–5).

When national identity is analysed as something ascribed to others, another useful perspective is gained (Table 1.3). Again, Catalonia has been studied in this respect (Linz, in Tiryakian and Rogowski, 1985, p. 209). Now the question was 'Which of the following conditions are necessary, so that a person could consider himself a Catalan?' (the question was also asked of Basques,

Table 1.3 *Catalan national identification, 1979*
The proportion saying that a certain condition is necessary for someone to consider him/herself Catalan, by identity chosen of residents
of Catalonia

Identity chosen	Condition		
	Live and work in Catalonia %	Speak Catalan %	Born in Catalan or descended from family %
Total	56.5	33.3	60.7
Spanish only	49.0	30.3	88.2
More Spanish than Catalan	64.9	32.7	89.2
As Spanish as Catalan	60.5	34.5	81.9
More Catalan than Spanish	64.1	45.5	71.8
Catalan only	51.5	27.0	77.2

Source: Adapted from J. Linz, 'From Primordialism to Nationalism' in
E. A. Tiryakian and R. Rogowski (eds), *New Nationalisms of the Developed West*
(Boston, London, Sydney: George Allen & Unwin, 1985), p. 209 (DATA survey).

Galicians and Valencians). The responses were then correlated
with identities chosen by respondents for themselves.

It is interesting to see that, despite the strong linguistic character of Catalan national identity, only one-third consider the
ability to speak Catalan to be a condition for someone to call
himself a Catalan. An ethnic criterion (Catalan descent/born in
Catalonia) is strongly favoured, especially by those who state a
Spanish identity, but a purely territorial criterion of 'living and
working in Catalonia' is also given by over half the respondents.
Linz concludes (p. 250), from a comparison of Catalonia, the
Spanish and French Basque countries, Galicia, and Valencia, that
there is less 'primordial' nationalism based on language or
descent in the regions of Spain than 'territorial' nationalism similar to that of the old 'nation-states', in which citizenship and
nationality come together as national identity. These distinctions
are similar to ethnic nationalism on the one hand, and official
nationalism (as used in this book) on the other.

Similar features are found in Scottish nationalism. Scottish
nationalists do not seek a 'Scotland for the Scots' or an ethnic

nation, but an independent government or state for Scotland. All who live and work in Scotland would be eligible for Scottish citizenship. This explains why some English people are Scottish nationalists.

It will be seen that we have moved some way from the biological and psychological discussion at the start of this chapter. We are now well into the complexities of modern national identity and political nationalism. What then is the place of human nature and the biological and psychological analysis of this subject?

Human nature and human psychology provide the necessary conditions for ethnocentric and nationalist behaviour, and such behaviour is universal. As with all human behaviour, it is a result of the interaction of genes and environment. In experimental psychology, groups can be observed displaying hostility to one another in certain circumstances. This is similar to group ethnocentrism and nationalism, but these groups perceive an actual ethnic or national identity which gives an added force to their ingroup/outgroup hostility.

We are not dealing with experiments, however, but with real societies. In these the groups are usually less clearly defined, and identities may be confused and multiple. There is not often in politics a clear ingroup/outgroup distinction, and national identities are often dual or even triple. In a class of American students I taught, there were many definitions of personal national identity. One student wrote:

Frequently, I am asked: 'What are you, really?' Everyone usually makes the general assumption that I am American but often feel they have to dig deeper.

My mother is Italian from both sides of her family while my father is a Russian-Jew from his. I consider myself Italian mainly because almost all of my mother's family live in and around Pittsburgh. Along with my mother and father I feel that my mother's family was responsible for raising me. I have learned Italian culture, heritage and some language.

Currently, I am studying the Italian language so I frequently do speak Italian with my grandmother who, luckily for me, does not speak a dialect.

I will always be proud of my Italian heritage and try to pass on what I know to my children. As for my Russian heritage

I still don't know much about it and no effort on my father's part to teach me has been made.

Identity and behaviour are partly genetic, but they are also shaped by context and choice. In politics they are resources waiting to be used by politicians and their supporters for their own advantage. Human nature provides the necessary condition for ethnocentric behaviour, but politics converts this into the sufficient conditions for nationalism as we understand it today.

2

Nationalism as Ideology

When people come to think about themselves and their position in society, their ideas are partly derived from their instincts (their nature), and partly from what they learn in their environment and from other people. Their *behaviour* is also in part instinctive, and in part the result of learning and environment.

Nationalism is both an ideology and a form of behaviour. It is of course in practice difficult to distinguish between the two, since the cause of the behaviour may in part be the ideology. As we have seen, ethnocentrism and nationalist behaviour is held by some to be partly instinctive. Giving it the name 'nationalist', rather than 'ethnocentric', focuses on the idea of the nation, and on the agenda which nationalism sets for action relating to the nation. This idea and this agenda makes nationalism a special kind of ideology and behaviour, though it is closely related to ethnocentrism. While it is possible to examine nationalist ideology and behaviour separately from ethnocentrism, and from ideologies and behaviour such as racism, we cannot escape from the fact that we are in the same broad area of human activity.

The idea of a nation can be considered as both natural and a product of the imagination. It is natural, if we accept the view of some sociobiologists, because it derives from the instinct of kin selection or ethnocentrism discussed in the first chapter. In this view, a nation has the function of an extended family, whether or not it is genetically related – though it usually is, in a broad sense.

Most writers on nationalism see the nation as a concept rather than as something natural. To them, nations are 'imagined communities', in Benedict Anderson's phrase (Anderson, 1983). People imagine nations, and their membership of these, because their minds are trying to make social constructs out of their relationship with other people. Of course, this approach does not help us to determine which nations are 'imagined', and how strongly. Nor does it place nationalism in a historical context. The idea of the nation and the idea of nationalism may be 'imagined' by many people with a minimum of prompting by political thinkers. But in its more developed form nationalism is an ideology, and this moves the focus from biology and psychology to sociology and philosophy. In these disciplines, an ideology is usually seen as a system of ideas, different from knowledge or science because it is not 'true', and because it contains a great deal of special pleading. Nationalism is an ideology which builds on the idea of the nation and makes it the basis for action. This action can be political or non-political. As this book is about politics, it is not necessary to delve deeply into cultural nationalism, or nationalism in sport, unless these types of nationalism have clear political effects. The difficulty of knowing what is, and what is not, political is particularly puzzling in the study of nationalism. Michael Billig, in *Banal Nationalism* (Billig, 1995), shows that nationalism relies on routine symbols and habits of language, especially in the media, for its continuing strength. But the votes cast for nationalist parties, or for independence or devolution in a referendum, are not clearly related to such nationalism.

For example, the most popular form of nationalist behaviour in many countries is in sport, where masses of people become highly emotional in support of their national team. But the same people may display no obvious nationalism in politics, such as supporting a nationalist party, or demanding home rule or national independence. Of course, most national teams represent states which have political independence, so their supporters' nationalism is official nationalism. In Britain, however, there are four national teams in international football: England, Scotland, Wales and Northern Ireland. This has led to some manifestations of social or even ethnic nationalism in a political form, as when Scottish supporters boo 'God Save the Queen' (the British, but also the English, national anthem), and sing their own unofficial anthems, 'Scotland the Brave' and 'Flower of Scotland', which are now played at international games. But Scottish football supporters do not seek political independence for Scotland more than other Scots, as far as is known, nor do they give massive support to the Scottish National Party. Yet a study of nationalism in politics cannot ignore such nationalist behaviour, because it underpins and heightens national consciousness, without which political nationalism would have no chance of success. Of course, the 'ideology' of nationalism involved here is minimal and is nearer to ethnocentrism than to political thought.

In the case of nationalism in sport we have three manifestations of nationalism: nationalist behaviour (perhaps biologically and psychologically derived – the 'animal behaviour' of the 'Soccer Tribe' (Morris, 1981)); a strong national consciousness (the 'imagined community' – the tribe is now the nation and its object of emotion the national team); and an ideology of nationalism (the learned sentiments of the national anthem with its patriotism and occasional xenophobia). These three components of nationalism recur time and time again in this study.

Where did the idea of a nation come from? And how did nationalism develop from that? These topics are the subject of much dispute among scholars, and in this work a particular interpretation will be given, which aims to be consistent with the rest of the argument. But other interpretations will be discussed which readers may find more convincing.

The idea of a nation is to be found as far back as the ancient world, although it is not clear that there was then what we understand as a nation today. Greeks and Jews in particular were conscious of their identity as peoples and acted to preserve their communities. In the case of the Jews, this was done throughout their prolonged 'diaspora' or dispersion throughout the world. While the Greeks retained their homeland, albeit under alien rule for many centuries, the Jews lost theirs until the twentieth century. The desire to return to the 'promised land' stayed with Jews throughout the centuries, and they repeated the prayer 'Next year in Jerusalem'. Zionism is the form of nationalism which in the late nineteenth century gave expression to this desire to rebuild a Jewish Homeland in Palestine. In 1917 the British Government in the Balfour Declaration promised to 'facilitate the establishment in Palestine of a national home for the Jewish people'. In 1948 the state of Israel was established, and in its declaration of independence it proclaimed 'the natural right of the Jewish people to be master of its own fate, like all other nations, in its own sovereign state'. The state of Israel would thereafter 'be open for Jewish immigration and for the ingathering of exiles'.

Here is an example of the idea of the nation and the ideology of nationalism existing over thousands of years, although taking a particular form (Zionism) only in the last hundred years. However, it should be pointed out that most writers take the view that nationalism is a relatively modern phenomenon, although having roots in the distant past (Kohn, 1944).

Not all nations are as clear-cut as the Greeks and the Jews. The historical record is very difficult to follow for most modern nations. What was a 'nation', or a 'people', or a 'race', at one period may disappear at another, or be merged with a larger community. Anthony Smith has come to the conclusion, after much study of nationalism, that nations have 'ethnic origins' (Smith, 1986). This means that we should not believe that nations have been produced only by modern developments, such as capitalism and industrialisation, as Gellner suggests (Gellner, 1983). Rather, they have origins in the ethnic groups of the earliest periods in history. This also pushes back the idea of the nation to the point where it was first expressed, rather than to the period when nationalist ideology was widely articulated ('the Age of Nationalism' in the nineteenth century).

We can see how this approach works when we look at the history of the Scottish nation. An early manifestation of national consciousness and nationalism is seen in the Declaration of Arbroath of 1320. This was a letter sent by a group of Scottish nobles and others to the Pope, seeking his support for the independence of Scotland, which was being threatened by England. The letter asserts the idea of a Scottish nation, and propounds an ideology which equates national independence for Scotland with freedom for the national community, itself seen as a natural right. Similar statements about nationality and nationalism can be found in nearly all parts of the world, but there are few which have survived in documentary form from such an early period (for a discussion of the Declaration of Arbroath and its significance in Scottish history, see Duncan, 1970).

The Declaration of Arbroath starts with a list of signatories, who may be considered the articulators of the idea of the nation and of nationalism. They are the counterparts of the Scottish nationalists of today, although in the fourteenth century they were a select group of landowners, church leaders and freeholders, rather than 'ordinary people' in a modern mass electorate. This is hardly surprising, as there was no such electorate in the fourteenth century. However, the function of articulating nationalism is performed by different people at different times, and even today only a minority of the Scottish nation is nationalist in the sense of articulating a nationalist ideology.

Much interest has been shown in the identity of nationalists: whether they come from a particular social class, whether they are intellectuals, and so on. It is not easy to get evidence for pre-modern periods, and the 1320 Declaration has been interpreted as the claim of 'a ruling elite group in defence of its property and privileges' rather than the claims of a nation-people to rule in some democratic way (Berry, 1981). Again, it is the difficulty of comparing modern nationalism with early nationalism that is involved here.

Nationalists are clearly idealists, since they propound the idea of the nation and the ideology of nationalism. They are also people with interests of their own to promote, whether it be feudal power in relation to a monarchy, or a material or psychic advantage as individuals or members of a group. So nationalist ideology is a justification for the pursuit of self-interest.

In some cases, nationalism verges on the irrational and may produce pathological behaviour. The study of 'the authoritarian personality' by Adorno and others (Adorno, 1950) linked personality traits with support for fascism. A later study of nationalism and personality (Forbes, 1985) has pointed out that the perception of differences between ethnic groups has more to do with the causes of nationalist behaviour than the personality characteristics of nationalists. So it seems that nationalism is not always peculiar or irrational behaviour but can be a rational response to particular circumstances, in this case the antagonistic interests of different nations. Even so, the excesses of nationalist (and xenophobic, racist, etc.) behaviour are not regarded normal or rational activity in a civilised society, and it seems sensible to regard such behaviour as pathological. How personality and environment bring about such behaviour is not clear.

If we look at the ideas and ideology of the Scottish Declaration of Arbroath of 1320 we can see clearly how the ideology of nationalism is created, why, and by whom. The signatories were a narrow elite, but they claimed to speak for 'the whole community of the realm of Scotland', not just for a narrow group (even if that was what they were). Of course they did not seek democracy, rather independence for Scotland, and 'freedom': 'For we fight not for glory, nor riches, nor honours, but for freedom alone, which no good man gives up except with his life.'

How did they come to think of the idea of a Scottish nation at all? We know that the people of Scotland were made up of various ethnic groups, such as Picts, Britons, Angles, Norse, Normans... and Scots. The Scots were only one group of incomers to north Britain (speaking geographically), but ultimately (by the eleventh century) they gave their name to the Kingdom of Scotland, formed from a union of earlier kingdoms of the Picts, Scots, Britons and Northumbrians (Angles).

The writers of the Declaration of Arbroath were not historians in any academic sense, yet they decided to describe the historical origins of the 'nation of Scots'. They thus first proclaimed a national identity and consciousness, something which is necessary for any nationalist ideology. Of course, this can be criticised as mere myth-making, not the truth. However, we are not concerned to discover what is true in nationalist ideas and ideology, but to point to the character of these ideas/ideology and their recurrence throughout history.

The nation of Scots, we are told,

> journeyed from Greater Scythia... dwelt for a long span of time in Spain... acquired, with many victories and untold efforts, the places which it now holds... In their kingdom one hundred and thirteen kings of their own royal stock have reigned, the line unbroken by a single foreigner.

Here is the identity of a people, albeit constantly on the move, and only finally settling in a homeland after displacing or conquering 'Picts, Norwegians, Danes and English'. What clinches the nation's position is the kingdom, and its 'non-foreign' line (though the Scottish kings were never purely Scottish). So a political structure, the state, gives form to the idea of the nation, and the desire for a nation-state or for independence as an existing nation-state is the strongest form of political nationalism.

Once the nation of Scots is identified, with its political expression, the Kingdom of Scotland, these 1320 nationalists seek to endow the nation with good qualities, which are threatened by foreigners. This invokes the psychology of ingroup–outgroup tensions, as threats to a mythological extended family, the Scottish nation, are identified. The special qualities of the nation are already seen in its successes over other nations, on the path to political nationhood in Scotland: in this regard, 'among other distinguished nations our own nation, namely of Scots, has been marked by many distinctions'.

It was obvious at this time of pervasive religious culture that such a nation must be 'God's People'. Certainly, the Jews had already proclaimed their Covenant with God, which included a 'Promised Land' in Israel, and the Scots would also be expected to be appointed by God as a favoured nation. And so it is:

> Their high qualities and merits, if they were not otherwise manifest, shine out sufficiently from this: that the king of kings and lord of lords, our lord Jesus Christ, after his passion and resurrection, called them, even though settled in the uttermost ends of the earth, almost the first to his most holy faith.

This special relationship of the Scots to Jesus would (it was hoped) not be lost on the Pope, to whom the letter was addressed. 'God's People' is a favourite idea of nationalists, and, apart from the Scots in the fourteenth century, Jews, Afrikaners and Mormons have used the phrase. Russia was 'Holy Russia'. Religion is a powerful reinforcement of the other foundations of subjective national identity.

When 'God's People' have a national church of their own this gives a strong institutional support to national identity and nationalism. Institutions tend to give rise to vested interests which are social and economic as well as ideological. The Scottish nation is closely identified with the Church of Scotland, and even before the presbyterian Reformation the Christian church was organised separately in Scotland. Thus the 1320 Declaration of Arbroath to the Pope sought national recognition for Scotland within the Roman Catholic Church as well as political independence for Scotland. This was to be granted by Rome. After the Reformation, the Church of Scotland was sharply differentiated from the Church of England within Protestantism because the former was presbyterian and Calvinist, while the latter was episcopalian and Anglo-Catholic in theology.

There are many other examples of churches as sustainers of nationalism: the Armenian and Georgian Christian churches; Moslems in Punjab and Pakistan and Buddhists in Sri Lanka in opposition to Hindus; Catholics in Northern Ireland in opposition to Protestants; Catholics in Poland, Czechoslovakia and Hungary in opposition to Russian Communists and Orthodox Christians. Even where churches are international, as with Islam and Roman Catholicism, they usually display national characteristics in the context of different nations.

Nations unite to face a challenge from foreigners. In the fourteenth century, as before and since, the challenge to the Scots came from England, at the time of the Declaration of Arbroath from 'that mighty prince Edward, king of the English', whose

> wrongs, killings, violence, pillage, arson, imprisonment of prelates, burning down of monasteries, despoiling and killing of religious, and yet other innumerable outrages sparing neither age nor sex, religion nor order, no one could fully describe or fully understand unless experience had taught him.

King Robert the Bruce managed to set the Scots free from these countless evils:

> Yet if he should give up what he has begun, seeking to make us or our kingdom subject to the King of England or to the English, we would strive at once to drive him out as our enemy... and we would make some other man who was able to defend us our king; for as long as a hundred of us remain alive, we will never on any conditions be subjected to the lordship of the English.

The Pope was asked to support the Scots' claim to independence in 'this poor little Scotland, beyond which there is no dwelling-place at all'. So the idea of the nation presumed the existence of a homeland, and no matter how humble or poor it was, the Scots sought to defend it from attack by the rich and powerful English. It is no surprise that even today Scottish nationalists refer with pride to the Declaration of Arbroath as an eloquent statement of Scottish nationalism and anti-English feeling.

Of course, the idea of the nation has developed over the centuries, even if its essence has not changed. During the French

Revolution in the late eighteenth century, the nation took on a new political meaning which linked nationalism to the aim of popular sovereignty. This meant that the nation was no longer to be passive in the government of the state, but was to be an active participant, without which there would be no legitimate authority. The signatories of the 1320 Declaration of Arbroath could have no concept of participant popular sovereignty, even although they linked the legitimacy of the king to the defence of the nation. Modern Scottish nationalism breaks with the existing governmental and state structure, while the fourteenth-century Scottish nationalists were defending their state and church from English attacks.

After the French Revolution nationalism became a revolutionary ideology, and the idea of the nation was for a time unsettling for most governments. The revolutionary aspect arose because the claim that the people were sovereign could not be accepted by the monarchs, aristocrats and merchants who ruled in nearly every state. Like democracy, this kind of nationalism was a political concept which sought to put all citizens on an equal footing, instead of excluding most from active membership of the state. It denied the legitimacy of a system of rule by social classes and status groups whose interests were not necessarily those of the whole nation. The idea of a nation now meant a community based on political equality and democracy, and democratic nationalism was the most powerful doctrine which spelled out why that was so, and how it was to be achieved.

As if that were not a big enough threat to the existing system of government, nationalism posed a second, equally disturbing, challenge to the state system. The idea of a nation was developed by some people along ethnic and linguistic lines, rather than according to democratic criteria. So while the revolutionary ideas of the French Revolution threatened monarchies and aristocracies in every state in Europe, ethnic and linguistic nationalists took this further and threatened the boundaries of states as well. This amounted to 'exclusive nationalism', since it excluded from the nation those people who were not ethnically or linguistically qualified to be members.

This involved a considerable amount of 'myth-making' about the historical credentials of the nation. Not every 'nation' in the Europe of the nineteenth century could point to a 'nationalist' document such as the Scottish Declaration of Arbroath, which had been drawn up in the fourteenth century. More common was an ideological construction by modern nationalists. Thus, Sabino Arana (1865–1903), 'had to invent a name, Euskadi, for the Basque country, design a flag for it, and construct an ideology which would justify the region's claim to independence from Spain' (Sullivan, 1988, p. 1). This ideology included a 'mythological' history of the Basque people and their descent from Noah. More complex were the nationalisms of the nations in the former Yugoslavia (Banac, 1984). For example, according to Banac, the Slovenes 'acquired a national consciousness only in the nineteenth century and...the Montenegrins, Macedonians, and Bosnian-Hercegovinian Muslims...are the products of twentieth-century mutations in South Slavic national affinities and are, indeed, still in the process of formation' (Banac, 1984, p. 23). To Banac, the whole national problem in what was Yugoslavia can be seen as the product of competing and incompatible nationalist ideologies, some medieval and some modern. The older 'Greater Serbia' ideology threatened the modern nationalisms of Slovenia, Croatia and Kosovo.

In the Developing World, apparently 'primordial' identities are often in fact the product of comparatively recent developments. Thus, according to Greenberg (1980, pp. 14–15):

> The Kikuyu, for example, whose coherence is now so important to understanding Kenyatta and nationalism in Kenya, had no certain identity before the imposition of British rule and the alienation of land to the settlers; distinctive groups like the Sikhs in India, Ibo in Nigeria, and Malays in Malaysia were barely conscious of their 'sameness' one hundred years ago. Even race, seemingly universal and 'primordial', central to the entrenched group conflicts in southern Africa and the United States, only became a basis for broad group identity and ideology in the mid-nineteenth century.

Even revolutionary France came under nationalist attack by those who on ethnic or linguistic grounds did not consider themselves to be part of the 'French nation'. Orthodox French revolutionaries, however, defined the French nation in terms of the citizenship of the French state, which made no ethnic distinctions. Rather it resulted from the 'social contract' which all could make. This was to prove a continuing problem for France in an age of ethnic nationalism, for Corsicans, Bretons, and much later Algerians and other 'non-French' colonials developed a non-French nationalism which would not rest content with citizenship of the French state. By the 1960s it also raised the question of whether Developing World immigrants (especially Moslems) to France who did not share the French culture could be considered members of the French nation. By the late 1980s this provoked a rise in anti-immigrant feeling, with strong voting for the National Front in cities such as Marseilles with a large immigrant population, and immigrants being attacked and even killed.

This is a problem for all states which are multiethnic in composition: that is nearly all the states of the world. Can 'equal citizenship' overcome ethnic and linguistic demands? If nationalism based on ethnicity and language is a powerful concept, how does the concept of a nation based on citizenship respond? An ideology of citizenship and the state which is not based on a single nationality can seek to establish a 'culturally plural' or 'multicultural' society, made up of several nationalities or ethnic groups each with the right to its own language, education, religion and so on. Or it can ignore these altogether and hope that the legitimacy of the state will be established through the support of all citizens without any recognition of minority ethnic and cultural rights. Only by achieving national homogeneity can such states hope to have much chance of success with this strategy, for it implies the assimilation (or at least integration) of minority ethnic groups to the majority national culture.

Once the idea of the nation and the ideology of nationalism became generally established in the political discourse of the world, they developed along lines which were to provide politics with its most powerful appeal to the emotions. Identity with a nation now appeared to be 'an inherent attribute of humanity', so that the idea of a man without a nation 'seems to impose too great a strain on the modern imagination' (Gellner, 1983, p. 6).

The 'Age of Nationalism' provides us with the classical statements of the nationalist ideology. Many of these texts have an archaic ring about them today, as well as a certain naivety. Nationalism never became a great system of ideas, as did liberalism or Marxism. But its influence on politics was even more important than these, if we look at the history of the modern world. Nearly all the wars of the nineteenth and twentieth centuries had their roots in nationalism, and all states now owe their legitimacy to some version of the national idea.

What is that idea? At its most abstract level, it seeks to place humanity in a context of time and place, rather than in terms of universal attributes. People belong to a particular nation, and are not cosmopolitan or nation-less. Philosophically, this is the opposite of the Enlightenment view of people as the same everywhere at all times (Berry, 1981). Various writers propounded the idea of nationalism in different European countries during the nineteenth century, and their influence on nationalist movements was great. They are particularly famous in connection with German, Italian and British nationalism, but their ideas spread to every part of the world, and inspired nationalists of all kinds.

Guiseppe Mazzini, the pioneer of Italian national unification, propounded the most exalted ideology of nationalism. For Mazzini 'nationality' was closely related to the liberal principles of liberty and equality, but was especially concerned with fraternity. Unlike the atheism of the French Revolution, Mazzini's ideology was highly religious, as the following typical extract shows:

> We believe, therefore, in the Holy Alliance of the Peoples as being the vastest formula of association possible in our epoch; – in the *liberty* and *equality* of the peoples, without which no true association can exist; – in *nationality*, which is the *conscience* of the peoples, and which, by assigning to them their part in the work of association, their function in humanity, constitutes their mission upon earth, that is to say, their *individuality*; without which neither liberty nor equality are possible; – in the sacred *Fatherland*, cradle of nationality; altar and workshop of the individuals of which each people is composed. (Mazzini, 1835, p. 47)

In this statement we can see an attempt to reconcile individualism, nationalism and internationalism in one package with 'nationality' as the core organising principle. Mazzini distrusted what he called 'nationalism' as having a 'narrow spirit' (Mazzini,

1850, p. 5), because it neglected the overall association of nations. In Mazzini's scheme, nations are equal in status, though each has a particular character and function to perform in a world harmony of nations.

In Britain, this liberal view of nationality found an echo in John Stuart Mill's writings. In *Considerations on Representative Government* (Mill, 1861), Mill proclaimed that 'Free institutions are next to impossible in a country made up of different nationalities. Among a people without fellow-feeling, especially if they read and speak different languages, the united public opinion, necessary to the working of representative government, cannot exist' (p. 361). It was this kind of thinking which led Victorian Britain to support nationalist movements in Europe, although it divided over that of Ireland. Mill himself was vague as to what constituted a nationality: his own Scotland is not mentioned as such, and the assumption was that Britain constituted a nationality, no doubt on the grounds of a common language.

German nationalist ideology also looked to language as the defining characteristic of the nation, but it had little of the liberalism of Italian and British national theorising. Johann Herder's writings predate the French Revolution (his major work on language and nationalism, *On the Origin of Language*, dates from 1772). Herder set the tone for German nationalism, which stressed the ethnic rather than democratic aspects of nationalism. The German *Volk* (people) is defined by its use of the German language, and the ancient origins of that language denote the ancient origins of the German folk or nation. Pride in one's language is a natural feeling, as is equally pride in one's nation:

What a treasure language is when kinship groups grow into tribes and nations! Even the smallest of nations ... cherishes in and through its language the history, the poetry and songs about the great deeds of its forefathers. (Herder, 1772, quoted in Barnard, 1969, p. 165)

Pride in one's nation and its language soon slides into assertions of national superiority, and Herder was particularly contemptuous of those Germans who used French instead of their native language (Edwards, 1985, p. 24). After Herder, a line of German nationalists developed the ideology of linguistic nationalism, and the superiority which the German language and literature gave to the German *Volk* (for example, Johann Fichte and Friedrich von Schlegel). The political importance of these ideas was seen in the growing strength of nationalism in Europe in the nineteenth century. Nationalist movements took root everywhere, some directed towards national unification (Italy and Germany), some to throwing off the rule of multinational empires (Greece, Belgium, Poland, Hungary, Serbia), and some to breaking away from long-established kingdoms (Ireland, Norway). All these had their national ideologues and heroes, and they copied each other. For example, Mazzini's Young Italy society (1831) was imitated by other national liberation movements throughout Europe (notably the Young Turks of the early twentieth century), and later in Asia and Africa (Young India, Young China, Young Burma).

Of course, ideas catch on only in fertile ground. Ernest Gellner has asserted that the condition for the emergence of the national principle and nationalist movements was the stage of development reached in some states in Europe (Gellner, 1983). According to him, their emergence from feudalism into centralised state government and their change from agrarian/mercantile societies to industrialised economies gave nationalism its chance to become the politics of the progressive forces in Europe, and later in the rest of the world, where similar circumstances occurred.

What is not clearly explained in this analysis is how nationalism developed in conditions which were not those of the industrialising societies. Many European nationalist movements seem to have been inspired by the ideology of nationalism whatever the condition of the economy. The appeal of nationalist ideology was intellectual and emotional as well as functional in an economic sense. Its political dimension was crucial: the aim was to escape from the domination of the 'other' and to establish self-government. Nationalism's roots in ethnocentrism explain the emotional strength it possesses in politics, which no socio-economic functional explanation is able to do.

The conditions favourable to the emergence of nationalism in its liberal forms (Mazzini and Mill) are not always present. Different conditions encourage other kinds of nationalist behaviour and different concepts of the nation. Pride in nation led to fascism in Italy and Nazism in Germany in the 1920s. 'Social Darwinism' linked natural selection to nations, with the idea that some nations were 'fitter' then others. Spurious biology led to racism, with claims that some peoples were genetically superior, and entitled to rule over others. There were ideologies of 'white supremacy', especially in the South of the United States (racial segregation) and in South Africa (apartheid), and an imperialist ideology of the 'White Man's Burden' in the British Empire. Almost everywhere there was anti-Semitism (an ancient attitude among Christians, but revived in the modern period, and linked to Nazism). The ramifications of such prejudices stretch into justifications for systems of slavery and castes, genocide, chauvinism and imperialism. Of course, there are differences between all these ideologies and the behaviour associated with them. Nationalism does not entail racism or genocide, but racism and genocide entail some form of nationalist ideology.

The idea of the nation and the ideology of nationalism at the simplest means the recognition of a people and its need for status, perhaps including its own state (the principle of national self-determination was accepted in theory by American capitalists such as President Woodrow Wilson and by Soviet communists such as Lenin and Stalin by 1917). Nationalism can take psychological, cultural or political forms: usually all three. Nationalist ideology can be left-wing, right-wing, constructive of new states or destructive of existing states. It can protect or destroy freedom, establish peace or lead to war. It is little wonder that it is difficult to tie down as a general phenomenon, and it is partly different in different periods of history. How historical change relates to nationalism is the subject of the next chapter.

3

The Evolution of Nationalism

For nationalism to emerge as a major force in politics, the conditions had to be right. These conditions may conveniently be divided into 'necessary' and 'sufficient' conditions. While ethnocentrism and an ideology of nationalism are both *necessary* for nationalist behaviour, the *sufficient* conditions for strong and widespread nationalism are more difficult to identify.

Writers on nationalism have provided us with a wide range of explanations for the rise of nationalism as a pervasive political force, and for the emergence of the nation-state as the most acceptable form of the state today. Writers on race and ethnicity have given us a related analysis of the conditions governing racial and ethnic politics. Case-studies of nationalist movements and ethnic politics provide a testing-ground for the hypothetical necessary and sufficient conditions for the emergence of nationalism and its political power in different contexts. In international relations, too, nationalism comes up in various forms: as a cause of conflict; as a source of opposition to the existing state system, in particular multinational states and empires; as opposition to international or supranational institutions and cooperation; and as a determinant of a state's power in international affairs. The conditions which strengthen nationalism in domestic politics may also strengthen it in international politics. At the same time, international circumstances have a strong effect on nationalism within states.

In the succeeding chapters, each of these subjects will be examined, and they all point to the general problem that historical change and different contexts in the contemporary world are exceedingly complex to study, and are the subject of widely divergent analyses. In some cases, these analyses have the character of general systems of thought or ideologies, as for example, Marxism, and 'universalist' or 'individualist' liberal thought. Both of these attack nationalism and seek to eliminate the context in which it thrives. Moreover, there is a fundamental difference between 'primordialists', who trace nationalism back to instinctive behaviour and the earliest societies, and 'contextualists' who see nationalism as the product of particular economic and social circumstances, especially those of modern times (a useful survey of both types of theory is found in *Theories of Race and Ethnic Relations*, edited by John Rex and David Mason, 1986). Leaving aside the controversial primordial type of theory, we can now go on to look further at the contextual conditions in which nationalism as we understand it developed from ethnocentrism, and ethnicity became nationhood.

This requires us to focus on three distinct, though related, facets of society: politics, economics and culture. Politics is essentially about power and authority. We are especially interested in the nature of 'the polity' (the state, principality, clan, etc.), and how it relates to 'the nation'. In particular, the politics of nationalism is about control over that state. Exclusion from power, and discrimination, affects particular nations in multinational states. Nationalism is a struggle to get power for the nation, against the forces that exclude and discriminate. This is encapsulated in the principle of national self-determination.

The focus on economics concerns the pursuit of wealth and how the economy divides people into occupational classes. Are there economic explanations for nationalism? Exclusions and discrimination can be economic as well as political, and will lead to nationalism if these are seen to be directed against particular nations.

Culture is about identity and status in terms of birth, family, language, religion, and so on. Ethnicity and nationalism are usually considered to be more clearly related to culture than to anything else. Thus national identity forms the basis of nationalism, and exclusions and discrimination operate against people whose national identity is unacceptable to the state or to other nations. It is probably true that ethnocentrism is universal, but nationalism is the result of particular patterns of political power involving nations in superior and subordinate positions in the state.

Most theories of nationalism seek to determine the relationship between politics, economics and culture which brings about the transition from ethnicity to nationalism. Table 3.1 summarises one way of analysing this relationship, which is similar to that of Gellner. The table indicates that we can look for an explanation for the rise of nationalism in the developments which have taken place in politics, in the economy, and in culture. The interactions between these three dimensions, at different periods of history, provide the key to the understanding of nations and nationalism.

For some theorists, these interactions are structured in such a way as to make one part (represented in the table by one column) dominant, as the ultimate 'reality' in the analysis. For example, Marxists and other economic determinists believe that social and political behaviour can be reduced to economic interests, particularly those of economic classes, sections, groups, and so on. Thus nationalism is seen as either a disguised economic interest, or in Marxist terms as 'false consciousness' which has misled people and stopped them pursuing their 'true' class interest.

Other 'reductionists' choose political power as their 'reality'. They see politics and the state as the producer of nations and nationalism. Economic and cultural identities and interests are ultimately subsumed under the primacy of political power (for this approach, see Breuilly, 1982, and Brass, 1985).

Nationalists, and some theorists of nationalism, are also reductionists. For them, individuals, the state and the economy are all ultimately dependent on membership of a particular nation. Where individualists seek to study the rights and duties of individual citizens in relation to the state, nationalists and some theorists of nationalism are concerned with the composition of the state rather than with the relationship between the state

Table 3.1 *Politics, the economy, and culture and nationalism*

Period of history	***Politics*** *Power/* *authority*	***The economy*** *Wealth/* *occupation/class*	***Culture*** *Identity/status,* *language, etc.*
Pre-nationalist	The pre-modern polity	The pre-industrial economy	Primordial ethnicity
Nationalist	The modern state	The industrial economy	Nationalism

(any state) and the individual. They thus pose prior questions – 'What is my nation?' and 'What is my state?' – before those posed by most political theorists. Before discussing rights, duties, and so on, of citizens, and the legitimate powers of the state, nationalists want to know what body of citizens, in terms of birth and culture, makes up the nationally legitimate composition of the state.

Behind the discussion of the relationship between politics, economics and culture there is a time factor. Contextualists assert that there was a 'pre-nationalist' period in which the relationships between politics, economy and culture were not conducive to nationalism. This was followed by a nationalist period, in which they were. In the pre-nationalist period, and in places today which share the conditions prevalent in that period, the state had not achieved its modern form of a centralised, sovereign and bureaucratic polity. Rather, it was a loose collection of sovereignties or power centres, as in feudalism or tribalism. The economy was agrarian or pre-industrial, and nationalism was found only as ethnocentrism, or as loyalty to clan chiefs, kings and princes.

To enter the period of nations and nationalism, with a world based on the legitimacy of 'nation-states', all three dimensions of politics, economics and culture had to be transformed, indeed constructed. Thus the polity had to become a centralised state, the economy had to be modern not feudal, and the culture had to replace ethnicity with something which can become nationhood. This is a 'constructionist' view of nations and nationalism, and implies that a non-national, non-nationalist alternative exists, and can be constructed.

This kind of account can be found in many theories of nationalism, especially that of Gellner (for a short monograph also on this theme, see Berki, 1986). It is typical of Marxist studies of the emergence of nationalism, and in later variations of Marxism such as the theory of 'internal colonialism', discussed below. These combine an analysis of economic conflicts in capitalist states with an explanation for nationalism. Marxists look especially at how nationalism affects different socioeconomic classes. Greenberg, whilst distancing himself from Marxist analysis and 'modernisation' theory, nevertheless concludes that 'identifiable forces in capitalist development carry forward and elaborate patterns of racial and ethnic domination' (Greenberg, 1980, p. 405).

For him, 'Racial domination ... is essentially a class phenomenon' (p. 406), and racist and nationalist ideology is to be explained mainly in terms of class interests, in particular, those of (white) commercial farmers, businesspeople, and industrial workers. These interests, however, are always changing, and may turn against racism and nationalism, although there is no universal process of modernisation which decrees that they will inevitably do so. Class analysis has gone out of fashion with the virtual demise of communist systems in the world, but 'false consciousness' is still a popular view of nationalism in sociology.

The transition from ethnicity to nationalism is represented in the third column of the table, that dealing with culture. Some theorists see this process as a fairly self-contained cultural process (they are reductionists in favour of culture). For them, nationalism develops from ethnicity through the articulation of the idea of the nation and the ideology of nationalism, and the rise of a national culture in a printed language, literature, national religion and education, and so on. Other theorists, who still stress the primacy of culture, see the process as related to developments in the polity and the economy. They point out that at first the role of the state was so weak that ethnic groups lived in virtual isolation from each other in an economy which was mostly agrarian and localised. As kingdoms expanded their territories, ethnic groups were united under one ruler, and the economy developed, with more trading across ethnic boundaries. In this context, the members of different ethnic groups developed a common culture, which made them into a nation. This culture typically consisted of a language, a religion, education and folk arts. For Karl Deutsch, a people or nation is 'a community of social communication' based on a common culture (Deutsch, 1966). In a more developed polity and economy this became a 'high culture', with universities, art, literature and music. Such was the cultural nature of the transition from ethnicity to nationhood.

While nations have their origins in ethnic groups, it is not easy to determine exactly how or when they arose. The prevailing view is that nations came about in the modern age because of a special combination of political, economic and cultural processes and events. There are many theories which explain the emergence of nationalism in the modern world, and well-known recent ones are by Karl Deutsch, Michael Hechter, Stein Rokkan, Ernest Gellner, Walker Connor, Benedict Anderson, Anthony Smith, Eric Hobsbawm, Tom Nairn and Liah Greenfeld. These are chosen because of their importance, and because they illustrate some of the arguments discussed above. A short summary of each of these theories is provided, as well as an opinion as to its merits and drawbacks. Of course, the reader will have to make up his or her own mind in the light of the discussion as to which is the most convincing theory.

There are many other theories about the emergence of nationalism in the modern world. Various 'Readers' and collections of writings on nationalism have been produced which give excerpts from well-known writings on nationalism and ethnicity (e.g. Hutchinson and Smith, 1994; Hutchinson and Smith, 1996; Woolf, 1996). There is even an *Encyclopedia of Nationalism* (Snyder, 1990).

Deutsch's Theory of Nationalism

Karl Deutsch, the American political scientist, wrote *Nationalism and Social Communication: An Inquiry into the Foundations of Nationality* in 1953, with a 2nd edition in 1966. It has become a classic in the study of nationalism, although it has its critics (e.g. Smith, 1983, p. 100), and it has not had many imitators in subsequent writings on the subject.

Deutsch was unusual in seeking to quantify and measure the elements of nationality, looking particularly at 'social communication' (common language and interpersonal transactions of all kinds). A people or nation is defined by the 'complementarity or relative efficiency of communication among individuals' (Deutsch, 1966, p. 188). Behind the reasoning of this theory was the then-fashionable 'systems theory' derived from cybernetics, with its measurement and use of 'messages' which sustain a system. Deutsch also represents the school of thought which sees nations and nationalism as the product of 'modernisation', the

> social mobilisation which accompanies the growth of markets, industries, and towns, and eventually of literacy and mass communication. The trends in this underlying process of social

mobilization could do much to decide whether existing national trends in particular countries would be continued or reversed. (Deutsch, 1966, p.188)

As Deutsch admits, 'this is largely a book on research and methods of research' rather than on nationalist movements. But it attracted attention to the basis of the nation as being a pattern of transactions which marked it off from other nations, thus broadening the focus from language to all kinds of social and economic data. It also asserted 'modernisation' theory, which was to prove so popular in the 1960s and 1970s, but which is now largely discredited.

When one looks at how particular examples of nationalism are treated by Deutsch, one sees the difficulty of relating such data to political movements. Thus, while Deutsch correctly plots the decline of the Gaelic-speaking and agricultural population of Scotland, he entirely fails to relate this convincingly to Scottish nationalism, which was based on other considerations. Nevertheless, an analysis of communication networks in Scotland, marking it off from England, would have been a good way to measure the functioning of the Scottish political system and its potentiality for nationalism.

Hechter's Theory of 'Internal Colonialism'

Michael Hechter's *Internal Colonialism: The Celtic Fringe in British National Development, 1536–1966* (1975) is another landmark contribution to the study of nationalism, especially in the British context. Hechter, an American, was, like Deutsch, attracted to the research methodology of providing quantitative evidence to support his thesis. He was also influenced by 'modernisation theory' or 'diffusion theory' which, like that of Deutsch, posits the view that 'from interaction will come commonality' and ethnic homogenisation (Hechter, 1975, p. 7).

Hechter, however, reacted against diffusion theory, and posited instead 'internal colonialism'. He maintained that modernisation and increased contact between ethnic groups within a state will not necessarily bring about ethnic unity, but will be just as likely to lead to ethnic conflict. This is because the inequalities between the regions in a country will relegate peripheral regions to an inferior position, leaving the core region dominant. The reaction to this in the peripheral regions will be hostility to the core, and if these regions are also national in character, this will take the form of nationalism. Thus Hechter saw Scottish, Welsh and Irish nationalism as the result of internal colonialism by the English core.

Hechter's book was published before the rise of Scottish and Welsh nationalism in the late 1960s, but he has published since on the subject (Hechter, 1985). The principal change between the two publications is in the nature of his 'cultural division of labour' theory. This theory states that in a situation of internal colonialism, there will be a social stratification of ethnic or cultural groups, with the core group occupying the best class positions and the peripheral groups the inferior positions. This corresponds to a 'colonising' nation and 'colonised' nations. Thus, in Britain, the English are the colonisers, and the Scots, Welsh and Irish the colonised.

Unfortunately for this theory, the facts seem to be at variance with such a division of labour. For example, Scots are not in practice relegated to inferior social positions in Britain, and Scotland has been as much an industrialised and imperial nation as England from the eighteenth century. This is not to say that there are not important regional inequalities in Britain, due to uneven economic development and to government and commercial policies favouring the south of England. All these have contributed to a rise in nationalism in Scotland and Wales.

Hechter took account of the criticisms levied at his theory (e.g. Page, 1978; Greenberg, 1980; Brand, 1985) and revised the 'cultural division of labour' thesis (a hierarchical stratification) as regards Scotland to a 'segmental cultural division of labour' (a vertical stratification) in which Scots occupy 'occupational niches' deriving from the distinctiveness of their national institutions, such as law and education. These may not be inferior positions to those found in England, since they include high-class occupations. So the group solidarity of 'colonised' nations and their assumed conflict with the colonisers is now called into doubt. By 1985 Hechter saw the capacity of nationalist organisations to attract support as being as important as the structure of internal colonialism (Hechter, 1985, p. 25). Nevertheless, his model remains a compelling one in many contexts (if not clearly in Scotland), and it will be returned to in the context of nationalisms in many parts of the world. The recurrence of a cultural division of labour in most multiethnic societies is particularly striking.

Rokkan's Theory of Regionalism

While not strictly a theory of nationalism, Stein Rokkan's work on regionalism in Europe with Derek Urwin (Rokkan and Urwin, 1982; 1983) is relevant to 'nation-building' and the problems of core–periphery relationships. It also deals extensively with 'the politicisation of peripheral predicaments' and 'the central response'.

Rejecting the 'diffusion' model of Deutsch, but not endorsing the 'internal colonial' model of Hechter, Rokkan and Urwin conclude that

> there is no simple centre–periphery polarity across culture, economics and politics. Peripheral predicaments and politicisation emerge out of the incongruity between cultural, economic and political roles, an incongruity which has existed on the continent as long as there have been states. While this remains unresolved, the potential for territorial problems remains, irrespective of the waxing and waning of individual parties or movements. (Rokkan and Urwin, 1983, p. 192)

It appears then, that it is a matter of degree whether the 'incongruity between cultural, economic and political roles' will lead to nationalism in particular situations. Rokkan has shown that students of nationalism ought to measure the degree of harmony between such roles in a state. They should then be able to predict that a strong mismatch between these roles will lead to nationalism.

Gellner's Theory of Nationalism

Ernest Gellner's Nations and Nationalism (Gellner, 1983) represents a type of theory which stresses the primacy of material conditions in shaping political thought and social change. In this it resembles Marxism, which Gellner nevertheless disavows. He proposes a fundamentally economic reason for the rise of nationalism. This is the development of 'industrial society', which took place in certain parts of Europe at the end of the eighteenth century, and then during the nineteenth and twentieth centuries throughout most of the world.

The connection between nationalism and industrialisation is that particular forms of polity and culture are required if industrial economic growth is to occur. These forms combine in the nation-state. Once industrialisation took off, the old states were generally unable to maximise their advantages and profits until they changed both their cultural life and their state structure.

In place of the feudal or agrarian society, with its diversity of languages, cultures and ethnic groups, there had to be a homogeneous society with an educational system for all. This education would train workers and managers for industry, and provide all with a common 'high culture'. It was necessary to have one common language in a modern industrial society, for the mobility and division of labour would come from that, and from the education that all received.

Gellner, unlike many other writers on nationalism, does not believe that nationalism happened because some European thinkers invented it and forced it on political systems which would have been better off without it. Rather, he believes that nationalism 'has very deep roots in our shared current condition, is not at all contingent, and will not easily be denied' (ibid., p. 56). This means that nationalism achieved its successes because it was appropriate for the needs of the time, rather than as an ideology which could be accepted or rejected intellectually in competition with other ideologies.

At this point, attention focuses on another necessary condition for nationalism, the changing structure of the state. The medieval European state was unsuited to the task which industrialisation demanded. It was generally weak at the centre, preferring to operate through semi-independent aristocrats and churches. While some monarchies, such as those of England, France and Prussia, began to reduce the power of the barons and the church in the name of royal 'sovereignty', there was little attempt to achieve a uniform culture within these countries.

Indeed, several languages continued to be spoken in most countries, and often the king himself was imported from a foreign land. George I of Great Britain, for example, came to the throne in 1714 from Hanover in Germany, and spoke German, not English. There was little public education, and most education went to aspiring churchmen, lawyers and landowners. This was often in Latin, a non-vernacular and pretty useless language as far as economic and social change was concerned. Only with a state education system in the vernacular, geared to the needs of industry, could progress be made. This meant a strong, centralised state, and a population free to work where it wished, without barriers of a feudal, religious or linguistic nature. The breakdown of the feudal state, and the emergence of centralised 'sovereign' authority was important for the development of nationalism, for it provided a strong state structure from which a homogeneous nation could be shaped. Control by the political authority from the centre over education, religion and law, swept away many local cultures or ethnicities, and replaced them with one large nation. In this way, 'nation-states' emerged. Where these were not formed, and the principle of 'one state, one culture' was denied, there was nationalist activity. While this theory applies particularly to the historic development of nationalism in Europe, it has clear relevance to new states (especially in the Developing World) which are not 'nation-states' in the sense defined by Gellner.

Gellner's theory is compelling, but it has its limitations. There is little here about the primordial roots of nationalism, and its powerful emotional appeal. Why should people be prepared to die for what is in this analysis an imperative of a rational economic and social system of industrialisation? Nationalist behaviour in its contemporary form is hardly explained in this theory. It has been called 'apolitical' (O'Leary, 1997) since it neglects the role of power politics in explaining nations and nationalism. It deals instead with the reasons why industrialising states adopted a national form in order to prosper, and the nationalism which was associated with that.

At one point, Gellner does address the question of the sharpness of nationalist conflict, but he relies again on a socioeconomic explanation. In the early industrial age, he says, wide social chasms and the uneven diffusion of industrialisation produced social conflicts, especially when cultural (i.e. national) differences marked off these chasms. When cultural differences did not correspond to class divisions, 'nothing much happened' (p. 121):

> Classes, however oppressed and exploited, did not overturn the political system when they could not define themselves 'ethnically'. Only when a nation became a class, a visible and unequally distributed category in an otherwise mobile system, did it become politically conscious and activist. Only when a class happened to be (more or less) a 'nation' did it turn from being a class-in-itself into a class-for-itself, or a nation-for-itself. Neither nations nor classes seem to be political catalysts: only nation-classes or class-nations are such. (Ibid.)

In this rather obscure passage, Gellner attempts to reconcile class analysis with nationalism, something which Marxists also seek to do. The main difference between Gellner's theory and that of most Marxists is that Gellner sees nationalism as the concomitant of any type of industrialisation, while most Marxists make nationalism dependent on capitalism as such. With the arrival of proletarian rule, according to Marx, nationalism becomes redundant. Gellner, on the other hand, does not see any future situation without nationalism.

Gellner's discussion of the matching of class and national divisions has a clear parallel in Hechter's theory of internal colonialism, with its 'cultural division of labour'. But, in his desire to establish the nation-state as the norm for modern society, Gellner has to reject 'multicultural society'. For him, a homogeneous culture, at least at the level of 'high culture', is necessary for modern states, although there may be room for innocuous folk cultures 'in a token and cellophane-packaged form' (p. 121). There is no place in his theory for cultural pluralism and 'consociational democracy', which tries to combine different national cultures within one state (see Chapter 9).

We can accept much of Gellner's historical analysis of how nation-states and nationalism emerged strongly at the time of industrialisation in Europe, when the breakdown of feudalism had taken place. It is more difficult to find in Gellner an explanation for the emergence of nationalism in pre-industrial times (e.g. Scotland in the Middle Ages, or England in Elizabethan times), and in non-industrialised countries in the Developing World. Moreover, nationalism arising out of 'post-materialist values' in 'post-industrial' societies (Inglehart, 1977) is clearly different from nationalism resulting from industrialisation. In all these contexts the conditions are different from those in nineteenth century nationalist Europe. Many nationalisms are found in countries which are largely agrarian, non-industrialised and non-centralised. A very important determinant of nationalism in the Developing World is the legacy of colonialism, and the independence movements directed against 'white rule'. Contemporary nationalisms have arisen in long-industrialised countries such as Britain, Belgium and Spain, which Gellner might have called nation-states. Something new seems to have happened there, outside Gellner's theory.

Nevertheless, Gellner's short book is a masterly study of the emergence of nationalism in history, and is a yardstick with which we can measure other writings on nationalism. It does not tell us all we want to know, but it gives us a clear theory relating nationalism to industrialisation, 'high culture', and the structure of the modern state.

Walker Connor: An Ethnonationalist

Walker Connor is an American political scientist who has engaged in a vigorous debate on nationalism with fellow academics since the 1960s. A specialist on the former Soviet Union, he pointed to its fatal national divisions when other political scientists were inclined to accept the official communist view that nationalism had been transcended by socialism. In the end it appears that he was proved right, since the Soviet Union has broken up along national lines.

The best source for his work is his collected writings, *Ethnonationalism: The Question for Understanding* (Connor, 1994), which includes his attack on American scholarship about nationalism, 'Nation-building or nation-destroying?', and on the prevailing confusion in terminology ('A Nation is a Nation, Is a State, Is an Ethnic Group, Is a ...'). Unlike Marxists, and most sociologists, Connor believes in the inevitable existence of nations throughout history and in the superior power of nationalism (as compared to economics, social class, etc.) to shape the world. He is an almost lone primordialist in the hostile environment of the social sciences, where contextualism and constructivism rule supreme. ('Contextualism' states that nations and nationalism are the products of particular historic and social contexts, and 'constructivisim' states that nations and nationalism are constructs of nationalists, not 'natural' (primordial phenomena). While he probably goes too far in this direction, since the actual history of nations is closely bound up in ever-changing contexts of a political and economic kind, Connor stands out as one of the few theorists who accept nationalism on its own terms, and as an inescapable fact of human nature. The advantage of this empathy is that he can understand and explain ethnocentrism (and its accompaniment, nationalism) wherever it occurs as a powerful force in human nature. He is not taken by surprise at its strength and recurrence, as have been so many social scientists. Unlike them, he does not reject nationalism; indeed, he favours it.

Benedict Anderson's Theory

Benedict Anderson's book, *Imagined Communities: Reflections on the Origin and Spread of Nationalism* (Anderson, 1983), is another recent major contribution to the study of the evolution of nationalism.

Anderson is more of a 'constructivist' and a 'contextualist' than a 'primordialist', but, unlike Gellner, he is concerned to explore the psychological appeal of nationalism, which is close to a primordial approach: 'What makes people love and die for nations, as well as hate and kill in their name?' (Ibid., dustjacket). Obviously, a purely functional approach such as Gellner's will not explain the emotions engendered by nationalism, yet Anderson does not go to the other extreme of a sociobiological or primordial interpretation. He takes a historical, rather than a timeless, universalist approach, so that nationalism is seen to emerge at a specific period in European history. Anderson's originality lies in his explanation of how and why people in certain circumstances come to 'imagine' themselves part of a nation, and why such an 'imagined community' has such a powerful attraction for them.

He first builds up a set of necessary conditions for the emergence of nationalism. These are partly material, and partly psychic. More subtly, he analyses the 'pilgrimages' which people make in their social and economic lives. It is these pilgrimages which define the boundaries of the nation, and lead people to identify with it and not with another social or political entity. Such pilgrimages may thus be taken to be the sufficient condition for particular nations to be 'imagined' and form the focus of nationalism. This seems to be a combination of Deutsch's community of communication, and Hechter's cultural division of labour.

The principal material precondition for nationalism, according to Anderson, is what he calls 'print-capitalism', meaning commercial printing on a widespread scale. It is this which spreads the idea of the nation and the ideology of nationalism, not only within one nation, but throughout the world. Through print-capitalism, vernacular languages are strengthened by the publishing of dictionaries and literature generally. In this way, nations are 'imagined' by many people, and linguistic nationalisms take root. Printing standardises languages, and also aids the development of capitalism and the centralised state. A sense of nationality flows from the common language and education which printing facilitates. But the emergence of nationalism also depended on some other 'modernising' processes, such as scientific discoveries and the exploration of the world. These broke down old ways of looking at society, and also broke the unity of Christendom and the Moslem world, with their associated international languages, Latin and Arabic. The monarchical state too, with its 'divine right of kings' and hierarchical authority structure, gradually gave way to rule 'by the people'.

At this point, Anderson links up with Gellner's theory, which connects nationalism with modernisation and the needs of the industrial state. But he goes further than Gellner by explaining the emotional power of nationalism. He draws attention to nationalism's appeal as a faith in an everlasting life through membership of a continuing nation. The nation represents the continuity of the extended family from one generation to the next. In an age of declining religion, with its belief in an afterlife, nationalism has a special appeal as a 'secular transformation of fatality into continuity, contingency into meaning' (p. 19). Anderson stresses the character of nationalism, not as a political ideology self-consciously followed, but as a cultural system with religious characteristics.

By pursuing the notion of 'pilgrimages' – essentially the pattern of social communication and 'life chances' of different peoples – Anderson is able to explain why nationalism has been found in every type of society in the modern world. The nation is often the social grouping which represents the boundary for mobility, both geographic and economic. This may be a matter of sharing a common language, or of being the object of differential treatment by the state. If an individual is identified as the member of a particular nation, this may give access to power and wealth, or conversely, discrimination and deprivation.

In the first instance, it is the state which determines which 'pilgrimages' can be made by members of different nations within it. Indeed, the state may decide who the members of the nations are. It does this to protect the interests of the powerful, and to keep other groups in a subordinate position. This is not necessarily anything to do with industrialisation (as in Gellner's theory), but is much more about political and social power generally. (For an extended treatment of the role of the state in shaping nationalism and the character of ethnicity, see Paul Brass (ed.), *Ethnic Groups and the State*, 1985; John Breuilly, *Nationalism and the State*, 1982, 1985, 1993).

This means that the development of nationalism can be analysed in almost any society, and not just in industrial society. For wherever a system of status and power divisions is based on nationality, nationalism is likely to flourish. This was the case in the multinational empires of Europe, and in the European colonies in America, Asia and Africa. In these areas, the imperial system confined the life chances or 'pilgrimages' of natives (including Europeans born there, known as 'creoles' in Latin America) to the colonies. Eventually, these natives saw themselves as members of a nation in rebellion against the imperial country. In this way, nationalism was born in the colonies. It was led by two groups, called by Anderson, 'pilgrim creole functionaries and provincial creole printmen'. The former were administrators and businessmen of native or creole origins, and the latter native/creole intellectuals and writers whose publications inspired national consciousness. Because of the policies of imperialism, they were cut off from advancement in the imperial home country and followed their 'pilgrimages', or careers, in the colonies, which they came to perceive as separate nations in rebellion against the imperial country.

A later refinement of the concept of 'pilgrimages' relates to 'official nationalism', which reacts against the new vernacular (in this book 'social' or 'ethnic') nationalisms. Fearing the break-up of the state through nationalist separatism, the old dynastic states begin a nationalism of their own. They try to impose a particular national culture on the whole state, and make that the condition for advancement, socially, politically and economically. Thus, the Russian Empire of the Czars instituted the policy of 'Russification', making the use of the Russian language obligatory throughout the Empire (this policy was also followed by the communists in the USSR). In the ex-colonies in Africa and Asia which gained independence after 1950, similar official nationalisms can be found, linking successful 'pilgrimages' in their societies to the adoption of a national language and culture sponsored by the state.

The title *Imagined Communities* points to the mental processes involved in nationalism. Members of even the smallest nation can never know most of their fellow nationals, 'yet in the minds of each lives the image of their communion' (p. 15). This is not a question of 'false consciousness', for there are, Anderson says, no 'true' communities larger than face-to-face primordial villages. All other communities are imagined.

Anderson introduces new perspectives into the study of how nationalism has evolved. But there is ambiguity in his definition of a nation and in his account of the conditions for the emergence of nationalism. Nations are no more 'imagined' than other social categories and identities, such as class, and defining what is 'real' rather than 'imagined' in social affairs is a cul-de-sac. And the social preconditions for nationalism are ambiguous. Printing could destroy nations as well as create them. Many languages and nations (or ethnic groups) have died or been weakened in competition with literary languages and nations possessing printing resources.

As for religion, it seems that it is not always replaced by nationalism, but may go hand in hand with it. We have seen that churches have reinforced nationalism in such countries as Ireland, Poland, Armenia, Israel and Iran. It is difficult, therefore, to relate the rise of nationalism to the decline of religion, except perhaps in some mainly secular societies. In some cases, religion and nationalism thrive together; in others, where a church is strongly supranational (as the Roman Catholic Church, or Islam), there may be tension between loyalty to religion and loyalty to the state or nation. However, even supranational churches can underpin nationalist movements against oppressive states which deny nationalism its free expression. Thus the Roman Catholic Church and Islam are closely involved with nationalism in eastern Europe and Asia.

Anderson's use of the idea of 'pilgrimages', points to the pattern of communication and social mobility as a powerful binding force in the consciousness and action of social groups (as Karl Deutsch did earlier). But there seems to be a prior question here: why do ethnic or national groups crop up so often in social stratification? Why do people seem to prefer their fellow nationals as companions on their pilgrimages, and why do states use nationality as a method of dividing power? Can there be something special about nationality which is not present in other social, economic and political divisions? Our final theorist, Anthony Smith, focuses on this in the ethnic origins of nationalism, and its special characteristics.

Anthony Smith's Theory of Nationalism

Anthony D. Smith's book *The Ethnic Origins of Nations* (1986) focuses on ethnicity as the precursor of nationalism, and gives an explanation of the transition from ethnic identities and loyalties to those relating to nations. For Smith, 'modern nations simply extend, deepen and streamline the ways in which members of *ethnie* [Smith's term for ethnic groups] associated and communicated. They do not introduce startlingly novel elements, or change the goals of human association and communication' (p. 215).

He is thus concerned to emphasise the continuity between ethnic identities and loyalties on the one hand and nationhood and nationalism on the other. In contrast, both Gellner and Anderson stress the essential *novelty* and *modernity* of nationalism. Smith does acknowledge the changes which made ethnicity into nationalism, and his explanations are similar to Gellner's and Anderson's. For example, the decline of religion, the rise of the centralised and bureaucratic state, as well as the pressures of the industrial economy are necessary for 'ethnie' to be mobilised and politicised into nations. But the 'new imaginings' and new thoughts (clearly a reference to Anderson's *Imagined Communities*) which lead people into national consciousness and nationalism are not really so new. Their essence can be found in pre-national communities at least as far back as Ancient Greece and Rome, although there was an ambivalence at that time about 'the masses' and their claim to be included in the 'ethnie'. Apart from this, Smith concludes:

> it is clear that modern nations and nationalism have only extended and deepened the meanings and scope of older ethnic concepts and structures. Nationalism has certainly universalized these structures and ideals, but modern 'civic' nations have not in practice really transcended ethnicity or national sentiments ... In terms of ends, as opposed to means, there is a remarkable continuity between nations and *ethnie*, nationalism and ethnicism; continuity but not identity. (p. 216)

Smith moves the study of nationalism back to the pre-modern period, as Hans Kohn did in *The Idea of Nationalism* (1944). But Smith sees more in common between modern nations and their precursors than Kohn did. At the same time, Smith talks of 'continuity but not identity' between 'ethnicism' and nationalism. Nationalism is more concerned with statehood or some form of self-government than 'ethnicism', which is less clearly political. Nevertheless, 'nationalism ... does more effectively what premodern ethnicists tried to do, that is, keep out foreigners and diffuse to their kinsmen the traditions and myths of their ancestors, using the modern mass education system' (p. 216).

Smith here echoes Gellner's theory of nationalism, where the latter speaks of the nation's education system and 'high culture' engendering cultural homogeneity. But Gellner saw this in functional terms: the means to economic efficiency in a developed industrial state. Smith, on the other hand, dwells on the traditional or pre-modern content to national culture, which has little to do with industrialisation. National myths, old languages, and so on, are the substance of nationalism as much as modernising communications and education, and Smith's theory is better able to cope with these than Gellner's (Smith and Gellner debated nationalism in public, shortly before Gellner died. See 'The Warwick Debate', *Nations and Nationalism*, vol. 2, part 3 (November 1996), pp. 357–88).

Where Smith seems to leave questions unanswered is regarding the transition from ethnicity to nationalism, and in the strength or weakness of particular nationalisms. 'Continuity, but not identity' between ethnicity and nationalism opens up as many problems as it solves, similar to those involving the connection between human nature and nationalism, or between ethnocentrism and nationalism.

Eric Hobsbawm: A Marxist Historian of Nationalism

Hobsbawm's name is very well-known throughout the world as a historian of social movements. He has also paid particular attention to nationalism, which he detests. He attacks the views of fellow-Marxist Tom Nairn (see below), who favours nationalism, especially in his native Scotland. In 1990 Hobsbawm published *Nations and Nationalism since 1780: Programme, Myth, Reality* (2nd edn, 1992), in which he supports the classic Marxist view of nationalism as 'false consciousness', and a 'bourgeois' construction, doomed to extinction along with that class. Indeed, he believes that the late twentieth century has witnessed the beginning of nationalism's final demise. Although he is no longer clearly an old-style communist, he certainly supports a non-nationalist, left-wing social and political system. Hobsbawm takes a cosmopolitan view of society, in which nations and nationalism have no positive role. He is anti-nationalist, having witnessed what he considers its evil ways in twentieth century Europe (in later books, *Age of Extremes* (1994) and *On History* (1997), he continues the attack).

The problem with Hobsbawm's approach is its *a priori* reasoning from Marxist principles. This makes it difficult for him to accept the facts. The end of the twentieth century has seen a revival of nationalism, and the collapse of communism. So, on two major counts, Hobsbawm seems to have got it wrong. But it would require a longer-term perspective, from the next century, to provide the proof of that.

Tom Nairn and the 'Break-up of Britain'

Tom Nairn published his book *The Break-Up of Britain* in 1977 (2nd edn, 1981). Nairn is (or was) a committed Marxist, who nevertheless considers nationalism progressive in Marxist terms, especially in Britain. He supports Scottish nationalism, if not necessarily the Scottish National Party (SNP), and predicted that it was going to break up the British state. He provides a wealth of theoretical and factual evidence for this view. His approach is mainly materialist, in that he explains nationalism as the result of uneven capitalist development, and Scottish nationalism in particular he attributes to the end of the British Empire and the discovery of North Sea oil. These gave the Scots a rational economic motive for going independent.

He was immediately attacked by Eric Hobsbawm in the pages of the *New Left Review* (1977) for the nationalist heresy in socialist thinking. Hobsbawm believed that socialism and nationalism were incompatible, in line with Marx. In fact, both Nairn and Hobsbawm got it wrong at the time of writing. Britain did not break up as predicted by Nairn, and nationalism remained a progressive force, at least in Britain, despite Hobsbawm. The debate between Hobsbawm and Nairn is of particular interest to those who want to study the treatment of nationalism in Marxism. It is conducted at a high level of theoretical abstraction, as well as political commitment, but with a rather remote connection to actual political events (e.g. the relative failure of both the Communist Party and the SNP in electoral terms).

Liah Greenfeld's 'Five Roads to Modernity'

Greenfeld's book, *Nationalism: Five Roads to Modernity* (Greenfeld, 1992), is often referred to in sociological discussions of nationalism. She maintains that 'nationalism lies at the basis of the world', because it is the 'constitutive principle of modernity' (p. 491). This is because modernity breaks down the old 'society of orders' and replaces it with an open, socially mobile one. In that society, nation and nationalism are essential ingredients, since they provide status and dignity, where previously these were based on aristocracy, the church, and wealth.

Greenfeld examines England, France, Russia, Germany and the United States of America (USA) for the development of national identity and consciousness over 500 years. She gives a very detailed 'sociological history', but not a Marxist nor other materialist one. Her book can be compared to another well-known work by the historian Linda Colley: *Britons. Forging the Nation, 1707–1837* (1992). Greenfeld is strong on social psychology and cultural history, but rather obscure as a describer of events. The terms 'modernity' and 'post-modernity' are slippery concepts, and nationalism does not necessarily belong with either (see Table 4.1, and pp. 82–3, below). One writer who places nationalism in a 'post-modern' or 'post-materialist' context is Ronald Inglehart (Inglehart, 1977). Both Inglehart and Greenfeld agree that a desire for status lies at the root of nationalism. The *politics* of nationalism and ethnicity do not emerge clearly from Greenfeld's book. But it is a marker in the literature on nationalism, nevertheless.

The theories discussed here are important to an understanding of nationalism, because they seek to explain how nationalism came to dominate world politics in the modern period. In comparison to the study of human nature and the study of political ideas, they stress the periodisation of history, and the particular contexts in which nationalism arose. They locate nationalism in time and place, rather than in the universals of 'ethnocentrism' and the 'idea of nationalism'. In the theories discussed in this chapter, it is apparent that developments in history are closely related to the emergence of nationalism in different parts of the world at different periods.

However, we are still some way from explaining these particular nationalisms. Once more, the 'necessary' conditions for nationalism in general are not the 'sufficient' conditions for nationalist movements to emerge and thrive. This means that we must go beyond the theories discussed so far to look for other explanations for the strengths and weaknesses of nationalist movements. We have to look at a variety of theories or explanations which focus not so much on the historical emergence of nationalism on the world scene as on contemporary nationalist political behaviour and the politics of cultural pluralism.

4

Ethnic and Social Nationalism

The idea of nationalism and the ideal of the 'nation-state' were not necessarily based on ethnicity. Rather they stressed the voluntary coming together of people in a state with a shared culture. That is how Gellner analyses the character of 'nation-states'. For him, ethnicity is not a 'given', but a construct of the state itself.

Yet in modern times, especially in the twentieth century, ethnicity has come to be more important in politics, and ethnic nationalism (or 'ethnonationalism') has been the distinguishing characteristic of one form of nationalism. This may be because ethnicity gives a higher status to citizenship, and therefore provides people more with a heightened sense of dignity than individualistic 'social' or 'civic' nationalism (Greenfeld, 1992, p. 490). In essence this is 'exclusive' nationalism, since it excludes from membership of the nation those people who do not share a common ethnicity, which usually means common descent.

A more open form of nationalism is what is here called 'social nationalism' (a more common term for it today is 'civic' or 'civil' nationalism). This is based on a shared national culture, but not on common descent. It is 'inclusive' in the sense that anyone can adopt that culture and join the nation, even if that person is not considered to be a member of the 'ethnic nation'. It is thus more individualist than collectivist in origin. 'Social nationalism' can be distinguished from 'ethnic nationalism' on the one hand and 'official (or state) nationalism' on the other, the latter being essentially based on patriotism, with no necessary ethnic or cultural basis.

These categories are in practice not always mutually exclusive, and their meaning can be further clarified by actual examples, which show how they can be applied in the contemporary world:

Ethnic nationalism: the nationalism of ethnic groups such as the Kurds, Latvians and Tamils, who define their nation in exclusive terms, mainly on the basis of common descent. In this type of nationalism, no one can 'become' a Kurd, Latvian or Tamil through adopting Kurdish, Latvian or Tamil ways. That is not to say that citizenship might not be available for 'non-ethnics', but there are usually tests and other restrictions for suitability.

Social nationalism: the nationalism of a nation which defines itself by social ties and culture rather than by common descent. This type of nationalism stresses the shared sense of national identity, community and culture, but outsiders can join the nation if they identify with it and adopt its social characteristics. Thus Scots, Catalans, Ukrainians and Russians accept as members of their nations those who do not ethnically belong, but who become Scots, Catalans, Ukrainians and Russians by joining the nation socially and culturally. There will probably be immigration restrictions in states formed as social nations, however. These will be officially justified on non-ethnic grounds.

Official nationalism: the nationalism of the state, encompassing all those legally entitled to be citizens, irrespective of their ethnicity, national identity and culture. Some states are correctly called 'nation-states' in the sense that the state is exclusively composed of an ethnic nation or a social nation. Most states, however, are multiethnic and multinational. For example, the United Kingdom consists of four nations (England, Scotland, Wales, and part of Ireland), but it is also possible to talk of a British nation and British nationalism. This 'official nation' and 'official nationalism' is based on British citizens and their patriotism. But there are also within Britain 'social nationalisms' in Scotland and Wales, with nationalist parties seeking statehood for these nations. In Northern Ireland, Irish nationalists seek the unification of Ireland, which would include all the population of the island, irrespective of religion and ethnicity. Nevertheless, there are strong ethnic overtones to the political discourse in Northern Ireland: there is a 'Loyalist or Unionist people' and a 'Nationalist or Republican people', whose characteristics are ethnic as well as religious (Protestant/Catholic) and political (British/Irish). There are some ethnic nationalists in Great Britain whose aims are

'England for the English', 'Scotland for the Scots' and 'Wales for the Welsh', but they are either on the extreme right of politics or are mainly interested in promoting cultural nationalism.

A state such as the USA is multiethnic and one social nation. While American nationalism might be considered to be no more than patriotism (official nationalism) rather than social nationalism, in fact it involves more than showing loyalty to the state. It means the adoption of American national culture, in language, education, the media and social behaviour. Thus patriotism and cultural homogeneity go hand in hand. Britain, too, while it has official nationalism, is in part an ethnic and social nation. There is much intermarriage between the ethnic groups, especially the Scots, Welsh, English and Irish (but not between Protestant and Catholics in Northern Ireland), so that their separate ethnicity is now somewhat indistinct. More defined is the ethnicity of the recent immigrants from the New Commonwealth, who are much less likely to intermarry with other ethnic groups. The 'social nation' in Britain is represented by the common British culture, especially its history and Royal Family, its media, education, business and politics.

Ethnic and social nationalisms pose a threat to any state which does not have a common ethnicity or a shared identity and culture. To overcome this, it must either become an ethnic nation-state, or a social nation-state, or a multinational state which guarantees ethnic or social rights to the nations within it. The last type of state will give official recognition to cultural pluralism, and its ideal constitutional form is consociational democracy (see Chapter 9). This is based on 'power-sharing' between the cultural groups (nations/ethnic groups/religious or ideological communities) in the state.

Why has *ethnic* nationalism come to assume such importance in contemporary politics? It may seem paradoxical that an apparently 'primordial' identity, pre-modern in origin, should be a hallmark of contemporary political behaviour. Primordial or instinctive behaviour is not bound by time, but its expression changes as the context changes. Thus what we have to understand in order to explain ethnic and social nationalism is a combination of timeless determinants of political behaviour and particular contexts. To make this task clearer, we return to the three-fold scheme used in discussing theories of the emergence and evolution of nationalism. For we can analyse separately the political, economic and cultural aspects, and their interactions, which make up an explanation for the emergence and importance of *ethnic* and *social* nationalism, in the same way as was done for nationalism generally.

Nationalism results from changes in the character of politics, the economy and culture. However, these changes lead to ambiguous results, and it is very difficult to predict that ethnic or social nationalism, rather than some other outcome, will follow these changes. Moreover, it is clear that nationalisms in different parts of the world relate to widely differing political, economic and cultural contexts. For example, in Table 4.1, the relationship between ethnic nationalism and 'post-industrial society' and 'consumerism' is not as obviously found in Developing World

Table 4.1 *Ethnic and social nationalism*

Politics *Power expectations/ capabilities*	Economy *Material interests*	Culture *'Psychic income'*

Democracy (self-rule)
Opposition to
  domination,
  discrimination and
  exclusion
	Uneven development
	and cultural division
	of labour
		Search for
		  identity and
		  status
		Increased
		  literacy

Nation-state Consociational democracy		

Nation-building
(v. imperialism, internal
colonialism)
		Increased
		  cultural
		  homogeneity

Consumerism (v. centralisation)	Decline of class divisions	Revival of ethnic cultures and/or

Post-industrial
politics (e.g. Green parties
and nationalist parties)
	Growth of
	  status divisions
		'Post-materialist
		  values'

State power v. divided nations	'Post-industrial society'	

ethnic nationalisms, for these have a different political, economic and cultural context. Their ethnic politics is based more on primordial 'communalism' than on a sophisticated type of democratic politics arising out of an advanced economy. The new intensity of ethnic politics in the Developing World can be explained only by modifying the model to take account of the different context to be found there. Even so, the *direction* of politics in the Developing World is towards those features, such as democratic politics rather than empire, and rising political consumer choice rather than monopoly. So the model above indicates a universal linkage between particular forms of politics, economy and culture. Once more, however, we are at the stage of specifying necessary rather than sufficient conditions, although we are all the time getting closer to the latter. When we examine specific nationalist movements in later chapters, we shall see to what extent this scheme is useful in particular cases.

Politics

In politics, the focus is on power, expressed in terms of authority and the challenge to authority. Those who achieve political power command political structures, most typically the state, but also a wide range of polities from empires to local authorities. In nation-states a nation wields power through the medium of the state. In a multinational state or empire, nations may compete with each other in a hierarchy of domination, discrimination and exclusion. These are the conditions leading to anti-state political nationalism.

Those who are not in power, but who are challengers to those in power, operate in some political systems through political parties, and in others through movements and terrorist organisations. In the politics of nationalism we have ruling national parties, opposition nationalist parties, nationalist movements, national liberation armies, and so on. Each of these relates to the nature of the state, as the focus of political power. Some nationalists seek to defend the state, others to overthrow it. The differences can be explained when one examines the ethnic nature of the state. If one ethnic group controls the state, then its nationalism is expressed as official nationalism or patriotism. Hence the ruling (to 1994) National Party in South Africa was essentially the party of the white Afrikaners, and the ruling (to 1994) United National Party in Sri Lanka was the party of the Sinhalese. But an ethnic group which does not control the state expresses its nationalism in opposition to the state. Hence, the African National Congress until 1994 was opposed to the structure of the South African state, and was banned by it from 1962 to 1989. The Liberation Tigers of Tamil Eelam ('Tamil Tigers') wage war on the Sri Lankan state. Such actions as the banning of parties or movements – the Tamil United Liberation Front (TULF) in Sri Lanka, the Palestine Liberation Organisation (PLO) in Israel – and the imposition of direct rule from Delhi on the Punjab, undercut the local moderate parties and make it more difficult to keep ethnic nationalism on a non-violent path. Instead, extremist or terrorist organisations tend to occupy the gap left by the absence of the more moderate, representative bodies.

In a state organised along 'consociational' lines, the situation is not as polarised. Ethnic nationalist parties, and ethnic sections of state-wide parties, are not anti-state, but seek maximum power within the state. Thus the Fleming and Walloon nationalist parties in Belgium, and the Fleming and Walloon Socialist and Christian Social Parties, seek the maximum power for their ethnic groups within the Belgian state on a consociational or 'power-sharing' basis.

Why has ethnic nationalism come to rival official nationalism or patriotism in politics today? A purely political explanation is not possible, as there are political, economic and cultural elements involved. But first, the political part can be isolated.

In politics the expectations of people have changed, and so have their capabilities. The ratio of expectations to capabilities provides the dynamic in politics generally, and nationalism is one result of this changed ratio (paradoxically, so is internationalism or supranationalism). What people have come to expect in most parts of the world is some form of democratic government: 'government by the people'. This expectation has been encouraged over a long period since the eighteenth century, but has quickened and heightened in the twentieth century. 'National self-determination' has been proclaimed as a right by politicians as widely separated in ideology as President Woodrow Wilson of the USA and Lenin and Stalin of the USSR, and more generally in the Covenant of the League of Nations and the Charter of the United Nations. But 'people' does not just mean any combination of individuals. A people has a collective identity based on something special. The more ethnic it is, the more special, for then it has exclusive membership. This gives it extra status and dignity, as Greenfeld shows (Greenfeld, 1992, p. 487).

The political capabilities of people have also changed. The multinational Empires broke up in Europe as a result of the First World War (1914–18), and in Africa and Asia after the Second World War (1939–45). War gave submerged nations their opportunity to achieve independent statehood, and those that could not be immediately 'liberated' waged bitter struggles for nationhood (e.g. Ireland v. Britain (1918–21), and Algeria v. France (1954–62)). The ability of these submerged nations to defeat powerful states marked the triumph of ethnic/social nationalism over official or state (imperial) nationalism. But it was of course the fatal weakness of the Empires at the end of war (wars caused as much by imperialism as by nationalism) that gave nationalism its chance.

The simultaneous rise of democratic expectations and the capability to achieve these through the overthrow of multinational empires was matched by the rise of nationalism within multinational states. Here, what was often involved was a nationalist reaction to domination, discrimination and exclusion. One aspect of this has been called 'internal colonialism' – the colonisation of subordinate ethnic groups within the state by the core ethnic group, giving rise to a 'cultural division of labour'. Internal colonialism and the cultural division of labour involve all three aspects of politics, economics and culture (see Chapter 3, under 'Hechter's Theory of Internal Colonialism').

The democratic expectation of self-government is as opposed to internal colonialism as it is to colonialism in the colonial empires. So as democracy grows in political attractiveness and is demanded for cultural communities, internal colonialism comes under attack. In this situation, many 'internal' ethnicities become mobilised politically against the state of which they are part, even when that state proclaims itself a 'nation-state'. Thus old-established states were by the mid-twentieth century threatened with break-up along with the world-wide colonial empires.

Expectations and capabilities linked both these contexts. The loss of Empire changed the expectations of many people in states that possessed such Empires, especially those groups whose position in the 'mother country' was one of a minority nation. Many Scots who are in total just under 10 per cent of the population of Britain, had looked to the British Empire for positions of power and wealth when these were not so easily obtained in England. When the British Empire dissolved, they found their career opportunities restricted. This meant that they had to restrict their careers more often to Britain itself, where they had to compete more sharply with the dominant English, even in Scotland. The same applied to the Basques and Catalans on the dissolution of the Spanish Empire, for they soon came into conflict with the Castilians who controlled the Madrid government when their overseas opportunities dried up. The more that internal colonialism and cultural division of labour existed within the mother country, the more political conflicts between the nations resulted.

Such nationalism may not be 'separatist', in the sense of isolationist, but may seek national participation in a wider polity than the old multinational state. This of course will only satisfy nationalist feeling if the new polity is able to act along consociational rather than majoritarian lines. It may be impossible to create such a polity. This was the fate of Nkrumah's African nationalism, Pan-Africanism. This sought the establishment of a 'United States of Africa'. Pan-Africanism, like Pan-Slavism in the nineteenth century and Pan-Arabism in the 1970s, foundered on the incompatibility of nationalism with a wider formulation of political and cultural identity. Nationalists in Scotland, Wales, Catalonia, the Basque Country and Corsica are very keen that their nations should join the European Union (EU) as independent members, but they may find that majority voting gives them as little protection there as in their existing states. It would give them international status, however, and as we have seen status is very important to nationalism.

Closely related to the modern desire for democracy is consumerism. People increasingly demand the right to choose for themselves what to consume, and by analogy how to live. They have been encouraged to do this by the development of capitalism (or, in socialist countries, the example of capitalism) and by the greater spending power available to most people in industrial countries. Thus consumerism usually means the demand by individuals and groups for material gain. They will decide what is the 'rational choice' for them in politics, and it may be that pursuing ethnic aims will appear rational if there is the prospect of material or some other gain (for an extended discussion of a 'rational choice' explanation of nationalist behaviour, see Tiryakian and Rogowski, 1985). In the most advanced 'post-industrial' societies, demands may go beyond economic gain to the satisfaction of 'post-materialist' values. Such values include civil rights, protection of the environment, and enhancement of such aspects of social status as ethnic identity (e.g. in language, religion, respect for the community, etc.). It seems that 'post-materialist' consumerism is closely connected to ethnic nationalism, but not to official nationalism (patriotism) (see Inglehart, 1977). 'Post-materialism' will be further discussed in the section on the economy.

In political terms, this kind of consumerism seeks the availability of rights such as the right of self-government, local democracy and cultural autonomy. Where ethnic groups are not territorially based, but consist of scattered individuals (as, for example, blacks in the USA), ethnic politics involves demands for preferential treatment for members of ethnic minorities, through programmes of affirmative action, 'clientelism', and so on. As Crawford Young has pointed out (Young, 1976, pp. 23, 34), ethnic groups are mobilised in 'quintessentially modern' political situations, not on the basis of some turning back to 'primordialism'. This is because ethnic politics is appropriate to contemporary politics, especially where there is 'cultural pluralism' and a 'cultural division of labour'.

While consumerism has been encouraged by the modern democratic state, it can thus also be turned against it. Demands for decentralisation and home rule for ethnic groups and social nations can be seen as consumer reactions against the modern centralised state (Sharpe, 1979, pp. 9–79). Paradoxically, when the state seeks to satisfy dissatisfied ethnic groups, as in programmes of regional economic planning to redress regional inequalities, or in the establishment of regional government agencies, it raises ethnic expectations further and demands for stronger home rule or affirmative action may follow.

In Gorbachev's USSR (i.e. from 1985 to 1991), *glasnost* (openness) and *perestroika* (restructuring of the state and economy) opened the floodgates to ethnic demands and capabilities to a point where many nationalities demanded independence or autonomy. The capability to articulate legitimately the expectations of the nationalities in the Soviet Union only became available when the Soviet state tolerated the formation of national 'Popular Fronts' and the expression of national demands at all levels of the state and Communist Party. Up till then (*c.* 1987), national expectations were low, and the capability to express them was circumscribed by an authoritarian regime. Thus the force of democracy and consumerism remained largely dormant until Gorbachev, and very soon took over completely, with the demise of the USSR in December 1991.

Similarly, the resurgence of nationalism in former Yugoslavia since the 1970s can be traced partly to political changes: the 1974 Constitution, which strengthened the powers of the national republics in the federal system; and the death of President Tito in 1980, which further weakened the central power and Yugoslav patriotism. The advent of free elections in the constituent republics, starting in Slovenia in 1990, led to the break-up of the socialist federation, for Serbia and Montenegro were unwilling to reconstitute the federal state along the looser, democratic lines demanded by the newly elected non-communist republics. (For further discussion of these cases, see Chapter 7.)

The examples of rising ethnic nationalism from authoritarian communist states point to the role of political vehicles such as parties, 'Popular Fronts', and semi-political cultural bodies like writers' and intellectuals' societies. For nationalism to flourish, nationalist bodies must be allowed to operate within the political system. A competitive party system with free elections will allow democratic and consumerist demands to be expressed, and these may take a nationalist form. All the new 'nation-states' which seceded from the USSR, Yugoslavia and Czechoslovakia did so because of elections, and (except for Czechoslovakia) referendums. A closed non-democratic system, on the other hand, or a democratic system based on majority rule which oppresses minority nations, will lead nationalism into underground and terrorist activities. Then a struggle ensues along non-democratic lines, in which the superior forces of the state are likely to prevail, unless a civil war breaks out, in which case there is a chance that the state will be defeated, as in Algeria (1962) and Ireland (1921).

These examples show that the state is as important an actor in nationalism as the ethnic groups themselves. The state may follow a number of strategies to preserve itself in the face of a nationalist threat. It will try to 'divide and rule' a nation which threatens it. Nations are not monolithic entities, but are split into factions, ranging from extremists and terrorists to state-allied 'unionists'. Only rarely does a nationalist movement achieve majority support in its own nation for a particular course of action, and the state is thus able to manipulate the factions of the ethnic nation to its ends. These strategies may work, or they may provoke further ethnic trouble, with perhaps the disintegration of the state. The latter is of course especially the case if free elections have been denied. The advent of multi-party elections in the communist countries in 1990 led to votes of over 90 per cent for secession in many of the USSR's and Yugoslavia's constituent national republics.

Multinational states and empires resisted nationalism at first, but those that did not see their subject nations/colonies secede through national self-determination/decolonisation, had two possibilities open to them. The first was to adopt a form of nationalism themselves ('official nationalism'), thereby seeking a new legitimacy for the state in a cultural homogeneity (i.e. a new 'social nation'). Thus the Russian Empire sought to make non-Russians Russian through Russification; Britain made many Scots, Welsh and Irish 'English' through Anglicisation. This was a kind of nation-building at a very late stage in the history of the state. New states in Latin America, Asia and Africa also sought to build nations out of ethnically diverse populations. It is significant that these exercises in nation-building have been only partially successful, and are particularly vulnerable to the rising demands of democracy and consumerism. The satisfaction of ethnic identity in political terms is one of these demands, and attempts at homogenisation are rejected, except where there is a clear payoff to compensate for loss of cultural identity. Internal colonialism is also attacked, and the demand is made by the subordinate nations for 'affirmative action' to redress social and economic national discrimination.

This usually leads to the adoption of an alternative accommodating strategy by multinational states (a category which of course comprises nearly all the states of the world). This strategy accepts cultural (ethnic/national) pluralism, and recognises it in the political system. Thus, the alternative to the homogeneous nation-state is the culturally plural state. This type of state varies constitutionally from a decentralised 'unitary' state such as Britain and France, to a 'confederal' or 'consociational' state such as Belgium, Switzerland, and Canada. Each multinational state has its own variation in constitutional and political terms to deal with its multinational character (for further discussion, see Chapter 9).

To sum up, the political explanation for the recent importance of ethnic nationalism is both general and particular. There is a general rise in democratic expectations and capabilities throughout the world, and this threatens multinational polities in particular; for one of the demands of consumers in a democracy is national self-government, and if the nation is perceived to be lacking in that respect, the state will come under nationalist pressure to change. The advent of free, competitive elections in the former communist countries of Europe released the force of nationalism to such an extent that it destroyed the existing states.

Thus particular developments, even events, control the politics of ethnic nationalism. A war, a change of regime, of government even, will release expectations and capabilities, or cause frustrations and resistance. Lenin, Stalin, Gorbachev, Tito, Thatcher and Trudeau, as state leaders in multinational polities, all provoked or released ethnic nationalism in their time. Nationalist parties and nationalist leaders for their part have also been important in organising responses from the ethnic grass-roots. Who won, and who lost, cannot be explained here (see the following chapters). There is no inevitability in the success of ethnic nationalism as compared to other political and social forces. Although ethnic politics may have become the leading force in politics in certain contexts, state, class and ideology match, and often overpower, ethnic nationalism in many cases, even if that may be seen now as a temporary victory. When such cases are studied in detail, the strengths and weaknesses of nationalism will be revealed.

The Economy

If politics is about power in relation to the state, the economy concerns material interests – of individuals, firms, trade unions, 'classes', regions, nations, and so on. These, of course, impinge on political power, and it is by seeking the connection between economic and political power that we can increase our understanding of nationalism. What features of the economy are conducive to ethnic and social nationalism?

We have seen in Chapter 3 that most theorists (e.g. Gellner, and all Marxists) link the emergence of nationalism in history to a 'stage' in economic development, namely, the rise of the modern industrial or capitalist state. That is what 'caused' nationalism in their view, since the 'nation-state' is seen as functional to that particular form of economy, and nationalism occurs when the establishment of the nation-state is blocked. The continuing strength of nationalism (and racism) is also 'explained' by economics, according to these theorists. They are 'reductionists', in that they reduce nationalism to economics: for them, there is always ultimately an economic explanation for nationalism, as there is for politics and culture generally.

Such theories are of course not accepted by everyone, yet there is evidence that economic factors and material interests are indeed closely connected with nationalism. If we focus attention on the rise of ethnic and social nationalism, how do economic explanations add to our understanding?

We have seen under the heading of 'Politics' that states may be organised in such a way as to give power to one ethnic or national group. This involves economic power if such a state is seen to be based on 'internal colonialism', with a 'cultural division of labour'. In such a state, the economic opportunities of ethnic and national groups are deliberately stratified, with one group on the top and others arranged hierarchically below it.

This takes the form of 'dominant' racism or nationalism serving 'class interests' (Greenberg, 1980). It may also lead to reactive nationalism among the colonised nations, who may seek to break away from the state which oppresses them, or at least seek to redress the unfavourable balance within the state through majority rule coupled with civil rights, or through consociational democracy, federalism, devolution, regional grants, and so on. Colonialism in general, of course, had a similar effect on the indigenous peoples of the colonies, who eventually sought independence from the imperial country.

A rise in nationalism, then, can be related to the economic consequences of the pursuit of a strategy of colonialism or internal colonialism, which leads to a nationalist reaction among the colonised. When such colonialism exists, a strong condition for nationalism is present, especially in an era of democracy and rising expectations, as discussed in the first section.

But it may be that no state of colonialism exists. Instead, what is likely to exist is some degree of 'uneven economic development': an economic stratification in a country which is not the result of an overt policy of the state, but the result of economic forces working 'naturally'. Thus in the world there are rich and poor states, through no merit or fault of their own, but because of the unequal distribution of the world's resources. Similarly, within a state there are rich and poor regions, with centres and peripheries in an economic sense (i.e. in relation to markets, natural resources, etc.).

The people of states and regions of states who feel 'relatively deprived' because of their economic situation can become politically restless in certain circumstances. They may demand changes to redress their perceived deprivation. On the other hand, they may become passive; their population may prefer emigration to rebellion, and they may become fatalists ('what is, must be'), especially where 'free market' ideas prevail.

Even in an economic system which is not one of internal colonialism, but is one of uneven development, there may be a form of 'cultural division of labour', though a less rigid one than in 'internal colonial' or 'racist' states. Rich and high-status people will generally belong to the richest regions, and poor people will be concentrated in the poor regions. A 'cultural division of labour' occurs when these regions are distinguished from each other on cultural lines as well as on lines of wealth.

Where people think of themselves in ethnic or social-national terms, and inhabit a territory which is differentiated on economic grounds from other such groups, then there is a high probability that nationalism will develop, given favourable political and cultural conditions. An example of this is the strength of nationalism in Scotland and the absence of nationalism in the north of England, although both areas are poor regions in Britain, at least on some indicators. The cultural division of labour is more marked in Scotland because Scotland is a nation, while the north of England is not, although it has (non-national) cultural distinctions from other parts of England.

It is not just the poorer regions that develop nationalism, how-ever. The rich regions may also be nationalist, if they perceive relative deprivation within the state on political and/or cultural matters. Thus, 'rich' Catalonia and the relatively prosperous Basque lands are nationalist because of what they see as their cul-tural and political deprivation in Spain, especially with regard to their national language and education; so too were the Baltic nations of Estonia, Latvia and Lithuania within the USSR, for similar (and other) reasons. In all these examples, deprivation has been largely overcome, but fears of internal colonialism (Spain) and post-colonialism (the Baltic states) remain strong.

Another way of looking at this disparity between the territorial distribution of economic resources in a state and its connection with nationalism is provided by Anthony Mughan (Mughan, in Sharpe, 1979). He divides power resources into two categories: *de jure* and *de facto*. The former derive from the constitution of the state (e.g. the right to vote), while the latter concern the qualitative differences between people (e.g. their wealth, educa-tion and so on). It is when these two types of power resource do not correspond for any one ethnic group that conflict develops. Thus a rich ethnic group which is not strong in political power will rebel, and try to change its political position. If the changes in the economy serve to reinforce an ethnic group's existing share of political power, then conflict is unlikely to occur. However, where ethnic groups gain or lose economic power while their political power stays constant or moves in the opposite direction, nationalism will develop. Mughan uses the example of Belgium to show how the rising economic power of the Flemings in a state dominated by French-speakers led to Flemish national-ism which demanded the reconstruction of the Belgian state along consociational lines based on ethnicity and language. The French-speaking Walloons, for their part, also became nationalist when their primacy in *de jure* constitutional and cultural power was shown to be out of step with their declining economic *de facto* power.

Where a relatively poor ethnic group stays in that position as the economy develops, nationalism will not occur if the *de jure* position of that group in the state relative to the wealthy group(s) remains correspondingly weak. Perhaps the low-key nature of Scottish nationalism compared to the virulent Flemish and

Walloon nationalism in Belgium in recent years can be explained by this theory. Through all the changes in the economy and politics, Scotland has remained weaker than England. Scottish nationalism took off strongly when the discoveries of oil in the North Sea off Scotland pointed to a relative shift in economic wealth in Britain towards Scotland. This led to demands for a reconstruction of the Constitution of the British state through devolution or federalism, and for its dissolution through Scottish independence. The relative decline in the Scottish economy after 1979 reinforced the correspondence between *de facto* and *de jure* power, and Scottish nationalism was only able to revive when the balance was again upset after 1987. Scotland's constitutional position seemed to deteriorate when the Conservative Government imposed unpopular policies on Scotland with only 10 out of 72 MPs in Scotland. Scotland seemed to be effectively disfranchised since its votes counted for nothing in the formation of British governments or their policies for Scotland. At the same time, the Scottish economy improved, and something of a cultural renaissance accelerated. So a disjunction between economic, political and cultural power took place, which contributed to a rise in nationalism. This interpretation corresponds with Stein Rokkan's analysis of regionalism as resulting from an 'incongruity between cultural, economic and political roles' (Rokkan and Urwin, 1983, p. 192).

When the focus turns to ethnic and national groups whose base is not territorial but within the labour force of a multicultural society, a similar economic explanation for nationalism, ethnic politics and racism is given by some theorists. In this context, the cultural division of labour operates within the economy to stratify individuals according to their ethnic origin: an ethnic-class system. Thus, black migrant workers tend to be at the bottom of the class hierarchy, for reasons related to the 'supply and demand' of their labour, but also because of their ethnicity and their class position in the country they came from (Indians and Pakistanis have different class origins from African-Americans). They are doubly discriminated against: economically as a 'lower class' in the labour force *and* culturally because they are ethnically different from the higher classes of the labour force (Miles, 1982; Enloe, 1973; Greenberg, 1980). This analysis has particular reference to ethnic politics and racism in cities, where ethnic groups compete for scarce resources in a modern economy. They compete in the economy as ethnic groups rather than as individuals to the extent that the state and the economy discriminates between them on ethnic lines (e.g. according to a cultural division of labour). This discrimination may be negative. (against their interests) or positive (in their favour). The former is a denial of opportunities on account of ethnic identity, ranging from the informal to the state-sponsored (e.g. apartheid), while the latter is typified by programmes of 'affirmative action' to favour disadvantaged ethnic groups (usually blacks) in the United States. In both contexts ethnic groups assert their identity for economic reasons; there seems to be a disadvantage in so doing in the former case, and an advantage in the latter. The alternative of assimilation is effectively blocked under an apartheid system based on skin colour, and so ethnic groups continue to assert their ethnicity. And there are political disadvantages present in a system of affirmative action, for not only will some members of the favoured groups prefer to seek assimilation or to compete on the same terms as members of other groups, but the groups not covered by affirmative action programmes may rebel against them as a denial of political equality.

These examples show that material, economic interests are at stake in ethnic politics, with groups and individuals seeking an advantage, usually by playing up their ethnicity to secure scarce resources. At the same time, there is an alternative strategy of assimilation, favoured in certain circumstances.

The relationship between the economy and nationalism is not static but dynamic. Indeed, as we have seen, it is the *changes* in political, economic and cultural relationships which give rise to nationalism. The technological changes which have occurred in the late twentieth century have altered the types of employment and the classes in the labour force in 'advanced industrial countries' (and to a lesser extent in other countries as well). The division of interest between the 'working class' and the 'middle class', which was reflected in class politics is no longer so obvious, as people see their interests increasingly in terms other than class. A great deal of political science is devoted to charting this development in political behaviour in western Europe and in North America. What is apparent is that while people still vote predominantly according to their assessment of their material interests seen in economic terms, they no longer do so in terms of class interests, if class is seen in dichotomous terms ('working class'/ 'middle class'). Thus in Britain, the Labour Party usually now gets under half the 'working class vote', and the Conservatives cannot rely on the 'middle class vote'. 'Non-class parties' such as centre parties, Green parties, and nationalist parties have gained many votes at the expense of the class parties in many countries. This change in voting reflects changes in the economy, and in the nature of material interests. As regards nationalist politics, it is the decline of class politics which opens up an increased potential for nationalist political behaviour, including nationalist voting.

Why should nationalism take the place of class politics, at least up to a point? In part the answer lies in the discussion above. Material economic interests *are* served by nationalism in certain circumstances, or can be seen to be served by it. This is especially true where a simple class division of interests is not present because of a cultural division of labour. But there is a more general reason for nationalism to eclipse class politics in many countries today, and that is the increasing importance in 'post-industrial societies' of 'quality of life' issues as compared to materialist or class issues. As Ronald Inglehart puts it:

> The values of Western publics have been shifting from an overwhelming emphasis on material well-being and physical security towards greater emphasis on the quality of life. (Inglehart, 1977, p. 3)

Non-materialist politics are, curiously enough, present in countries which are either 'pre-industrial' or 'post-industrial'. In both cases, nationalism occurs strongly today, although pre-industrial societies are not considered by commentators such as Gellner to display nationalism. Today, countries in the Developing World which have not yet industrialised nevertheless display nationalism or ethnic divisions rather than class divisions because class has not yet developed widely as an alternative cleavage.

Post-industrial societies, on the other hand, have gone through the industrialising phase, and are now apparently entering a 'post-industrial' phase where 'post-materialist values' compete with material interests. These values tend to focus on such things as the quality of the environment and on civil rights and cultural matters. Economic or class interests are not strongly articulated because there is a high degree of economic and physical security in these societies.

In place of class divisions come status divisions. Clearly, this is one possible explanation for nationalism arising in advanced 'post-industrial societies', for it is only when class divisions fade that status divisions such as identity, language, culture and nationality can assume major importance. Thus nationalism is likely to occur when the class cleavages of industrial society are weak, and this can be both before and after the main period of industrialisation.

Culture

Culture differs from economy as 'psychic income' differs from financial income or material interests. 'Psychic income' refers to those things which satisfy the mental and spiritual needs of human beings; material interests are those things which are readily quantifiable in cash terms, such as incomes and jobs. Of course, it is impossible to draw the line in any precise manner: money can buy culture, and jobs can be obtained in education and the arts.

Culture also reintroduces the discussion of status and class. Culture is more linked to status, while material interests form the basis of class. Essentially, class refers to an economic situation, while status involves identity, prestige, inner satisfaction, and so on.

Nationality and culture are almost synonymous. This is because both include a sense of social identity, a language, education, religion, the arts, science and so on. While some culture may be cosmopolitan, many of its attributes are national. For nationalism, the place of culture is vital. Without a national culture there would be little left of nationhood, certainly of ethnic and social nationhood (state or official nationalism, on the other hand, may be multicultural). Thus in the formula 'Politics + Economy + Culture = Nationalism', there is a special weight for culture.

What changes in culture have been conducive to a rise in ethnic and social nationalism? And what changes have been contrary to such nationalism – that is, conducive to official (state) nationalism or cosmopolitanism? Is the balance today favourable to nationalism, or against it?

The search for identity in the conditions of the modern world has led to increased ethnic and social nationalism in some cases, and increased official nationalism and cosmopolitanism in others. Why this ambiguity? In part it is the result of the different characteristics of economic systems which have developed. Gellner pointed to the imperatives of the industrial state in the emergence of nationalism: homogeneous national cultures within one state go hand in hand with industrial economies, according to him, and are indeed necessary to them. Thus a social and cultural identity flows from the needs of the economy, and is promoted by the state.

As we have seen in the previous discussion of Gellner, there is ambiguity here. If Gellner is right in his general approach, then as the economy internationalises, the national characteristics fade into cosmopolitan ones, and with them fade the national cultures. To some extent that has happened, and nationalism has weakened at the state level. However, it is difficult to explain sub-state ethnic and social nationalism from Gellner's theory. His theory postulates that as the state economy predominates over local and regional economies, so too state identity, state culture and official nationalism will predominate over ethnic and social identity, culture and nationalism. Yet what we are faced with is the opposite: the rise of ethnic and social nationalism in opposition to state nationalism.

Of course, this may be a temporary reaction to an inevitable centralising process, and ethnic and social nationalism may face ultimate defeat by state nationalism, or cosmopolitanism ('globalisation'). Yet when we examine the strength of culture in nationalism, we find that it seems as powerful as politics and economy, and that in the conditions of sudden change in the modern world people turn to their ethnic and (nearest) social culture as a defence against deprivation in politics and material interests. This is not a throw-back to ancient ways, but a very up-to-date way of defending personal and group interests. It is also dependent on modern cultural developments which, contrary to Gellner's theory, do not contribute to state homogeneity, or state nationalism. As Dogan and Pelassy put it in *How to Compare Nations*:

> The development of media, transportation, school enrollment, or urbanization paradoxically does not necessarily favor a

homogenization of society. Indeed, these very elements that objectively unify styles of living at the same time provide minorities with the means of subjectively recognizing themselves as conscious entities. (Dogan and Pelassy, 1984, p. 52)

So what we should look for in explaining how cultural developments have contributed to the rise of ethnic and social nationalism, in opposition to state nationalism or cosmopolitanism, is the presence and strength of a substate educational system, with its associated intelligentsia, a substate media system, and a set of cultural organisations which support the local language, arts, historical studies, and so on, as a distinct culture of the ethnic or social nation.

These things have of course been well studied in the *history* of nationalism, but there are *contemporary* developments which have led to renewed cultural nationalism. First, there has been a big increase in literacy, through the spread of education to all people. The opportunities to promote national culture have steadily increased with the spread of mass publications, and these are often accessible to nationalists, unless the state exercises censorship and monopolises printing (as in most authoritarian states). There has also been an immense spread of the broadcast media, notably television. If there is a national language which has been suppressed or discouraged by the state, linguistic questions are likely to be a rallying point for ethnic and social nationalism, and will get exposure in the press and broadcast media. A separate Welsh language TV channel was granted in 1982, after a hunger-strike by the Welsh Nationalist President, Gwynfor Evans.

All this has led to competing messages reaching people, and competing cultures arriving right inside the home, where before perhaps only one culture was dominant. One of these cultures is that of the ethnic and social nation, no longer 'home-bred' but systematically refined by national cultural leaders, many of them 'cultural nationalists'. They articulate to the widest possible audience the claims of the nation to cultural autonomy and survival. This gives confidence to those disposed towards nationalism, since they become aware of the nation's cultural identity as something valuable and respectable, and not something to be ashamed of in the face of the culture of the state or cosmopolitan culture. They are able to share their national identity with opinion leaders, and to learn from them what their national culture is, and how it should be defended.

Most minority nations feel that their culture is under attack from the state, which usually identifies with the majority nation or with a synthetic state culture. This leads to a sense of cultural deprivation among many in the minority nations. 'Relative deprivation' is closely linked to nationalism, and can take the form of political, economic or cultural deprivation. Cultural deprivation in the context of nationalism is experienced when discrimination or insult takes place on account of a person's national identity, language (including accent), religion, habits, tastes, and so on.

This occurs most frequently, of course, when face-to-face contact takes place between dominant and dominated nationals, but it is also experienced collectively, and at a distance, as when linguistic or educational usages are imposed officially on all citizens by the state. These emanate from the capital city, through laws or regulations, but they are often left to fellow nationals to enforce. All this leads to a sense of cultural deprivation, and this kind of deprivation is at least as important in explaining nationalist behaviour as its more celebrated counterpart, relative economic deprivation. Examples of cultural deprivation in motivating nationalism abound throughout the world, and two examples from Scotland illustrate it. Billy Wolfe, Chairman of the SNP from 1969 to 1979, writes in his autobiography, *Scotland Lives* (Wolfe, 1973, p. 8), that in the British Army

> I was constantly exposed to the English middle-class assertion that the anglicised (they called it 'the civilised') Scot was the best kind of person in the world (a world in which only English was spoken).

Another former leading figure in the SNP, Jim Sillars, recalls that when he served in the British Navy, 'I could understand them but they either could not or refused to understand me' (Sillars, 1986, p. 11). In Portsmouth (naval base) people 'delighted in taking the mickey by refusing to understand a single word I said'. Years later, his first speech in the House of Commons after his election in 1988 was greeted with taunts from English Tory MPs,

'Speak English!', which no doubt strengthened his cultural nationalism.

These are nationalists who point to personal cultural deprivation to explain their nationalism. Collective cultural deprivation also leads to nationalism, and is present when cultural organisations and educational bodies fight for the national culture against assimilation with other cultures and education systems. Thus the Educational Institute of Scotland, the largest teachers' union in Scotland, ran a press advertising campaign in 1988 against the 'Anglicisation' of Scottish education through the introduction of reforms patterned on English practice. Cultural deprivation also motivates nationalism in the former Soviet Republics, Belgium (especially Flanders), Quebec, Wales, Corsica, Catalonia, the Basque lands, and many other nations. Any nation whose identity is based on language, religion, education or the Arts, and which is faced with threats to its culture, is likely to react with nationalism.

Is cultural nationalism on the increase, or is it merely a losing battle against assimilation and cosmopolitanism? As we have seen, the technological opportunities for cultural nationalism are increasing, in publications and broadcasting. These can assert national cultures, and if there is a 'cultural division of labour', then material interests will reinforce cultural ones: class and status will be combined. Moreover, the 'search for identity' and the pursuit of 'psychic income' are features of 'post-materialist society'.

Culture matters more as class and materialism decline in significance as the focus of political conflict. This may be because class interests are now less salient since they have been transformed into sectional interests. Nationalism cuts across class and sectional interests, and it can only succeed when classes and sections lose their ability to command supreme loyalty. In cultural nationalism people unite to pursue something different from personal, sectional or class interest – their status as members of the nation.

The apparent decline of class conflict in many modern societies gives nationalism its opportunity, and the rise of cultural nationalism shows that cultural conflicts are as important as economic ones. While much is ambiguous about the changing nature of politics, economy and culture and how such change contributes to the rise of ethnic and social nationalism, the weights in the equation have shifted from those which favoured official state nationalism and cosmopolitanism to those which emphasise ethnic and social nationalism. But such preconditions for nationalist behaviour are only made into strong political nationalism by the activities of nationalist movements and parties, to which we now turn.

5

Nationalist Movements and Ethnic Politics

In this chapter, the focus is on the forms of nationalist movements and ethnic politics, and the nature of their support. The aim is to give a historical and geographic perspective to the study of nationalism. There is also a discussion of the nature of nationalist political behaviour, the social characteristics of nationalists, and the circumstances in which nationalist movements and ethnic politics succeed or fail. In the next three chapters, case studies are given of nationalist movements and ethnic politics in different parts of the world today.

Forms of Nationalism and Ethnic Politics

Pre-Nationalism and Ethnic Politics

For most writers on nationalism, nationalism is a modern political ideology which can be found only from the late eighteenth century. In this view, nationalism belongs in the period of 'modernity' which is based on industrialisation and the philosophy of the Enlightenment (Gellner, 1983; Greenfeld, 1992). For other writers, however, 'national consciousness', is traced back to ancient times (Kohn, 1944), and nations are held to have 'ethnic origins' (Smith, 1986).

It seems that many of these distinctions are rather artificial. There are clear examples of pre-modern nationalism in Scotland, England, France, and among the Jews, although there was no clear political role for 'the people' until the ideology of democracy took root after the French Revolution. Thus 'national self-determination' and 'popular sovereignty' as explicit

89

principles had to await the era of representative government and democracy.

It is also the case that many 'nationally conscious' nations did not seek statehood until modern times. For example, it was the Zionist ideology of the late nineteenth century which made many Jews support the aim of a 'national home' in Palestine. But Jews had always been highly nationalist (or at least ethnically exclusive) during the period of the 'diaspora' (dispersal throughout the world).

'Official nationalism' through nation-building is found in the pre-modern period in western Europe, with states such as England, France, Spain and Portugal consolidating their hold over the people with appeals to patriotism, and with the construction of national languages, literature, educational institutions, and so on. Here, the 'state' preceded the 'nation', and nationalism meant nation-building.

In most other parts of the world nations remained largely at the ethnic and social level. Nationalism was not 'official', since states did not usually seek to be national in character. Rather, they were either multinational or multiethnic empires, kingdoms, and so on, or, in what is sometimes called the 'Developing World' today, 'tribal' or 'communal' politics. In these states, imperialism and ethnic politics, rather than nationalism, predominated.

It is possible to view some contemporary Developing World politics as 'pre-nationalist', since in these tribalism and multi-ethnic states are to be found. However, the fact is that nationalism is a world-wide ideology today, and it influences the Developing World as much as the 'Western' and 'Communist and Post-Communist' Worlds. So it is impossible to isolate politics in the Developing World from the effects of the nationalist ideals of self-determination and cultural homogeneity. Thus 'pre-nationalist' politics properly belongs to a *period* before the spread of nationalist ideology, rather than to *places* in the world today.

Classical European Nationalism

As we have seen in Chapter 2, the ideology of nationalism seems to have originated in Europe. It then spread throughout the world in the nineteenth century. But this nationalism, even within

Europe, has been held by some to be divided into a 'western' and an 'eastern' form. The 'western' nationalism is ethnically inclusive in that it is based on a 'social nation' which could encompass more than one ethnic group. It is essentially about the cultural homogeneity of the state, and the common citizenship of those sharing that culture. 'Eastern' European nationalism, on the other hand, is ethnically exclusive and is focused on the nation as a community of common descent, language and religion. In 'western European nationalism', the existing citizens of a territory are acceptable as members of the nation, and could form a 'nation-state'. In 'eastern European nationalism', only those with the correct ethnic credentials have the right to live in a territory and be the citizens of the nation-state (for an account of these nationalisms in the contemporary world, see Michael Ignatieff, *Blood and Belonging: Journeys into the New Nationalism*, Ignatieff, 1993).

The forms taken by nationalist movements in Europe set the pattern for nationalisms throughout the world. The inclusive nationalisms are more liberal and democratic, and do not engage in genocide, transfers of population, etc. The exclusive nationalisms are intolerant and often lead to authoritarianism. Examples of the former are Irish (but not in Northern Ireland), Scottish, Catalan and Norwegian nationalisms, and of the latter, Bulgarian, Turkish, Serb, Croat, Tamil and Sikh nationalisms.

Of course, these categories are not rigid, and there is a case for saying that the distinctions are largely false. All nationalisms are both partly inclusive and partly exclusive. In Northern Ireland, exclusive nationalism prevails, in that Protestants are seen as a 'community' apart. Yet they would be included in a united Irish nation-state. 'Greater Serbian' nationalism is both expansive beyond Serbia as now constituted and exclusive in its strategy of 'ethnic cleansing'. In the centre of Europe, German nationalism is a combination of ethnic nationalism, based on language and the concept of *Volk* (Germans of common descent), and social or official nationalism based on citizenship of the German state, whatever form that takes (otherwise known as 'traditional' nationalism based on the 'lesser' German nation or *kleindeutsch*, which does not include Germans in Austria or Switzerland).

During the nineteenth century various strategies of nationalist movements became apparent:

Unification Movements

The unification of the German nation and of the Italian nation in the late nineteenth century was accomplished through war and conquest of existing states. Usually a core state (the Kingdom of Prussia in Germany and the Kingdom of Sardinia in Italy) expanded its power over other states which constituted the 'nation', and either annexed them or left them virtually powerless (as Bavaria in Germany or Venetia in Italy). This type of nationalism is also called 'Risorgimento' (rebirth) nationalism, after the Italian nationalist movement, and it combined the aim of national unification with liberal ideals of democracy and freedom from oppression (for a useful account of the forms of nationalism, see Alter (1989), whose scheme is partly followed here).

National Secession Movements

In most cases, nationalism led to the break-up of existing states, not their joining together in one large nation-state. So nationalist movements in Ireland, Greece, Poland, Serbia and Norway, for example, achieved independence for their nations by breaking away from Britain, the Ottoman Empire, the Russian Empire, the Austrian Empire and Sweden, respectively. Today, national secession movements are still active in Europe: in Scotland, Wales, the Basque country, and Corsica, and were successful in the early 1990s in Yugoslavia, the USSR and Czechoslovakia, when no fewer than 21 new states were formed from these. Of course, these secession movements vary greatly in the intensity of their nationalism and in the degree of popular support given to them, and it is difficult to predict which ones will be successful. Usually a regime change at the centre of the multinational state is required before a secession is successful. But Ireland broke away from Britain largely as a result of the actions of Irish nationalists, even if the outcome of the First World War could be considered a regime change for the British Empire.

Reform Nationalism

This kind of nationalism occurred in Japan in the mid-nineteenth century, and in Turkey in the early twentieth century. It was also seen in part in China, Egypt and Persia (Iran) after 1921. As with 'risorgimento' nationalism the aim was national 'rebirth', but it was confined to an existing state, and the nationalists were the traditional ruling class, not a new anti-establishment group. The strategies were economic modernisation, the defence of national identity, and independence from foreign control. Thus the Japanese, Turks, Chinese, Egyptians and Persians fought off European imperialists and established modern nation-states. Reform nationalism took different forms: in Japan it was focused on the Emperor; in Turkey on the Young Turks and secularisation; in Persia on the Shah. All were 'nationalists' in their antipathy to foreigners and their sponsorship of a national language and culture.

Integral Nationalism

Integral nationalism differs from 'risorgimento' rationalism in its belief that one's nation is superior to all others, and may even be the result of biological natural selection. 'Risorgimento' nationalism, on the other hand, is liberal in its attitude towards other nationalisms, believing them to be equal in status, even if their claims may be mutually incompatible (e.g. *irredentism* is a form of nationalism which lays claim to the territory of another state).

Integral nationalism is an absolutist ideology (the absolute loyalty to the nation is demanded), and in politics is clearly linked to totalitarian, fascist, and Nazi forms of government. Its main examples are Mussolini's Italy, Hitler's Germany, Franco's Spain, and Action Française in late nineteenth-century France.

Colonial Nationalism

In the European colonial empires (especially the British, Spanish, Portuguese, Dutch and French) a nationalism developed among the European settlers, which led to the independence of the colonies from the mother country. The Americans showed the way in 1776, followed by the Spanish and Portuguese in

Latin America in the early nineteenth century. By the late nine-teenth century, Canadians, Australians, South Africans (both British and Afrikaner) and New Zealanders had displayed their nationalism in new nation-states, even if this was often tinged with a 'dual identity' with the mother country.

The most recent examples of colonial 'settler' nationalisms are the French Algerian nationalists of the 1950s and early 1960s and the British Rhodesian settlers, with their 'Unilateral Declaration of Independence' in 1965. These settlers were seek-ing secession in order to maintain their own internal (racist) hegemony at a time when the mother country wanted to liber-alise the situation. Both these 'colonial' nationalisms failed, when the metropolitan power successfully asserted its authority (unlike the earlier examples), although this led to the triumph of anti-colonial nationalism (see below).

The settlement of Israel by Zionist Jews in the twentieth cen-tury provides an interesting hybrid between colonial nationalism and integral or exclusive nationalism. The colonisation of Palestine was based on an ancient ethnic claim to its homeland by the Jews. The native Palestinians are inclined to view the Israelis as settlers, which makes Palestinian nationalism more akin to anti-colonialism, and Zionism similar to 'Risorgimento' nationalism.

Anti-Colonial Nationalism

Anti-colonialism is the last form of nationalism dealt with here. The emergence of indigenous 'national liberation' and anti-colonial movements in the British Empire corresponded with the spread of nationalist ideology from Europe. Thus, unification and Risorgimento nationalisms were to be found in the colonies of Africa and Asia. So too was 'Pan-Africanism' and the complex mix of religion and nationalism in Asia.

Given the existing colonial state structure at independence, the nationalists of the new 'nation-states' had to preserve boundaries which reflected the boundaries of colonial power rather than cul-tural or national divisions. Thus nation-building, irredentisms and secessions were permanently on the agenda of nearly all these new states. Now nationalism did not usually mean anti-colonialism, except in the form of hostility to 'dependency' on the former colonial powers (re-categorised as 'neo-colonialism'). Instead it meant interethnic disputes, communalism, and sometimes genocide. In this situation, the development of political parties along ethnic lines, and of ethnic 'liberation armies', subverted the stability of the states which had succeeded the colonies. Only ethnic accommodation and 'consociational democracy' seemed to offer a way out of this predicament.

Consociationalism and Multiethnic Politics

The twentieth century has seen an attempt to make democracy compatible with a 'culturally plural' society. This represents an alternative to the classic aim of nationalism, which was to form a 'nation-state' out of one homogeneous nation or ethnic group.

The Swiss were the first (from the Middle Ages) to show the way to combine several linguistic and religious peoples in one highly decentralised system of government. Later, from the 1970s to the 1990s, the Belgians federalised their state to give equality to the Flemings and Walloons. From the 1940s, wherever one state contained several nations or ethnic groups, and sought to establish democratic government on the basis not of majority rule but through consensus between minorities, then some form of consociationalism was adopted. Such attempts were made in Lebanon, Yugoslavia, Nigeria, Malaysia, Sri Lanka, India, Northern Ireland and South Africa. The success rate has not been high, as many of these experiments collapsed, or were not properly attempted in the first place. However, most of these multicultural states are still trying to produce another version of consociationalism, for that model of government remains the main democratic alternative to the nation-state in conditions of territorially based multiculturalism (for an extended discussion, see Chapter 9).

Within a nation-state, there may be ethnic minorities whose claims cannot be met by territorial consociationalism. These are groups who do not possess a territory they can call their 'home'. They are usually recent immigrants, marked off from the rest of the population by their ethnicity and social class. A multicultural or multiethnic society of this kind exists in most Western states, including the United States, Canada, Britain, France and Germany. Ethnic politics has developed in these countries, and it differs from nationalism in that the ethnic groups accept the constitutional structure of the state. They seek to use the constitution to their advantage, through their votes (occasionally but not usually forming ethnic parties), pressure group activity, and promoting legal changes to outlaw discrimination, provide for 'affirmative action', minority language/religious/educational rights, and so on. The more pronounced these demands are, and the bigger the minority groups, the more the state will tend towards consociationalism on the basis of non-territorial individual and group rights. The working-out of a political form to take account of this type of multicultural society is still in its infancy.

The Social Origins of Nationalists

Who is likely to be a nationalist, or to support a nationalist movement? In the previous discussion, we have seen that nationalism is found in many different contexts, both in history and across the world. It can be divided into 'official nationalism', 'social nationalism', and 'ethnic nationalism'. Thus it can be espoused by the governments of states, and by those who seek to overthrow these governments. While the theories discussed in earlier chapters have examined the general political, economic and cultural conditions in which nationalism emerged and evolved, they have not clearly pinpointed the nature of nationalist support nor the reasons for the political successes and failures of nationalist movements. Without nationalist activists, organised in nationalist parties and political organisations, nationalism would be largely ineffective politically.

'Nationalists' should not be defined as one homogeneous group. Even if we focus on nationalist parties alone, we can distinguish between nationalist leaders, activists, party members, and those who merely vote nationalist in elections. All of these differ in their social characteristics and political motivation. Moreover, what can be called nationalist political behaviour is found beyond the confines of nationalist parties and organisations. It is also to be seen in other parties, in trade unions, and in cultural bodies. In particular, European socialist and Green Parties now support devolution to regions and nations, and sometimes total national independence (e.g. the Scottish Green Party).

So we must extend our analysis to these. Finally, the interaction of nationalists with those who do not display social or ethnic nationalist behaviour (and who may be actively anti-nationalist in that sense, though they may be 'official nationalists') to a large extent determines the characteristics of anti-state nationalists and whether their political actions will succeed or not.

All this seems to imply that few, if any, generalisations can be made about nationalists and their political behaviour. But that is not really the case. There is often common ground between the many studies of nationalist movements, even if the contexts of these are very different. This gives some hope that a general theory of nationalist political behaviour is possible.

One study which generalises about the social origins of nationalists across nations is by the Czech historian Miroslav Hroch (Hroch, 1985). Hroch's work has been widely used by students of nationalist movements, and he shows that nationalist movements in nineteenth-century Europe drew support from different social groups at different phases of their development. In the first phase, the cultural one, some members of the middle and upper classes developed an interest in national history, language and culture, and supported organisations devoted to promoting these. No clear political aims were voiced at this stage. The second phase, however, involved people of a similar social type in voicing political demands for home rule, usually in pressure groups rather than in nationalist parties. This mobilised support for nationalist demands in the people as a whole. The third and last phase saw the establishment of nationalist movements as mass movements, with nationalist parties and political organisations. The most extreme nationalists were now satisfied with nothing less than total political independence for their nation, and their support was broadened to include the mass of the people. These phases of nationalism are linked by Hroch to the phases of economic and cultural change in the countries concerned.

Hroch's categorisation of the phases of nationalist movements is useful, and has been applied to other cases. Hroch was examining the nationalist movements of the 'smaller European nations' in the nineteenth century, and it is not clear that his analysis is as applicable to contemporary politics, or to non-European contexts. It can be said that while his conclusions are still relevant, the phases of nationalist activity today are less clearly separated. In contemporary nationalist movements, these phases have been largely compressed into one. All nationalist movements today are mass movements, at least in aim, and the division between cultural, political and economic nationalism is not a matter of development over time, but a division among nationalists. To that extent it remains true that cultural, political and economic nationalists can be distinguished socially from each other.

In contemporary nationalist movements, cultural nationalists are usually drawn from the education world or the creative arts, especially writing and broadcasting. Here we can see that a vested interest in nationalism is involved, for the livelihood of such people is bound up with the nation's identity. Teaching a national language, writing it and broadcasting it, brings such people economic gains and a reason to favour nationalist political behaviour, though not always to the point of supporting a nationalist party. Usually nations possess educational and cultural institutions, even if they do not have statehood or autonomy. Workers in such institutions are the backbone of nationalist movements. They are not recognisable as being economically deprived but may be considered part of a 'segmental cultural division of labour' in Hechter's terms (Hechter in Tiryakian and Rogowski, 1985, p. 22). This means that their occupations are identified with the nation, and that they defend their economic interests in a way which can be described as nationalist political behaviour.

Nationalists are also drawn from the ranks of the economically deprived, and their poor economic position may lead to nationalism even if their occupations are not 'national' in any cultural sense. For example, industrial workers threatened with unemployment may be nationalist if it seems to them that their nation has been discriminated against by the state. Once more, the 'cultural division of labour' is involved, and even 'internal colonialism', if members of a nation perceive themselves to be exploited by the dominant nation. It might be predicted from the theory of internal colonialism that those who suffer most economically and socially from such colonialism would be the most nationalist. But such people may perceive their deprivation in class rather than national terms, and may prefer to support a socialist party rather than a nationalist one. Nationalist parties find it difficult to get working-class support where socialist parties offer remedies for their economic complaints, but the credibility of such remedies varies according to the political context. In general, nationalists tend to come from intermediate social positions, rather than from the ranks of the poor or the rich, who are more attracted to 'class parties'.

Paradoxically, the 'cultural division of labour' leads to nationalism or racism among those who assert their economic superiority over other nations or races within the state. In racist societies, dominant classes sustain their power and economic advantages through racist economic and social practices and a racist state structure (Greenberg, 1980). But even in non-racist states, dominant economic-cultural groups may resent having to subsidise the poorer nations in the state, and may seek political independence for their nation so that they can keep its superior resources to themselves. Examples of these 'wealthy' nationalists are to be found among the Flemings in Belgium, the Baltic nations in the former USSR, the Catalans and Basques in Spain, and those Scots who proclaimed in the 1970s and 1980s that the new-found wealth off Scotland in North Sea oil made them 'rich Scots' compared to 'poor Britons'.

It must always be remembered, however, that only a proportion of any nation exhibits strong nationalist behaviour. What that proportion is depends on the particular circumstances of the situation. In most cases, the divisions among nations are as important as their features of unity, and this is particularly true of elite groups in the nation. There are three main types of elite: the **political** elite, encompassing politicians, civil servants and the military; the **cultural** elite, especially teachers, writers and clergy; and the **economic** elite, comprising businesspeople and trade union leaders. Each of these reacts differently towards nationalism and towards the central state. As we have seen, where there is a strong national culture, the cultural elite is likely to be nationalist. The economic elite is likely to be the least nationalist, especially if its links with wider markets and firms are strong. The position of the political elite is crucial, and it is only when it fragments that nationalism is able to make progress. Even so, there is always a segment of that elite which remains loyal to the state, or which exploits the state from within on behalf of the nation, without going over to the nationalist side. The balance here is a shifting one, and the centre may be so unsympathetic to nationalist demands that some centrist 'go-betweens' find their role unviable, and turn towards nationalism. This was, for example, the case in Ireland after 1916, when nearly all members of parliament (MPs) and local officials in the South of Ireland supported the break from Britain. It has also happened recently in the Basque country, Catalonia, and the Baltic nations of the former USSR. In these cases the hostile reaction of the state was as important to nationalist behaviour as the demands of the nation itself.

While these observations about the links between occupation and nationalist behaviour provide a general context for the study of nationalism, it is by no means clear that nationalists are related in any systematic way to the social structure, although there are tendencies towards regularities. In Scotland, most nationalist activists are employed in Scottish cultural, educational and local government institutions; in small businesses; or are self-employed. They are rarely managers or employees in large firms. Perhaps this is because the large firms, and their associated trade unions, are less identified with the nation than with the state and the international economy, and they may fear that nationalism will threaten their prosperity by setting up trade barriers and extra taxation. They are also strongly connnected to Conservative parties, which have a unionist predisposition. However, it is not possible to predict how many people in a given social category will behave in a nationalist manner, until other political factors are taken into account.

These can only be discovered in the history of each nation. For example, nationalists in different parts of Spain differ from each other in social characteristics, according to the histories and economies of their nations, and because of the policies of the Spanish state towards them. Nationalists in Catalonia are distinctly more middle class and wealthy than many nationalists in the Basque country. In the latter nation, industrialists have traditionally supported the Spanish state as an internal free market and external protection for their trade. In the late nineteenth century they achieved the abolition of the customs barrier between the Basque country and the rest of Spain, and with it most of Basque autonomy. The decline of the Spanish Empire in the twentieth century and the suppression of Basque culture by General Franco (in power, 1939–75) converted many Basque businesspeople to the nationalist cause. Today, Basques are divided politically along class and ethnic lines. Immigrant and urban workers tend to support the Socialists, the middle class the moderate nationalists (PNV), and the urban unemployed and small farmers the separatist Herri Batasuna Party (HB) and its associated paramilitary body ETA (Keating, 1988, pp. 214–17; Sullivan, 1988). The more prosperous Catalans are not as drawn to extreme nationalism, and there is no equal counterpart to ETA and HB in Catalonia (Keating, 1988, p. 225).

This is related to the more repressive policies of the Spanish state towards the Basques than towards the Catalans. Basque nationalists were able to gather support from many people before 1975 as they strongly opposed the unpopular Franco regime. The threat of Basque separatism provoked an attempted military coup in Madrid in 1981 which had the aim of reversing the decentralising Constitution of 1978. This shows how nationalism within a state can lead to an extreme centrist reaction, even though the ruling nationalist parties in the Basque lands and Catalonia are autonomists rather than separatists.

Religious leaders are prominent in nationalist movements in some cases. This may be because religion is a strong national identifier, as in Poland and Armenia, or because church leaders are relatively free to express political dissent in authoritarian regimes (e.g. South Africa under apartheid). Writers and scholars are also notable nationalists. In 1989 the writer Vaclav Havel became President of Czechoslovakia, and the musicologist Vytautas Landsbergis the President of Lithuania.

The presence of immigrant workers complicates the pattern of political behaviour. On the one hand, they often provoke nationalism among the indigenous workers. On the other hand, these immigrant workers swell the vote for state-wide class parties (usually socialist). Thus in Catalonia and the Basque country, the Spanish Socialist Party gets much support from the large number of workers who have moved there from other parts of Spain. Similarly, in the Baltic nations of Estonia, Latvia and Lithuania, the Russian immigrants at first opposed Baltic nationalism and were largely loyal to the USSR and the Communist Party of the Soviet Union. After the Moscow 'coup' of August 1991, Russians in the Baltics were almost as keen to secede from the USSR as the Baltic ethnic nationals. Socialist and other governing parties in western Europe, and even some in the former Communist Party of the Soviet Union (CPSU), responded to nationalist demands by granting moderate home rule forms of government, thereby seeking to contain nationalism through concessions. This can be considered a form of nationalist behaviour by non-nationalists, though cynics might say it is just a devious way to defeat the nationalists without really granting any power to their nations. This strategy, however, tends to backfire when nationalist demands escalate as frustration is felt.

Nationalist Political Behaviour

The extent of nationalist political behaviour is difficult to determine, for it is found not just in nationalist parties and organisations but in other parties and organisations as well. However, the nationalism of these other bodies is usually a reaction to the demands and successes of the self-confessed nationalists, and it is best to concentrate on these in the first place.

At one end of the spectrum, nationalists seem to encompass all those expressing national identity, ethnocentrism and some kind of economic and social interest in the nation. It is all too easy when discussing nationalism to assume that all Scots or Catalans or Tamils share a common nationalist political behaviour, especially when nationalist parties are doing well in elections, or when extreme nationalist organisations are hitting the headlines in campaigns of violence. Commentators in the newspapers and in broadcasting copy the nationalists themselves when they 'reify' the nation by attributing to it a single will, which is in reality not present. The nation is always divided into the wills of particular individuals and groups, and its political behaviour is similarly divided. In the nation there are nationalists and anti-nationalists, and divisions among the nationalists themselves, with separatists and autonomists often forming their own parties. These divisions are a source of weakness for nationalism, despite its great strength in politics throughout the world. For they can allow the anti-nationalists or official nationalists to 'divide and rule' a nation in many cases. If a nation were truly united, its will might be irresistible. But there is never 100 per cent nationalist behaviour in any nation with one aim. The opposing 'unionists' use official nationalism to combat the unofficial. nationalists, seeking loyalty for the state through an appeal to patriotism, expressed in state symbols such as the flag, army and national anthem. This clash of nationalisms emphasises the pervading appeal which nationalism has in modern politics, and such conflict is in effect a form of international relations, but with only one side possessing full statehood (see Chapter 10 for further discussion of nationalism in international relations).

The nationalist movements which aim for total independence seek to destroy existing states, while other forms of political activity, even Marxist revolutionary movements, usually leave the boundaries of the state intact. Only the nationalists who fought for the establishment of independent states in place of the colonies left the existing boundaries alone. This often meant that later a new set of nationalists, representing the 'nations within the nation', came to press for self-government within or outside the newly independent states, for example, the Ibos in Nigeria who sought to establish the state of Biafra.

The apparently intractable and non-negotiable nature of the nationalist demand – national self-determination – makes nationalist political behaviour seem a different kind of political behaviour from that of any other, at least regarding the territorial integrity of the state. That is why it is so feared and resisted by state governments everywhere. Yet the reality is that there is a wide spectrum of demands within nationalism and nationalist politics, and a wide variety of modes of political behaviour, from terrorism to constitutional electioneering. The politics of nationalism is a complex interchange of forces both between nationalists and others, and between nationalists themselves (for this, see particularly Brass, 1985). Each plays for the support of the wider public, and each deploys its own resources and exploits its opportunities.

The case studies which follow illustrate these political manoeuvrings and their results. Each can be analysed according to the general features involved. First, the resources generated by the nationalists themselves can be analysed: their ability to organise, to gain support, and to influence governments and international opinion. Here, the degree of division among the nationalists, involving perhaps several nationalist parties, nationalist organisations, terrorist organisations, and so on, is relevant. The more divided they are, the more they can be resisted. Second, the political context in which the nationalists operate ultimately determines their success or failure. The degree of dominance by particular nations in the state, and the degree of exclusion of non-dominant nations from power and full citizenship determines the type of nationalism which is present. Depending on the type of resistance they meet from the state, nationalists may have to fight to the death for their aims, or they may face an 'open door', or any situation between the two. An authoritarian state may suppress nationalist movements while a liberal state will allow them free expression within the law. But even these categories can vary over time in the nature of their responses. In the USSR, Stalin took a very different approach to the 'Nationality Question' from Gorbachev, but even Gorbachev took a Moscow view of the nationalities, and sought to repress them. In liberal-democratic Britain Thatcher and Major were unyielding on Scottish and Welsh devolution compared to Callaghan and Blair. Only the political histories of these countries can explain why such changes occurred in the fortunes of nationalism.

So we have both a 'bottom-up' and a 'top-down' view of the politics of nationalism and ethnicity. In the former, the nationalists themselves provide the resources, but in the latter their capability is determined by the whole political environment in which they find themselves, especially the response of anti-nationalists at home and in the central government. What determines the 'variables' and the result of the interaction between these is the central question in this study. In the case studies, there will be discussion of these variables, and of the results of nationalist political behaviour. The complexity of each case means that the discussion is necessarily brief and simplified. No definite conclusions can be offered, rather an indication of the features which are related to the theoretical models introduced in this book.

6

Nationalism in the Western World

The following case-studies provide a brief discussion of contemporary nationalist and ethnic politics in different parts of the world. These are the cases which have been the most prominent in recent years, and are the most obvious tests of the theoretical models discussed in this book. Of course, many other cases could be discussed, as well as parts of the world where nationalism appears to be less prominent in politics. It would be desirable to cover all the cases in the world, for a general theory of nationalism should be comprehensive as well as comparative. However, the agenda for this book is already over-filled with the cases considered here. Other cases of nationalist movements must be assumed to share most of the features of those discussed here. Where nationalism seems to be barely present at all (an unlikely scenario) the necessary conditions for nationalist politics as described here should be lacking.

Western Europe

Nationalism in Europe has revived generally since the 1960s, after a period of apparent quiescence in the aftermath of the Second World War. Nationalist parties or movements which have had a considerable, though variable, impact on contemporary west European politics are to be found in Britain (Scottish, Welsh, Irish, National Front, British National Party), France (Corsican, Breton, Basque, National Front), Spain (Catalan, Basque, Galician), Belgium (Fleming, Walloon), Italy (S. Tyrolean, Northern League), Switzerland (Jura), and Germany (Republican Party, Neo-Nazis).

There is also a related political movement, 'regionalism', which can seem to shade into nationalism where linguistic or cultural characteristics define the region. Some writers treat nationalism and regionalism as the same subject (e.g. Keating, 1988), and it is certainly difficult to draw a line between them in some countries. Here, the case-studies focus on explicitly nationalist movements, and exclude 'regionalisms' such as those of the Mezzogiorno in Italy and Andalusia in Spain. In Italy, the Northern League and the South Tyrol People's Party are both ethnonationalist and regionalist, sometimes even secessionist. While the distinction between nationalist and regionalist is to some extent a false distinction as far as the economic and territorial aspects of the subject are concerned, it is a real distinction when the cultural and ideological dimensions are considered. Regions are not nations, since they do not fulfil the necessary conditions for nationhood. Regions are strictly, and ideologically, *part* of a nation, not nations in their own right. In the same way, regionalism is not nationalism.

Is there any general explanation for the revival of nationalism in Europe? And what are the particular features of these nationalist movements? After the war, the map of Europe was drawn up by the superpowers, and the principal political division was an ideological and military one, that between communism on the one hand and the capitalist West on the other. At that time, all the political, economic and cultural resources of the continent were fully occupied with recovery and with the conditions of the Cold War.

By the 1960s, recovery was well under way, and expectations were also changing, both about internal politics and about the international world. There was a higher degree of security, both economically and militarily, for most people, and this made room for the alternative politics of culture and consumerism. Democracy was extended to include greater participation, and more parties were formed, which picked up votes as older party alignments loosened. This opened the way for nationalist parties to enter elections in opposition to the state-centred parties.

At this time too, the state began to institute regional policies to try to redress the economic imbalances between the rich and poor parts of the country. These regional policies led to the establishment of government development agencies within historic nations such as Scotland and Brittany, which fuelled expectations and increased the identity of these nations within the state structure, although that was not intended. However, such policies were for a time seen as unsuccessful, and nationalist parties were able to exploit their failure in redressing the territorial imbalances in the economy (Keating, 1988).

The post-1945 nationalist parties varied greatly in character and strength. The Scottish National Party, whose origins go back as far as 1928 but which had never won many votes, was one of the first to be markedly successful in elections, winning 30 per cent of the Scottish vote in the election of October 1974. The Welsh Nationalist Party (Plaid Cymru) rose to 11.5 per cent of the Welsh vote in 1970. Both of these parties dropped considerably in support thereafter, then revived in the late 1980s. In the 1997 election the SNP won 22.1 per cent of the Scottish vote, and 6 MPs. Plaid Cymru won 9.9 per cent of the Welsh vote and 4 MPs. The electoral threat to the major parties was sufficient to make them concede devolution to Scotland and Wales in the mid-1970s (the Conservatives under Margaret Thatcher changed their minds in 1976), although this was made subject to referendums in 1979 with a special rule that 40 per cent of the electorate should vote 'Yes'. In the event, this test was not passed in either nation, and in Wales there was a 4:1 vote against. Thus it appeared that the nationalist parties had failed to mobilise their nations, and that the central state had revealed the divisions therein, while appearing to concede to nationalist pressures. Labour remained committed to devolution, and when it returned to power in 1997 proposed a Parliament for Scotland and a non-legislative Assembly for Wales. Referendums in September 1997 in Scotland and Wales endorsed these proposals, by 74.3 per cent in the former, and by 50.3 per cent in the latter.

In fact, the centre in Britain never really conceded much to nationalism, since the form of devolution offered retained most power in the capital. This was apparent to most at the time of the referendums in 1979, and contributed to the low turnout and 'Yes' vote. The Scottish and Welsh cases show that the 'bottom-up' view of nationalist political behaviour applies well in the initial stages. A strong nationalist party with good electoral support will usually bring about concessions from the centre, but the centre will exercise its constitutional power and political ingenuity to confuse the nation and meet its demands only halfway. Thus 'top-down' politics prevails unless the pressures and resources from below are maintained or increased. In the case of Scotland and Wales, these pressures and resources largely evaporated for several years, to be revived again in the late 1980s. By this time, however, the Thatcher Conservative Government refused to concede anything to nationalism, and the nationalist pressures from below were largely contained. That is because the Opposition Labour Party was able to act in a nationalist fashion while gathering in its traditional class vote. Many Scots and Welsh voters hoped to get their socioeconomic and nationalist demands satisfied by supporting Labour, and believed they could deliver as the British government. If that were not possible, however, the potential for increased nationalist voting remained, and was already in evidence by 1988, when the SNP won the Glasgow Govan by-election from Labour. Labour and the Liberals joined in the Scottish Constitutional Convention in 1989, and produced a stronger devolution scheme, including tax powers, which formed the basis of the Labour Government's legislation after 1997. The SNP boycotted the Convention, since it excluded consideration of independence, but was prepared to join in the 'Yes, Yes' campaign in the 1997 referendum on the two questions: one relating to setting up a Scottish Parliament, and one related to its tax powers. Both questions got large affirmative majorities (74 per cent and 64 per cent respectively).

The SNP and Plaid Cymru were unusual in the politics of nationalism in having succeeded in winning many votes in elections (though never a majority), and in being the only credible nationalist parties claiming to represent their nations. Only in Catalonia and in Euskadi (the Basque country) after 1975, and in the 'Nationalities' of the Soviet Union and Yugoslavia since 1989, have nationalist parties been more successful electorally. Popular support for nationalist parties in Catalonia and Euskadi goes back to the late nineteenth century. Their electoral activities were interrupted by the Franco regime from 1939 to 1975, when they were proscribed. Even in Catalonia and Euskadi, however, the nationalists have been split into several parties, especially in the latter, where the moderate Basque Nationalist Party (PNV) is estranged from the more separatist Herri Batasuna (HB), and from the left-wing Euskadiko Eskerra (EE).

At the first Basque 'autonomous' (regional) election in March 1980, Basque nationalist parties won 64.2 per cent of the vote, divided among four parties. The largest, the PNV, won 37.6 per cent, followed by 16.3 per cent for Herri Batasuna. The PNV won 43 per cent of the vote in the 1984 Basque elections, HB 15 per cent, and EE 8 per cent. At the 1986 'autonomous' election, the PNV split, with Eusko Alkatasuna (EA), a right-wing splinter party, taking 15.9 per cent of the vote. The PNV was reduced to 24 per cent of the vote. In total, Basque parties won almost three-quarters of the vote in 1986 in the regional election, but only 52 per cent at the Spanish general election. In the Basque Autonomous Community, the PNV was forced into a coalition with the Socialist Party in order to keep HB out of government. Nevertheless, the PNV has been the main governing party in Euskadi (Basque country) since 1980, even if it won only 35.6 per cent of the vote and 22 of the 75 Basque Assembly seats in October 1994. In the 1996 Spanish general election it won 5 seats in the lower house, and agreed to support the minority Popular Party (PP) Government, with the promise of concessions on stronger devolution, which were duly delivered in 1997.

In Catalonia, too, the nationalist Convergence and Unity Party (CiU) is the leading party in Catalan regional elections, increasing its vote in regional elections from 27.6 per cent in 1980 to 47 per cent in 1984 and 46 per cent in 1988 to form the government of Catalonia. In regional elections in November 1995, the CiU won 41.0 per cent of the vote and 60 out of 135 seats, down from 71 in 1992. In Spanish elections, however, the PNV and CiU have done worse and the Socialists and Spanish parties better, which indicates that nationalist voting is lower in state-wide elections than in regional (national) elections. Thus in the 1996 Spanish elections the PNV won 25.9 per cent of the Basque vote (35.6 per cent in the 1994 regional elections) and CiU 30.0 per cent of the Catalan vote (41.0 per cent of the 1994 regional election vote). Nevertheless, the 5 Lower House and 5 Senate seats of the PNV in 1996, and the 16 Lower House and 8 Senate seats of the CiU in that election were crucial in propping up the PP Government, and in return these autonomous communities gained more tax powers. For a summary of these elections, see Tables 6.1 and 6.2.

Nationalist parties in other parts of western Europe have won fewer votes, and many have similarly had to compete with other

Table 6.1 *Catalan elections*

	Autonomous elections				Spanish elections (Congress of Deputies)			
	1992		1995		1993		1996	
	%	Seats	%	Seats	%	Seats	%	Seats
CiU	46.2	70	41.0	60	33.0	17	30.0	17
PSC-PSOE	27.5	40	24.8	34	36.2	18	39.8	19
PP	6.0	7	13.1	17	17.7	8	18.2	8
ERC	8.0	11	9.5	13	5.3	1	4.2	1
IC/IC-EV	6.5	7	9.7	11	7.7	3	7.8	2

Key

CiU: (Convergence and Unity). Right-of-centre nationalist (led by Jordi Pujol).
PSC-PSOE: (Catalan-Spanish Socialists).
ERC: (Esquerra Republicana de Catalunya). Regionalist party.
IC or IC-EV: (Communist Left). Catalan version of IU (United Left).
PP: (Popular Alliance).

nationalist parties representing a choice between total separation or autonomy, and between socialism, liberalism and conservatism. Obviously such a division weakens the nationalist cause, but success or failure in gaining concessions from the state is determined also by the intensity of the nationalism involved, and by the reaction of the centre. Nationalist voting makes the government of the state responsive if it is dependent on electoral support from its constituent nations, whether through state-wide parties with strong national wings, or when small nationalist parties hold the balance of power in central legislatures.

This introduces the whole picture of party politics in the state and in the nation. For it is not just the nationalist parties who determine the political agenda, though they may place the nation's claims on that agenda. The other parties must respond, and how they do so is crucial, since in all the cases mentioned here the nationalist parties by definition do not possess majority support or representation in the state.

State-wide parties may split into national wings under pressure from nationalism. In Belgium, the Socialist, Christian Social and

Table 6.2   *Basque country (Euskadi) elections*

	Autonomous elections				Spanish elections (Congress of deputies)			
	1990		1994		1993		1996	
	%	Seats	%	Seats	%	Seats	%	Seats
EAJ-PNV	28.5	22	29.8	22	25.6	5	25.9	5
PSE-EE	19.9	16	17.1	12	26.1	7	22.1	6
HB	18.3	13	16.3	11	15.5	2	12.7	2
EA	11.4	9	10.3	8	10.4	1	8.5	1
PP	8.2	6	14.4	11	15.6	4	18.9	5
IU-EB	1.4	—	9.1	6	3.5	2	4.1	—
UA	1.4	3	2.7	5	—	—	—	—

Key

EAJ-PNV: Euzko Alderdi Jeltzalea-Partido Nacionalista Vasco (Basque Nationalist Party). Moderate, centrist.
HB: Herri Batasuna. Political wing of ETA (Euskadi ta Askatasuna). Extreme nationalist.
PSE-EE: Partido Socialista de Euskadi/Euskadiko Ezkerra (Basque Socialist Party).
EA: Eusko Alkatasuna. Right-wing breakaway from EAJ-PNV.
PP: Partido Popular. Moderate conservative party.
IU-EB: Izquierda Unida. Left-wing party.
EA: Eusko Alkartasuna (Basque Solidarity). Radical nationalist but non-violent party. Allied to EuE (Euskal Ezkerra; Basque Left).
UA: Unidad Alavesa (Alavan Unity). Stands for the rights of the province of Alavesa.

Liberal Parties split into Flemish and Walloon wings after 1965, and fought elections on their own platforms. This meant that nationalism could be expressed as much through them as through the nationalist parties, the Volksunie (Flemish Nationalists) and the Rassemblement Wallon (Walloon Nationalists). The nationalist parties were unable to muster more than a fifth of the vote in their nations, and peaked in the mid-1970s. This did not mean that nationalism declined in Belgium. Rather, the old parties took over the nationalist claims and proceeded to federalise Belgium along linguistic and national lines.

In Belgium the central government became highly responsive to national claims through the splits in the major parties and, after the constitutional changes, devolved powers to the national communities and regions (the distinction between the powers of communities and regions in Belgium is broadly between cultural and economic matters; in both cases the nations are the basis of the division, except for Brussels, which is bilingual and has a regional council only, cultural matters being shared between the French and Flemish Community Councils).

In Britain and France, the major parties did not split, but MPs and Deputies from the nations acted in a more nationalist or decentralist way. This evoked a governmental response, especially when left-wing parties were in office. The Labour Party in Britain and the Socialist Party in France became converted to decentralisation in the 1970s and introduced devolution legislation. In Britain the Labour Government was unable to achieve the qualified majority required to pass its schemes at referendums in Scotland and Wales in 1979, but achieved majorities at the referendum in September 1997.

In France, a general scheme of regional assemblies was introduced in 1982, with a special statute for Corsica, where nationalists had been extremely active. Brittany, however, was not given special treatment, perhaps because its nationalist activity had faded in the late 1970s. Its nationalist voting remained under 5 per cent. In Corsica nationalist and 'autonomist' parties have regularly won around 15 per cent of the vote in regional and local elections in the 1980s and 1990s. The extreme nationalists (CCN) boycotted the first regional elections in 1982, but the autonomists (UPC) won 10.6 per cent of the vote and 7 seats. Another nationalist party (PPC) won 2 per cent of the vote, and one seat. In the 1984 regional elections in Corsica the nationalists (ex-CCN, now MCA) won 5 per cent of the vote and 3 seats, as did the autonomists (UPC). In the 1992 regional elections nationalist parties won 25 per cent of the vote and 9 out of 51 Assembly seats. But they were deeply split among themselves, and by 1995 in local elections the nationalist total had dropped to 14.4 per cent. Most voters continued to support the 'French' parties, and it was through these that nationalist and regionalist demands were channelled to Paris. There are no Corsican nationalist parties represented in the French Parliament, and in the 1997 elections they did not even stand. Thus, unlike the position in Catalonia and the Basque Country, when regional elections were introduced to Corsica the nationalists were unable to take control. Instead, the centre and right-wing parties reaped the benefit of nationalist pressure and Socialist reforms, and now also acted in a nationalist way on behalf of Corsica.

In Corsica, as in some other parts of Europe, there was a background of violent non-constitutional nationalism, expressed in bombings, kidnappings, killings and robberies. Welsh language extremists, the Irish Republican Army (IRA) and Ulster Defence Association (UDA) in Northern Ireland, ETA in the Basque country, and Swiss Jura separatists were also violent nationalists who posed a direct threat to the authority of the state. Extremist nationalism is probably the result of frustration with the effectiveness of constitutional methods, from the nationalist point of view. Where nationalists form a permanent minority, as in Northern Ireland up to now, they have no hope of winning a majority in elections. Thus one source of legitimacy is denied them. They are also faced with intransigent central governments who resist the 'break-up' of the state. A political tradition of violence is invariably found in such areas: for example, banditry in Corsica, and Fenianism and militant Orangeism in Ireland. In such a political culture, force seems a natural method to achieve political ends.

While violent nationalism hits the headlines throughout the world, it should be borne in mind that only a tiny minority of a nation indulges in such actions. But there may well be passive support from a much larger number, and the political impact is great. What the central state seeks to do is to eliminate the terrorists or to marginalise them by getting the support of the moderate nationalists. Thus in Northern Ireland, the British Government in 1974 sought to defuse militant Irish nationalism by establishing a power-sharing Executive, including the constitutional nationalists (the Social and Democratic Labour Party). But when this Executive was set up, it was soon killed off by an Ulster Unionist backlash in another example of 'direct action', a general strike. Now the emphasis is on talks to deal with the constitutional future of Ireland, but the militant Sinn Fein party is not as acceptable to the Unionists as the SDLP, because of its links with the Irish Republican Army. Similarly, the Spanish state has had to support the moderate Basque National Party (PNV) against the extremist Herri Batasuna and the paramilitary ETA.

Even so, the bombings continue, perhaps because HB and ETA have not shared in governmental power in Euskadi.

Contemporary European nationalism is peculiar in that it occurs in states which seemed to be well-established and stable. Most people by the 1950s had regarded Britain, France, Belgium and Spain as 'nation-states', rather than as multinational states. It thus came as a big surprise when Scots, Welsh, Bretons, Flemings, Basques, and so on, came to voice nationalist demands, and to achieve a big political impact in the 1960s and afterwards.

Are there any general explanations for this? Inglehart has pointed to the changing political culture in advanced economies, or 'post-industrial societies', with popular support for 'post-materialist' values. He has shown that support for nationalist parties in Belgium in the early 1970s was heavily drawn from people with such values (Inglehart, 1977, pp. 234–43). Green Parties are also in favour of regional autonomy, with the Scottish Green Party supporting Scottish independence. At the same time, paradoxically, 'post-materialists' tend to favour supra-national integration, for example in the European Community. What they do not show great affection for is the traditional centralised state, nor the traditional class or religious parties. This can be termed a cultural explanation for nationalism, but it is also an explanation based on changes in the economic and international environment. In the case of Europe these changes had brought about a high standard of living and international peace and security, leading to less dependence on the state.

Despite these affluent conditions, nationalist movements express discontent with the economic and political systems. They see their nations as disadvantaged economically within the state, and their political rights denied under an over-centralised constitution. Their success in altering these systems has been remarkable in recent years. For this we must look to *regime changes*, which have provided the opportunity for decentralisation policies. In Spain, the Franco regime, which had repressed the nations within Spain, was replaced by a democratic system in 1975, and it proceeded to introduce home rule. Democratisation and devolution in Spain were seen as two sides of the same coin. In France too, the advent of a new-style Socialist rule, after years of centralism of both right and left, opened the doors to regional devolution. In Belgium, the regime changed when the political parties split into Fleming and Walloon wings. This led on to constitutional reforms which split the government of the country on linguistic grounds. In Britain, the upsurge of Irish Republican nationalism in Northern Ireland was the result of a regime change. After 1968, the Northern Ireland Unionist Government of Terence O'Neill was forced into conceding civil rights to Catholics. This upset the status quo of Unionist domination, and opened the way for more virulent Nationalist activity. Then the British Government suspended the Stormont Parliament and Government in 1972, which created a constitutional vacuum in which Nationalists and Unionists turned increasingly to illegal, violent actions. In contrast, Scottish and Welsh nationalisms were rendered comparatively weak in the absence of a marked regime change. Devolution failed to go through in the 1970s and 1980s, largely because the grassroots nationalist pressures were insufficiently strong to support it, and the centre remained relatively static. In 1997 a breakthrough occurred with the advent of a Labour Government and a favourable vote for devolution in the Scottish and Welsh Referendums. Elsewhere in Europe, the decentralisations of the 1970s and 1980s have largely satisfied moderate nationalist demands. It remains to be seen whether these changes will be stable, or will lead on to further demands and separation.

Quebec

Nationalism in Quebec has posed a major threat to the political system of Canada since the 1960s. The Parti Québécois (PQ), founded in 1968, won the Quebec Provincial election of 1976 with 41 per cent of the vote and 71 out of 110 seats in the Quebec Assembly. It remained in office until 1985, when the Liberals were returned. In the meantime, the PQ had promoted its aim to make Quebec a separate state, on the formula of 'Sovereignty-Association', which meant that some links with the rest of Canada would be retained. However, even negotiations on the basis of this formula were rejected by the Quebec electorate in a referendum in 1980 by 59.5 per cent to 40.5 per cent, on an 84 per cent turnout. Although the PQ was essentially the party of the French-speaking population, they were on that occasion split equally between 'Yes' and 'No' (Fitzmaurice, 1985).

The next phase came when an attempt at constitutional reform (the Meech Lake Accord of 1987) failed to get the ratification of the Provinces in 1990 (see below). Yet another attempt failed when it was decisively rejected in a Canada-wide referendum on 26 October 1992. This led to a revival of Quebec nationalism, and the PQ won the Quebec elections in September 1994, with 77 of the 125 seats, but with only 44.7 per cent of the votes. The PQ proceeded to hold another referendum on sovereignty, albeit with Quebec in 'economic and political partnership' with the rest of Canada. On a 93 per cent turnout, this was narrowly defeated by 50.6 per cent against to 49.4 per cent in favour (30 October 1995). While this was obviously a disappointment to the PQ Government, it was also a clear signal that Quebec nationalism had risen in strength since the 1980 referendum.

The case of Quebec shows that nationalist political behaviour can be a most unpredictable political force, although its foundations may be long term. The French-speaking population of Canada, concentrated in Quebec, but also strong in Acadia (New Brunswick) have always constituted a separate nation within Canada, and they rarely intermarried with the non-French-speaking immigrants. Some, however, supported Canadian nationalism and were Founding Fathers of the Confederation, so there was always some ambiguity as to which of the two nationalisms meant more to the francophone elites. The mass of the francophone population, however, felt itself to be the object of internal colonialism in a Canada dominated by English-speakers of British extraction. The Canadian Constitution in its federal structure (known in Canada as 'confederation' – the most decentralised form of federation) protected the francophone population with religious and linguistic guarantees. These were underwritten by the British Parliament until 'repatriation' of the Constitution in 1982.

What brought about the sudden rise of Quebec separatism in the 1960s, its equally sudden decline in the 1980s, and its revival in the 1990s, is still something of a mystery, even to Canadians. Many despaired of Canadian unity when the PQ achieved power, while the PQ in its turn was taken aback at its electoral defeats in the 1980 referendum and in the Quebec election of 1985. But its revival in 1994 was not sufficient to produce a mandate for sovereignty in the referendum of 1995.

There is agreement among most observers that the rise of Quebec nationalism was largely the result of social and economic changes in Quebec in the 1960s: the 'Quiet Revolution'. This was a form of 'modernisation', with a growing urban economy and secularisation. The passivity of the French population under British rule, encouraged by the Catholic Church, came to an end, and a new generation asserted its civil rights, which included the right to national self-determination, the sole use of the French language in Quebec (including the English-dominated Montreal and suburbs), and control over the economy. Some Quebec nationalists in the Front pour la Libération du Québec (FLQ) turned to violence, and in 1970 a Quebec government minister was murdered, and another kidnapped. This led to emergency powers being introduced in Quebec.

All these social and political developments can be considered a regime change, although they took place under the Quebec Liberal Party, which had indeed encouraged the 'Quiet Revolution'. The eclipse of the Liberals in 1974, and of the PQ in 1985, was the result of electoral choices which related as much to how these parties had governed as to any verdict on nationalism. The Liberals were tarnished by scandals in the 1960s and early 1970s; the PQ failed in economic management when it was in power.

Regime changes also occurred at the centre which profoundly affected the strength of nationalism in Quebec. Pierre Trudeau, the Liberal Prime Minister of Canada virtually continuously from 1968 to 1984, though a French-speaker from Quebec, was a Canadian 'official' nationalist who sought the unity of Canada through bilingualism and strong central power. His policies seemed to threaten Quebec, since bilingualism there could mean the weakening of the French language (Laponce, 1985), and centralisation was at odds with Quebec independence. In this regime change then, Quebec nationalism flourished as a reaction to aggressive Canadian nationalism.

The revival of nationalism in 1989 was related to the establishment of a free trade area between Canada and the United States (another regime change). This made the Canadian economy less important to Quebec than its links with the USA (the same was true of the western provinces). So there was an element of economic rationality in supporting an independent Quebec within a free trade area with the USA. Quebec nationalists could assuage fears of economic isolation under independence, just as the Scottish nationalists could with their slogan 'Independence in Europe'.

The Canadian system of government has been fundamentally changed to take account of moderate Quebec nationalism, represented by the Liberals. It is less comfortable with the PQ, whose counterparts in the Federal Parliament, the Bloc Québécois, paradoxically formed the official Opposition after the almost total wipe-out of the Progressive Conservatives in the federal elections of 1993. Yet Quebec remains within the Canadian federal structure and its unilingualism has been checked, if not overcome. Its national identity is now recognised (if not constitutionally finally ratified), but it is not clearly accepted by the English-speaking population. Canada is one state and two nations.

The lesson of this case for nationalist parties is that their electoral support can be highly volatile and dependent on the effect of the electoral system, even if the underlying nationalism is strong (it is not usually predominantly separatist, however). Other political parties can capitalise on nationalism and engineer regime changes which satisfy moderate nationalist feeling and keep the nationalist parties out of power. The PQ tried to take Quebec out of Canada, but failed to convince the Quebec electorate, let alone the rest of Canada. The defeat for nationalism which the 1980 referendum seemed to represent resembled that sustained by the SNP and Plaid Cymru (PC) in Scotland and Wales in 1979. But in both cases, there was a second chance. Quebec nationalism revived under the auspices of the Liberals in the 1980s, and under the PQ Government after 1994, just as the Labour Party took over much of Scottish and some of Welsh nationalism in the same period and proceeded to legislate for devolution when it came to power in 1997. These cases show that the variable fortunes of nationalist parties may disguise a steady advance in nationalism in other parties.

At the same time, the nationalist parties can revive if they can demonstrate potential economic advantages of independence to the voters. The case of Quebec shows, contrary to Gellner and other theorists of modernisation, that ethnic differences can prevent the emergence of a 'nation-state', even under the conditions of an industrialised society and a long-established state. Modernisation within an ethnically-divided society may increase nationalism, and not just at the early stages of development, but in mature economies.

Ethnic Politics in the USA and Britain

'Ethnic politics' refers to the politics of 'ethnic groups' or 'ethnic minorities'. While a broad interpretation of 'ethnic group' would include 'ethnic nation' as used earlier, the contemporary political usage is much narrower. In this context, ethnic groups or minorities do not usually possess a defined territory, and their aims differ from those of 'classical' nationalists in that they do not seek 'national self-determination' within a national territory. Rather, they seek protection and advancement for the group, and especially for individuals in the group, within an existing state. Only rarely do they form ethnic parties or secession movements. Instead they tend to work through pressure groups, community action associations, and established multiethnic political parties.

Members of such ethnic groups tend to be recent immigrants, or inhabitants of states with a special history of slavery, indenture or forced migration. Thus in the USA nineteenth-century immigrants such as the Irish and Italians were typically engaged in ethnic politics. Today, Hispanics and Asians are beginning to occupy a similar position in some parts of the USA. Blacks, most of whose forebears were slaves, straddle the categories 'ethnic' and 'race', but with no clear distinction other than that of skin colour. In Britain, 'ethnic minorities' are either black or Asian, with no distinction usually being made between the two.

Many other countries have different types of ethnic politics, such as politics relating to 'guest workers' in Germany (usually Turks or Slavs), or to Moslems in France (usually from Algeria and Morocco). It is also reasonable to include long-established pockets of minority populations as 'ethnic' rather than 'national' where no nationalist aims or viable nationalist movements have developed. Of course, this gives rise to the criticism that ethnic groups are really failed nations, since their credentials as nations have failed to be successfully established (Hobsbawm, 1990).

Here, however, attention is focused on the 'non-nationalist' politics of ethnic groups.

Even so, ethnicity, race and nationalism are linked. Black African nationalism is found not only in Africa but also in the USA and in Britain. While there are connections between the two, the contexts are of course different. In the USA, social and political change after 1945, and especially after the Korean War, led to a strong civil rights movement, which achieved considerable success in the 1950s and 1960s, after a fierce struggle. In Britain, black immigration from the Caribbean and immigration from Asia (mainly India and Pakistan) produced similar pressures for civil rights when these groups became politically active in the 1960s.

These developments fit in with the features associated with the rise of nationalist movements generally, such as the political mobilisation of the nation at the grass-roots and a 'regime change' at the top. In Britain and the USA, the black and Asian populations gradually rose in social status and started to organise effectively; the government changed the constitutional and political system in response, thereby providing the opportunity for further political action.

There are links between black African nationalism and black nationalism in the USA. The example of the newly independent black states in Africa was encouraging to oppressed blacks in America and Europe. In the USA, many black nationalists see themselves today as 'African Americans' and stress their roots in Africa. A few have even identified with Africa entirely, and have returned there. Most, however, assert their nationalism as US citizens, but they also support special black institutions such as black churches, schools, colleges and business firms. The extreme expression of black nationalism was the Black Power movement, which in the 1960s spawned a violent wing, the Black Panthers. This made no progress in the 1970s, and by the 1980s Black nationalism was essentially constitutional in its methods.

Blacks in Britain (whose African origins are usually mediated by residence in the Caribbean islands) similarly assert their rights in terms of British citizenship. Their nationalism is mainly concerned with the promotion of black cultural identity in a 'multicultural' British society. There is hardly any African-British nationalism, nor has there been a Black Power movement in Britain.

Black nationalism in the USA and Britain is related to the larger pattern of ethnic politics in these countries. Ethnic groups seek a variety of political objectives including 'civil rights' ('equal opportunity', or the abolition of adverse ethnic and 'racial' dis‑crimination), advantages for their group ('positive discrimina‑tion'), and a share in party organisation and government (reserved places). It is clear these different strategies are not exactly consistent, either in philosophical or practical terms.

In the USA and Britain, 'race' and ethnicity are usually dis‑tinguished from one another, with the former label applied to 'blacks', 'browns' and 'yellows' of ultimate African and Asian ori‑gin, and the latter applied to other ethnic groups, usually European in origin. While there is little scientific basis for the distinction between race and ethnicity, the political distinction is a strong one, as we shall see.

'Race relations' in politics in practice means the relationship between citizens of different skin colours. 'Ethnic politics', on the other hand, conventionally concerns white or near-white ethnic groups of European origin in the USA such as Irish, Italian, German and Latin-Americans (Hispanics). These are not official or rigid distinctions, nor are they likely to be permanent in poli‑tics. For some writers, 'race' should be replaced by 'ethnic group' (Miles, 1982), and 'good race relations would be ethnic relations' (Banton, 1983, p. 397). The distinction made by Banton is that 'race' denotes an exclusive ethnic group based on colour, while an 'ethnic group' is a voluntary association based on beliefs about a common heritage. Ethnic competition is thus more open and acceptable to liberal thinkers than racial competition. It is of course very difficult (but maybe not impossible) to transform exclusive 'racial groups' based on colour into inclusive 'ethnic groups'. Nor is it always the case that ethnic groups are in prac‑tice inclusive (open to all).

Legislation on civil rights and race relations in the USA and Britain is vague about who is covered (the Scots and English are included in British race relations legislation by implication), but the original political intention is clear: to protect blacks and Asians from continuing white oppression and discrimination. This pinpoints the essential political difference between the 'pol‑itics of race' and 'ethnic politics'. Nearly all blacks in the USA and Britain share a heritage of slavery. This dominates their political position to this day, and has largely determined their economic and social status. European, Asian and Latin-American immigrants came as free citizens, and have experienced fewer difficulties in establishing a favourable economic and social status. Thus black politics is directed at redressing the legacy of slavery, and ethnic politics is about achieving gains for ethnic groups in what is for them a relatively open and competitive political system.

It is significant that only blacks have espoused nationalism along the lines of 'Black Nationalism'. That is because the channels of ethnic politics were largely closed to blacks, on account of the background of slavery, and because of colour discrimination. The 'melting-pot' of the American nation has been quicker to melt the different (white) ethnic groups than it has been to melt the blacks with the whites. And since the 1960s it has largely ceased to melt the ethnic groups too, preferring to stress ethnicity along with equal citizenship in the 'American Dream' of the 'Land of the Free' (Glazer and Moynihan, 1975).

The 'melting-pot' was always an inept image where colour was concerned. There is no way that colour distinctions can be eliminated. Non-colour ethnic distinctions can be changed or ignored, but this will only happen in certain circumstances. As in the other case-studies, we find here that ethnicity predominates as a political interest where class, religion and territory are comparatively weak as social divisions. This condition has been found at various times in American and British political history.

The first manifestation of ethnic politics in the USA and Britain was the organisation of immigrant groups by the political parties into voting blocs. Irish, Jewish, Italian and German immigrants to the USA in the nineteenth and early twentieth centuries retained a strong ethnic identity as long as it was difficult for them to assimilate to the predominant 'Anglo-Saxon' American nation. And even when assimilation was possible, many preferred to continue to stress an ethnic identity in order to benefit from the political share-out of jobs and services. In the absence of a comprehensive merit system of recruitment to public employment, patronage was brokered by ethnic leaders, who in turn delivered the votes of the group to the party. Even today, American politicians make direct appeals to ethnic groups in order to win votes, and some residue of patronage along ethnic lines still persists.

In Britain, the 'Irish vote' and the 'Jewish vote' have historically occupied a similar position in the political system. These went to the Liberal and Labour Parties, for the Conservative Party primarily represented the Anglican and English establishment. Today, these ethnic groups vote much more according to social class, as the barriers to their social advancement have been reduced. Even so, Catholics are heavily skewed in their votes to the Labour Party, irrespective of class. This is not so much a matter of Irish ethnicity (a weak identity among many Catholics in Great Britain) as of political opportunism. The Labour Party offers an avenue to power for Catholics which is still not available in other parties. Jews, on the other hand, have largely deserted the Labour Party for the Conservatives as they have grown more prosperous, despite some anti-Semitism amongst right-wingers. Such views are outweighed by the ideological congruity between 'New Right' Conservatism and the Jewish business ethnic, bolstered by the great economic success of many Jews in British society (Alderman, 1983; 1989).

Most attention in Britain is now paid to the 'black vote' and the 'Asian vote', which goes heavily to the Labour Party (Anwar, 1986). The political influence of that vote is not great, however, since the British political system does not encourage ethnic politics. That is because there is less pride in diverse ethnicity in Britain than in the United States, for the country does not see itself as an immigrant nation. There is a more centralised and bureaucratised governmental structure in Britain, which leaves little room for patronage to ethnic groups such as at the level of state and local government in the USA, where ethnic pressure is most easily wielded. The British party system is made up of parties of a predominantly class character, with ideological, not sectional, programmes.

The American party system, on the other hand, is decentralised and non-programmatic, and is in reality a coalition of numerous interests. In this system, there is easy access for ethnic groups, and a 'log-rolling' political process whereby groups support one another to get legislation passed in the interests of all of them. A disciplined party system, such as that in the British Parliament, does not allow for this.

The log-rolling process is not always possible when there are political conflicts between ethnic groups. Black groups are unable to cooperate with white racist groups such as the Ku Klux Klan and right-wing American groups which stress white interests. More complexly, Black nationalists and Jews have come into conflict for a variety of reasons. Although both Blacks and Jews engage in ethnic politics as historically disadvantaged groups, the present social and economic position of most Jews is well ahead of Blacks. In particular, Blacks are often in subordinate face-to-face situations with Jews, as tenants of Jewish landlords and as employees in Jewish shops and businesses. This emphasises a cultural division of labour between them.

An international dimension is also involved. The Jewish lobby in the United States has been very successful in keeping the USA on the side of Israel in Middle East politics. Israel had ties with Apartheid South Africa in trade and defence procurement which Blacks naturally objected to. In addition, Black Moslems, who are a type of Black nationalist movement, side with their co-religionists in the Middle East against Israel. This is one example where domestic and international factors shape ethnic relations (see also Chapter 10).

The big question for ethnic groups in American and British politics is how far they should seek a separate identity and how far they should work within parties and organisations with a multiethnic or non-ethnic character. In both the USA and Britain ethnic parties have been almost totally absent, although an Islamic Party of Britain was formed in 1989 to represent the peculiar interests of Moslems held to be neglected by the other parties. It made no progress. Instead, Blacks have sought a political role in the mainstream political process, including direct representation in non-ethnic parties. Thus, the Labour Party was faced with a demand for a 'Black Section' in the late 1980s. This was rejected in 1988, yet an affiliated 'Black Socialist Society' was granted in 1990. This did not satisfy the advocates of formal Black Sections.

In the USA, ethnic groups work through the Democratic and Republican Parties. The constitutional structure inhibits the establishment of minor parties generally but, as we have seen, a more fundamental reason for the absence of ethnic parties is the relatively open nature of the major parties to pressure groups, especially at the state and local government level. There are now many black mayors of American cities, usually Democrats, and ethnic groups play a large part in state politics. In Congress, however, blacks are a tiny group, and state-wide elections for the Senate favour 'White Anglo-Saxon Protestant' (WASP) candidates over 'ethnic' candidates. That is because it is impossible for any one ethnic group to carry the election over such a wide territorial area. When an ethnic candidate is put up, the other ethnic group voters tend to prefer a 'WASP' as more neutral and more 'American'. In a presidential election especially, a Bush has an advantage over a Dukakis.

Despite this, there has been a revival of ethnicity and ethnic politics in the USA, and signs of increased ethnic political activity in Britain too. Why is this? Black political activism in both countries spearheaded the new consciousness of ethnicity. The response of the state in the USA and Britain was to concede 'civil rights' and, in the USA 'positive discrimination' ('affirmative action') through quotas for blacks in education and public employment. This legitimation of ethnicity encouraged other ethnic groups to follow the Blacks in their search for roots, their new-found ethnic pride, and their political activism (Martin Kilson in Glazer and Moynihan, 1975). So ethnic politics revived as a channel of influence in American and British democracy after a period of quiescence since the first wave of mass immigration ended in 1924 in the USA and in 1914 in Britain (mainly Irish and Jewish). Since the 1950s, 'Black' (Caribbean and Asian) immigration to Britain produced the pressures for civil rights which the long-established Black population produced in the USA in the 1950s and 1960s. The later (from the 1970s) mass migration to the USA of Hispanics from Latin America and of Asians from Indo-China and the Philippines has added a new dimension to US ethnic politics.

The successes of Black politics in the USA in the 1960s produced a reaction among whites in the 1970s and 1980s, pushing them towards the Republican Party. In Britain, too, many white voters in the working class turned away from the Labour Party to support the Conservative Party in areas such as London and the West Midlands of England where blacks and Asians were numerically strong and politically influential in the Labour Party. The Conservative Party has been careful to avoid an overt appeal to white racism, and Enoch Powell's and Norman Tebbit's anti-immigrant stance was officially renounced. Nevertheless, both

Labour and Conservative Governments passed a series of laws to restrict New Commonwealth (black) immigration from 1962 onwards. This was in contrast to the liberalisation of US immigration laws at that time. In the USA, the strict quotas imposed on non-European immigrants since the Chinese Exclusion Act of 1882 were relaxed in 1965, when civil rights legislation made discrimination on account of colour embarrassing in the context of immigration controls.

In Britain, there has been some working-class support for the extreme 'nationalist' politics of the National Front and the British National Party, but these parties have made negligible gains in electoral terms, and the National Front contested only 4 seats in the 1997 general election, with an average vote of just over 1 per cent. This is in contrast to the National Front in France, which has had considerable electoral success. For example, its leader Jean-Marie Le Pen stood in the 1995 President elections and won 15 per cent of the vote in the first round. The *Front National* (FN) won 35 National Assembly seats in 1984, but the change in the electoral system from PR to Second Ballot meant the total loss of its seats by 1993. It won control of four towns in the south at local elections by 1997, however, including Toulon (population, 437,000). The basis of the FN vote is anti-immigrant feeling, especially in areas with large numbers of immigrants from North Africa. But it also appeals to former Communist voters and others suffering social deprivation. The British National Party (BNP) put up 54 candidates in the 1997 general election with the policy that people of non-European origin cannot be absorbed into the British population. Only 3 of its candidates won over 5 per cent of the vote, and its vote overall was under 1 per cent. National Front and BNP activists cause considerable communal tension and some violence, and the more general urban violence in British and American cities since the 1960s has contributed to the political polarisation between urban whites and blacks.

The failure of the Labour Party until 1997 to keep much of its white working-class vote in London and the areas of England with a strong Black or Asian immigrant population is partly the result of the Party's local identification with that population. This has repelled working-class whites who fear a Black presence in housing, education and employment as a threat to their economic position. There are thus clear 'class' reasons for racism in Britain (Miles, 1982).

Despite anti-immigrant 'white politics' in the Conservative Party, many Asians are attracted to it as the party which best represents the strong shopkeeping interest in the Asian community. Private education is popular with Asians who can afford it, on account of their religious preference for single sex schools and their intense desire to obtain top educational qualifications. All this draws them away from the Labour Party to the more middle-class and private enterprise-oriented Conservative Party. So that party has to satisfy both white and Asian ethnic political pressures. In practice, it does this by officially avoiding ethnic issues in its election campaigns, concentrating instead on individualism and enterprise. On the ground, however, the politics of racism is important in sustaining the Conservative vote in some parts of Britain, and some Conservative candidates play on this.

Ethnic politics are more important in the USA and Britain today than they were a generation ago. That is first of all because of the political successes of blacks under the American civil rights legislation of the 1960s, leading to increased ethnic awareness in other groups. In Britain, mass immigration from the New Commonwealth in the 1950s and 1960s produced similar pressures for civil rights legislation and multicultural education. There followed a reaction in Britain in the form of immigration controls and racism.

The political culture of the USA is more favourable to ethnic politics than that of Britain. Britain is also less receptive to multiculturalism, seeing itself not as a 'melting-pot' of immigrants, but as an old-established 'nation-state' essentially English in character. The inappropriateness of this for the increasing non-English, non-white population of Britain has led to the development of ethnic politics since the 1960s, but the satisfying of ethnic demands in Britain seems likely to continue to be more difficult than in the USA for cultural and political reasons.

7

Nationalism in the Former Communist States

Perhaps the biggest surprise for students of nationalism in recent years has been the sudden upsurge of ethnic nationalism in the former communist states, especially in what was the Soviet Union, Yugoslavia and Czechoslovakia. In the space of a few years, nationalist movements arose, and considerable ethnic violence has occurred, especially in Croatia and Bosnia-Hercegovina (ex-Yugoslavia) and in Azerbaijan, Chechnya and Georgia (ex-USSR). Some of this occurred while these states were still communist, and yet it seems incompatible with the philosophy and practice of communism, in which nationalism is supposed to disappear, to be replaced by patriotism and 'proletarian internationalism' (see Connor, 1984). The complexities of Marxism need not detain us here, but the failure of Marxism to understand nationalism is significant. Marx and Engels predicted that national boundaries would, like the state, under socialism wither away, to be replaced by the solidarity across the nations of working people. Lenin espoused the doctrine of national self-determination when nationalism appeared to be stronger than socialism in defeating the Russian Empire. Once established, the Soviet Union was to suppress the nationalist movements within it which were seeking independence from Russia, but it did grant a sort of federal system with republics constituted along the lines of 'nationality'. National liberation movements abroad were supported wherever capitalist empires were the object of attack. Stalin espoused 'socialism in one country' as against Trotsky's internationalism and the 'Austro-Marxist' view of nationality as pertaining to individuals and not to territory

(Hobsbawm, 1990, pp. 7, 33). This soon developed into 'Great Russian Chauvinism'. Many western political scientists in the past were prepared to follow the official view of the communist governments that they had indeed solved the 'Nationality Problem', or at least had harnessed it in a way which was supportive of the communist system (e.g. McAuley, in Harding (ed.), 1984). By the end of the 1980s a completely new picture was emerging.

The Former USSR

By 1990 in the USSR several of the Soviet Republics were in turmoil with nationalist demands for independence, mass demonstrations, rioting, violence, bloodshed and deaths. The troubles ranged geographically from the Asian Republics such as Kazakhstan and Uzbekistan, the Caucasus (Armenia, Azerbaijan, Georgia) and Moldavia (now Moldova) near the Black Sea, to the Baltic Sea (Estonia, Latvia, Lithuania). While these areas might be considered peripheral regions of the USSR, the appearance of a Popular Front in the Ukraine coupled with mass demonstrations in support of the Uniate Catholic Church there marked a spreading of nationalist sentiment to a core Republic. The Russians themselves were affected by nationalism, and reacted against the claims of the 'nationalities' (Russians were not considered officially to be a 'nationality' themselves). Organisations such as Pamyat (Memory) and Interfront were formed by Russians, the former including anti-Semitic elements, and the latter aiming to protect ethnic Russian interests in the non-Russian republics. In June 1990, the Russian Republic declared its 'sovereignty' within the Soviet Union, following the example of nearly all the other republics. While this was certainly nationalism of a kind, it can only be understood in the context of the other demands which were being made at that time by the republics and reforming Soviet politicians, and which were now being granted. The main one was the democratisation of the political system, with the granting of competitive elections. Once this was agreed to, the voters could choose leaders who were not communists, or were communists with a nationalist programme, namely to achieve sovereignty or even independence for their nations. At first, as in June 1990, this 'sovereignty' was thought to be compatible with remaining part of the USSR. It was when the USSR itself imploded after the failed coup of August 1991 that all the constituent national republics of the USSR went all the way for independence, leaving only a shadowy Commonwealth of Independent States in its place. The three Baltic states refused to join that organisation.

What explanations can be given for this type of nationalist behaviour? There is something in common between these nationalisms and the ones discussed in the previous chapter. They have all arisen in the context of old-established states, which had already experienced nationalism since at least the eighteenth century, but which had apparently achieved political stability by the 1950s. However, the political systems differed greatly, with liberal democracy and free elections being the context for the western European nationalisms (except Spain before 1975), and communist authoritarianism the basis of the Soviet and Yugoslav systems. Moreover, it would be difficult to point to a 'post-industrial' political culture as contributing to the latter nationalisms, as shortages rather than affluence marked their economies. Yet it could be said that expectations were rising there too, particularly as regards civil rights, and that this resembles the 'post-materialism' in the west which contributed to nationalist political behaviour. In all cases of nationalism, issues of domination, discrimination and exclusion are combined with an increased sense of national identity and aspirations for democratic self-rule.

One obvious feature in common in the former communist states is that regime change seems to be the most important factor. The sudden rise of nationalism in the USSR and Yugoslavia coincided with a profound crisis in the system of government, coupled with rising expectations on the part of the constituent nations.

Under the leadership of Mikhail Gorbachev, the USSR began in 1985 to embark on a profound change in its political system, encapsulated in the words *perestroika* (reconstruction) and *glasnost* (openness) (Gorbachev, 1988). Included in this change was a new freedom to express political views and to participate in the political system in organisations competing with the Communist Party. This permitted nationalist political behaviour where previously it was repressed. In particular, it allowed the election of nationalist politicians in competition with the official Communists (CPSU), and in some cases (e.g. the Baltic nations) the election of nationalist or nationalist-supported governments. These asserted the right of secession granted in the Soviet Constitution. A throwback to the philosophy of Lenin and Stalin with its proclamation of the right of national self-determination, this clause in the Soviet Constitution was now activated by several nationalities under Gorbachev. However, the Soviet President resisted the implementation of this right by insisting on procedures for secession which would effectively veto it except on terms dictated by Moscow. Thus national self-determination for the constituent nations of the Soviet Union was to involve the consent of the Soviet Union as whole. It is important to note that Gorbachev both *encouraged* and *repressed* nationalism in the Baltics and elsewhere, e.g. Russia itself. This inconsistency was to prove his downfall, for he unleashed the forces which would destroy communism while remaining committed to communism himself. Thus a non-communist USSR was an impossibility, as was Gorbachev's place in such a state.

Gorbachev instituted the policy of *glasnost* (openness), which led to a revision of the official history of the Soviet Union. For example, the Nazi–Soviet Pact of 1939, which included the plan of annexation to the USSR of Estonia, Latvia, Lithuania and Moldavia, was officially revealed in 1989. This destroyed the legitimacy of the USSR as far as the Baltic nations were concerned. Commemorative nationalist protests in the annexed Republics were held, and one such demonstration in August 1989 was reported to have involved about two million people linking hands between the three Baltic capitals. Soon nationalist demonstrations in Moldavia, Armenia, Georgia and Ukraine attracted the support of hundreds of thousands.

Gorbachev's other policy of *perestroika* meant the reconstruction of the economic, constitutional and political structure of the Soviet state, including the position of the 'nationalities'. The Soviet Union's Constitution already recognised these nationalities in its federal system of 15 Republics and various 'autonomous regions', which were based on national identities. But these Republics and regions were subject to Communist Party 'democratic centralism', which meant that no real autonomy existed. These territorial political units did, however, provide a formal structure of government for the nationalities, and a system of political and economic preferment for local elites within their Republics. This was to prove an essential resource for nationalism under Gorbachev's more open regime, for local Party leaders whose powers had been curtailed under the centralising rule of Yuriy Andropov (1982–4) were eager to reassert their authority under Mikhail Gorbachev.

Gorbachev was primarily concerned to reform the overall Soviet system with a view to increasing economic efficiency, but his programme also included greater decentralisation, especially in economic and budgetary matters (Gorbachev, 1988, p. 299). He did not expect that his new regime would unleash a series of ethnic disorders and nationalist claims, yet he could not easily repress these under *glasnost*. He no doubt hoped to harness popular energies for his reforms by giving greater independence to the nationalities, and he put nationalistically inclined Party leaders into positions of power where they appeared to be reformers. In his clean-out of the 'old guard' he also cleaned out many wedded to the old ideas of centralism. Thus many Communist Party leaders in the Baltic Republics were new appointments who showed a sensitivity towards the nationalist demands of the Popular Fronts. In Lithuania, some of them broke away from the CPSU in December 1989 to form an independent Lithuanian Communist Party.

In other parts of the Soviet Union, Gorbachev's modernising appointments offended the local nationalists. In Kazakhstan, the local party leader was sacked in 1986 and replaced by a Russian. This provoked Kazakh nationalist rioting. Gorbachev's appointments were not designed to produce nationalism, rather to produce economic and political reforms. But the effect was to stimulate nationalism generally.

This gave an opportunity for nationalists who were more akin to those in the West to express themselves and be elected to office. While the new Gorbachev regime tolerated this, it opposed the breakaway of the Lithuanian Communist Party from the CPSU, and the declaration of independence by the Lithuanian Parliament at the end of 1989. He similarly denounced Latvia's and Estonia's declarations of independence in 1990. At the same time, he upheld the constitutional right of the republics to secede, although only on terms laid down by the

USSR Constitution and implemented by the Soviet authorities. As the Baltic governments now rejected the legitimacy of this Constitution, conflict was inevitable. Economic sanctions were imposed on Lithuania, which retaliated with economic sanctions against Russia.

Two features of the conflict between the USSR and the Baltic nations were particularly difficult to resolve. One was military. The Baltic region was important for the Soviet armed forces, and independence for the Baltic nations threatened the security of the USSR. The army was also worried about desertions of non-Russian personnel, which could spread to other nationalities. The other difficult feature was the strong presence of Russians in the Baltic countries, especially in Latvia and Estonia, representing their social and economic interdependence with the USSR. Russians manned many factories in Latvia and Estonia, which were geared to serving the Soviet economy, having been financed by Moscow.

Here were strong features of 'internal colonialism' and a 'cultural division of labour', leading to 'anti-colonial nationalism'. As an 'imperial' power, the USSR was not prepared to lose its territory without a struggle, and in the absence of official support from the centre the 'nationalities' were in a weak position. Moreover, other states were not inclined to aid the break-up of the USSR if this jeopardised the improvement in East–West relations which had already led to the liberation of the eastern European nations. So the conditions in international relations were not ripe for a new state settlement involving the loss of territory for the USSR, especially as German unification within the western orbit was already threatening to tilt the balance of power against the Soviet Union. Yet when it came, the break-up of the Soviet Union was quickly accepted in the international community, and the new states were recognised. That is because there was no alternative: the USSR had itself dissolved, without external pressure. Some ambiguity remained: Nagorno-Karabakh in Azerbaijan was claimed by Armenia and civil war ensured, with Armenia eventually predominant; Moldova was also in turmoil, with a Russian secessionist republic (Dnestr), and a desire on the part of the majority ethnic Romanian population to become part of Romania. While Russia, Ukraine and Romania supported their client populations, the international community stood aside. By 1997, Moldova had stabilised, with Russian withdrawal, autonomy for Dnestr, and a Referendum decision in 1994 to stay apart from both Romania and Russia. Similarly, when Chechnya revolted against Russia, it was the Chechens' actions that forced Russia to grant virtual independence within the Russian Federation in 1997.

By the end of 1991, all the Soviet nationalities had declared total independence, including Russia. All had held referendums at one time or another on the subject of constitutional change, although it is not always clear what they had voted for. For example, the Russian Federation voted by 71.3 per cent in March 1991 to approve a draft Union Treaty, but by December that year the USSR was dissolved and Russia was an independent state. Boris Yeltsin, the first democratically elected (June 1991) Russian President and opponent of Gorbachev was happy with this outcome, which was not sanctioned by any referendum in Russia. Yet Russian independence was inevitable after Ukraine voted overwhelmingly (90 per cent) for independence on 1 December 1991. This meant that the old Soviet Union was effectively stripped of most of its members.

There can be no denying the proposition that nationalism caused the downfall of the Soviet Union, but it could have survived if the political leaders had taken different decisions at different times. At first, even the most nationalist leaders in the Baltics, such as Vytautas Landsbergis of Lithuania, did not expect to achieve independence for their countries, and were seeking reform of the USSR along admittedly extremely decentralised lines, with 'sovereignty' for the republics. This was too much for Moscow, and Gorbachev appeared to sanction the force that was used to overrule the Lithuanian Government. Lithuania appeared impatient with the progress towards 'sovereignty', while the other Baltic governments, Latvia and Estonia, seemed to be prepared to compromise on independence in the short term. Moscow laid down that referendums on independence should be held, with at least two-thirds of the electorate in agreement. If Russians were included in the electorates of the Baltic countries (particularly Latvia and Estonia where they are numerous), then independence might not be carried. 'Ethnic nationalism' entered in when Latvian and Estonian Congresses were set up in 1990, elected by the citizens and their children of Latvia and Estonia in 1940. This electorate excluded later Russian and other immigrants. However, the full franchise Supreme Councils were the most important bodies, and were dominated by nationalists and members supported by them. This division between 'ethnic' and 'civic' nationalism is ever-present in the Baltics and in eastern Europe generally (see Ignatieff, 1993, pp. 3–6; Smith, 1991, pp. 9–13), but it would be simplistic to say that only one variety (the ethnic) is present there. All of the former Soviet republics are multiethnic, and large numbers of the non-titular (i.e. minority) nationalities voted with the majority for independence from the USSR. In Ukraine, for example, Russians voted overwhelmingly for Ukrainian independence in the referendum of 1 December 1991. And, although there have been barriers (mainly language tests) to Russians becoming citizens of the Baltic states, most would like to do so. For their part, the ethnic majorities are naturally suspicious of the Russians in their midst, given the history of annexation and repression since 1940, but the signs are that a 'civic' nationalism is making ground against 'ethnic' nationalism (Rose, 1997; Nairn, 1997). This makes sense, since the alternative of 'ethnic cleansing' is disastrous in domestic and international terms. All the European former Soviet Republics wish to be on good terms with the European Union, and indeed the Baltics and probably others would like to join. Other institutions such as the Council of Europe and the Organisation for Security and Cooperation in Europe (OSCE) have an influence on all these new states, since most are members. Ethnic nationalism is largely unacceptable to these bodies, if that means discrimination or redrawing boundaries. That is not to say that tensions do not exist between Russia and its former partners in the USSR, for claims are frequently made by Russian politicians and by Russians in general that Russia has the right to intervene to protect Russians in other states. (Miller *et al.*, 1998, p. 192, gives 30 per cent of MPs and 26 per cent of the public saying the government should threaten military action if necessary to protect the rights of Russians in neighbouring countries).

Generalisations about nationalism in the former Soviet Union are difficult to make, because of the considerable differences between the nations, between their nationalist movements, and between their relationships with the USSR. A vast literature has been written since 1990 to describe all these complexities, but it should be noted that very few of those now writing on nation-alism thought it important before the late 1980s, when it erupted on the scene in eastern Europe.

It could be said that nationalism was at first latent rather than explicit. Economic autonomy was the first demand, followed by the right to make the national language official. These were generally granted to the Republics in 1989. While Republican national flags and anthems were banned until Gorbachev came to power, education in the native languages was never eliminated. It is true that a Russification campaign was continued from Czarist times, under the banner of 'Soviet patriotism' and com-munist solidarity, but education in non-Russian languages was never stopped, and many spoke these languages at home, if not at work (Motyl, 1987). The result was that when Gorbachev opened up the Soviet system to nationalist demands, language and religion became a focus for nationalism in the politics of the Republics. In Estonia Russians went on strike in 1989 in protest against proposed voting qualification laws which would discrimi-nate against them on grounds of length of residence. No doubt they were encouraged to do so by some centrist elements in the Communist Party, and Moscow declared the law unconstitutional. Tension has continued after independence, but it is not as great as was feared, for the citizenship laws have become more open and the Russians are happy to stay on as residents (Rose, 1997).

The national conflicts are not just between the non-Russians and the Russians. They are also between the non-dominant nationalities themselves. A bitter struggle erupted in 1988 between Armenians and Azeris over the region of Nagorno-Karabakh, an Armenian enclave in the Azerbaijan Republic, which had been allocated to Azerbaijan in 1923. Armenia demanded the incorporation of this region into Armenia, while Azerbaijan refused. Considerable violence broke out in both Republics, with many deaths in Azerbaijan. Azerbaijan set up a commercial blockade to put pressure on Armenia. Moscow inter-vened to restore order and refused to sanction any boundary change. Instead, in 1989 it introduced 'direct rule' from Moscow over the Nagorno-Karabakh region, in the manner of British direct rule in Northern Ireland since 1972, and Indian direct rule in Punjab in 1987. At the end of 1989 Moscow restored the region to Azerbaijan. It seemed to be just as unable to pacify the nationalists on both sides as the British and Indian Governments with their direct rule. In 1994 a multinational peace-keeping force was sent under the auspices of the OSCE, and peace talks took place between Armenia and Azerbaijan, but there is no permanent ceasefire. In March 1996 the Karabakh Armenians declared their independence, but in effect nothing changed, and an international peace-keeping force keeps an uneasy peace.

Other interethnic conflicts erupted in 1989 in Georgia between Abkhazis and Georgians, and in Moldavia (Moldova) between Moldavians, Ukrainians and Russians. A feature of these conflicts is that the rise of one nationalism usually produces a reaction from others. Georgian nationalists, under the virtual mandate given them by Gorbachev's policy of increasing the power of the national Republics, proceeded to promote the idea of the ethnic unity of Georgia and to play down the contribution of other ethnic groups to Georgian culture and history. They aimed to make Georgian the official language, and to extend the Tblisi State University into the non-Georgian region of Abkhazia. This provoked a violent nationalist response from the Abkhazis, whose language and culture is distinct from the Georgian. Thus the price of unleashing Georgian nationalism under *perestroika* was to upset the balance between the Georgians and the non-Georgians. This type of situation is common throughout the world, where one nationalist upsurge begets another, either in imitation or in reaction.

In many of these cases, too, there is again present a cultural division of labour, with ethnic groups differentially placed in the labour market. But this time the 'core nation' may play no part, and internal colonialism is absent. Armenians typically engaged in profitable trading in Azerbaijan. This gives rise to resentments, expressed for the first time openly as nationalism in the conditions of *glasnost*. But the Russians and the Soviet state were not directly involved in this cultural division of labour.

The form nationalism takes varies with the type of political culture. Mass demonstrations and violence erupts in areas where participative institutions are weakest; more sophisticated areas with a history of self-rule such as the Baltic Republics tend towards constitutional action, although they too saw huge crowds demonstrating and 'illegal' declarations of independence, followed by economic and military sanctions from Moscow.

The presence of long-standing religious animosities affects nationalist behaviour. Moslem–Christian divisions correspond to national divisions in many areas of the former Soviet Union, as for example Azeri–Armenian and Abkhazi–Georgian. Shia Moslems everywhere have become more militant since the Iranian Revolution of 1979, and this has affected Soviet Moslems too, exacerbating ethnic and linguistic conflicts. Religious differences in the Baltic nations, in contrast, are not as extreme as these, but are important, with Catholic Lithuanians and Lutheran and Orthodox Latvians and Estonians in opposition to Russian Orthodox. So there is a strong cultural input into the different nationalisms of the Soviet republics.

Although cultural nationalism was acceptable to Moscow, up to a point, secession and the redrawing of boundaries were ruled out, as were laws discriminating against non-nationals. Moscow ruled in 1989 that the unity of the Communist Party of the Soviet Union must be maintained, although the Lithuanian Party later seceded. It also laid down that the Russian language must be given equal status with the national languages as the official language of the Republics.

The clash between nationalists and the centre was perhaps the most difficult problem facing Gorbachev, and threatened either a break-up of the Soviet Union or the repression of the nationalist movements. In the event, both took place. A further regime change, this time in the direction of a reaction towards centralisation and authoritarianism, would have made it very difficult, if not impossible, for nationalist politics to survive as long as the political and military elites stayed loyal to the centre. But the failure of the August 1991 Moscow coup, which had these aims, sealed the fate of the USSR and the success of the secessionists. Nationalism filled the void left by the total collapse of communism at the centre of the Soviet Union, but the ground had been prepared from at least the late 1980s by Gorbachev's policies and the failures of the USSR to perform efficiently and to democratise in time.

It can be seen that in the pre-Gorbachev USSR the 'top-down' explanation for the capacity for political nationalism seems to be the most important. Without a regime change at the top, nationalism could not be expressed in politics, as the system until 1985 was authoritarian and repressed overt nationalist behaviour. Gorbachev changed the Soviet system and the further regime change after the 1991 coup set the seal on Soviet communism. The limits to nationalism in the USSR had been set by the Communist Party at the centre, and when that changed, and then collapsed, the door was open for the alternative nationalist solution.

But next in importance is the scale and intensity of the 'bottom-up' nationalist behaviour, once it was allowed to express itself. That such nationalism gathered a very wide social spectrum of support, even surpassing Western nationalist movements, indicates that authoritarian political regimes can suppress nationalism but cannot eliminate it. The explanation for this 'bottom-up' nationalism is to be found partly in the 'internal colonialism' of the Soviet state, with its strong 'cultural division of labour'. In particular, Russians were claimed by non-Russian nationalists to be exploiting them through centralised planning and forced industrialisation, which took their resources away and gave them to the rest of the country. This took the form of the introduction of heavy industry in some areas and the extraction of primary resources in others. The purpose was to serve the interests of other parts of the country, and it often damaged the environment and economy of the nationalities. Russians migrated to get employment in the better-off Baltic Republics, and often took the best jobs. Such migration threatened the ethnic balance of the population, with Latvians comprising only half of the population of Latvia. Russians, in reply, resented subsidising the poorer Nationalities in the Soviet Union, and many sought independence for themselves. Sudden or extensive changes in an economic system often lead to nationalism if these changes can be associated with differential economic gains for different ethnic groups.

Equally as important as the economic explanation for nationalism is the political and cultural dimension. Political mobilisation occurred when elections became free and nationalists could compete openly with the Communist Party. It finally released the expression of the democratic will when multi-party elections were allowed from 1990, and communists were defeated by nationalists or autonomists.

The cultural aspects were clearly manifested in linguistic nationalism, national religion, and in the numerous symbols of the nation such as the flag, national anthem, dress, myths of history, and so on. 'Russification' had offended national sensibilities from the late nineteenth century, and the policy continued under communism, with some significant concessions to national languages and cultures. All these complaints were to come together in Gorbachev's regime change, which provided the crucial opportunity for their expression.

Yugoslavia and its Breakaway Nations

Some of these features are also found in the former Yugoslavia, where until the death of Tito in 1980 the regime was largely authoritarian, especially with regard to separatist nationalist aspirations. After Tito, the leadership of Yugoslavia became much weaker, with a collective Presidency consisting of one representative each of the six Republics and two Autonomous Provinces. The Chairman was taken from each in turn. Each Republic and Province had a veto in the federal decision-making process, and many economic functions were devolved to them and to self-managing enterprises, leaving the central government economically weak. Even before the death of Tito, the 1974 Constitution had established most of this decentralisation, and so provided a framework for nationalist activity once the restraint of Tito's power was removed. One of the 1974 changes was to remove the Province of Kosovo from the control of the Republic of Serbia, except for some residuary powers. This was to prove a major cause of nationalist conflict between the Albanians and Serbs in the 1980s. Thus regime change in Yugoslavia also provides a key explanation to the initial upsurge in nationalism.

But why was nationalism apparently waiting to arise, when the opportunity was given? For this, we must return to 'bottom-up' explanations which have proved useful in other case-studies. First, an economic explanation. Nationalism feeds on economic discontent, and channels it into a nationalist perspective. It does this especially when there is regional uneven economic development, and where there is a cultural division of labour and many immigrant workers. Both the Soviet Union and Yugoslavia were economies in dire trouble with shortages, uneven development and a strong tinge of 'internal colonialism'.

Then again there is a cultural explanation for nationalist behaviour. Each nation in Yugoslavia claimed either a language, or a culture, and often a religion, and certainly a historic memory, which years of communist rule had failed to eliminate, and may have actually encouraged. Just how these relate to national identity and nationalism is extremely complex and ever-changing (Banac, 1984). In Yugoslavia, the competing national ideologies of the Serbs, Croats, and Slovenes were present from the foundation of the Yugoslav state in the 1920s, and continued to cause division under the communist regime. In particular, the 'Greater Serbian' nationalism is centralising and intolerant of the other nationalisms in Yugoslavia.

It was also hostile to liberal democracy when the other republics moved towards that from 1990, with competitive elections. Even after Serbia instituted multi-party free elections in 1990, the voters returned the communists to power, as they did in neighbouring Montenegro. The split between communist and non-communist republics, as the result of multi-party elections, was too much for the Federation of Yugoslavia, which quickly split apart. Only Serbia and Montenegro continued the Federation, and the remaining four republics proclaimed their independence, backed by popular referendums. That, however, triggered a double reaction from Serbia: direct intervention to stop secession in Slovenia and Croatia, and support for new Serb Republics within Croatia and Bosnia-Hercegovina. The ensuing civil wars and 'ethnic cleansing' plunged the area into catastrophe from which it is only now emerging, in large part because of international intervention by the (US-led) North Atlantic Treaty Organisation (NATO) and the European Union (EU). As in the Soviet Union, decisions at the centre (Belgrade) were not up to the task of preserving the federation. Slobodan Milosevic, the Serbian communist President, would not agree to a further decentralisation of Yugoslavia, and sabotaged the conventions of the Federal Presidency whereby the Croats and Slovenes had a right to the chair of the Presidency in rotation. And he undermined the new states of Croatia and Bosnia-Hercegovina by supporting the rebel Serb republics there with federal arms and money. So a political impasse built up between Serb/Yugoslav communists and Slovene, Croat and Bosnian nationalist democrats.

Behind the politics was a cultural division between the parts of Yugoslavia. This might have been contained had a more accommodating approach been used. As in the Soviet Union, language differences have always been accepted and encouraged in Yugoslavia, up to a point. There was no one official Yugoslav language, and Serbo-Croat, Slovene and Macedonian were recognised as official and equal languages, with minor languages regarded as equal in the Regions in which they were used. However, Croats did not always wish to be joined linguistically to Serbs, and Serbs and Albanians fought bitterly over their respective rights in the Autonomous Province of Kosovo, part of the Republic of Serbia. After it broke away, Croatia rejected the Cyrillic alphabet of the Serbs and proclaimed Croatian as a separate language from Serbian. In Bosnia, however, it was impossible to produce a separate language for the state.

It was Kosovo which, in the most recent period, first showed that nationalism had reemerged in Yugoslavia as a major political problem. From the start of the 1980s, the ethnic Albanians who make up a majority of the province demonstrated for greater autonomy, with some desiring incorporation with Albania. By 1988 the minority Serbian population had mobilised in reaction, and had found a champion in Serbia's Communist Party leader, Slobodan Milosevic, who demanded the total incorporation of Kosovo in Serbia. The issue was marked by violence, strikes and deaths in Kosovo, and threatened to break up the federation. It was compounded by the reaction of the other Republics, who fear the dominance of Serbia, which accounted for 40 per cent of the total population. Slovenia and Croatia in particular voiced dissent against Serbia in the Central Committee of the federal Party in 1989, and sought greater independence in the federation. The Slovenian Communist Party Central Committee pressed for constitutional changes which would give Slovenia the right to secede from the federation, a claim rejected by the Yugoslav Presidency, even though the Slovenian leaders at first said that they had no intention to exercise the right. However, in 1990 the Slovenian Communist Party seceded from the Yugoslav Party, and took up a more separatist stance. The reason for this change was that competitive elections in Slovenia had made the politicians more responsive to nationalism, if they hoped to be elected. It was also apparent to Slovenians that Serbia was moving in a 'Greater Serbian' direction, which threatened the interests of Slovenia. Thus independence looked a more attractive proposition, especially in a changing eastern Europe of non-communist states linked to the European Community. Despite these last-minute moves by the communists to satisfy nationalist opinion, multi-party elections in Slovenia and Croatia in April and May 1990 resulted in the election of non-communist, nationalistically inclined governments. These proceeded to declare themselves in favour of virtual independence for Slovenia and Croatia, a course of action hotly contested by the Yugoslav Presidency, now virtually unrepresentative of the Republics concerned. At the same time, Serbia dissolved the Kosovo legislature, which had also declared its independence, and reincorporated Kosovo and Vojvodina, the largely ethnic-Hungarian autonomous region in the north, into Serbia. This was a clear signal to the rest of Yugoslavia that Serbia was intent on extending its power into the areas populated by other ethnic nations. When Slovenia, Macedonia, Croatia and Bosnia-Hercegovina held competitive elections in 1990, nationalists replaced communists in power, and proceeded to hold referendums on independence. These were carried overwhelmingly, but in Bosnia the Serbs did not vote, which meant that one-third of the population had not consented. That was a recipe for disaster, for the Serbs in Bosnia wanted either the continuation of Yugoslavia or a separate Bosnian Serb Republic, preferably linked to Serbia. This led to the proclamation of such a republic, civil war and 'ethnic cleansing' in which Serbs, Croats and Moslems fought to establish an ethnic territory of their own, at the expense of the other ethnic groups. An effective ethnic partition took place, along Serb, Croat and Moslem lines, which despite international intervention has not been entirely reversed.

In Croatia, on the other hand, after an initial Serb success in driving out the Croats from 'Serb territory', the Croatian government reclaimed most of the territory for the state, again with some international support. Slovenia was largely ethnically homogeneous, and had no trouble in establishing its nation-state, after a short-lived skirmish with federal troops in June-July 1991. Macedonia did not fare so well, as its very name aroused the opposition of its neighbour, Greece, which claims a monopoly on the name 'Macedonia'. Greece imposed economic sanctions on the new state, but a compromise was reached whereby the name of the new state was to be 'The Former Yugoslav

Republic of Macedonia' (FYROM) for UN and other international purposes. Even so, Greece objects to the use of Macedonia in the title at all. Another problem for Macedonia is that only two-thirds of the population is ethnically Macedonian, with around a quarter Albanian. These voted overwhelmingly for autonomy in 1992, and have objected to the use of the Macedonian language in the new state. So Macedonia is faced with a double external threat: from Greece, and from Albania backing ethnic Albanians in Macedonia.

While these national questions in Yugoslavia have a long history, their intensification in the 1980s and 1990s is thus the result of recent developments. The 1974 constitutional changes and the death of Tito in 1980 have already been mentioned. Failures in the Yugoslav economy became severe in the 1980s, and their effects were unevenly felt. At one end of the scale, Kosovo is one of the poorest parts of the country, while at the other end, Slovenia and Croatia are the richest. These differences are relatively large when compared to those in the states of the European Union.

Uneven regional development, coupled with corresponding cultural divisions, provided fertile ground for nationalism. The constitutional structure and the political culture determine the form which that nationalism will take. The nationalism of Slovenia and Croatia is linked to the demand for greater democratisation and liberalisation, while that of Kosovo and Macedonia is based on ethnic exclusiveness. Serbia harks back to its historic dominance of the state ('Greater Serbia').

The power of the centre to resist these nationalisms was peculiarly weak in Yugoslavia, with little in the way of 'official nationalism', especially in the absence of the charismatic leader, Tito, and his control of the army. The state held together through a form of consociationalism, whose tensions were greater than such a system could bear. The introduction of multi-party elections after 1990 was the crucial regime change which allowed non-communist, nationalist governments to be elected to power in the constituent republics of Slovenia, Macedonia, Croatia and Bosnia-Hercegovina. These governments aimed at some form of independence for these nations, although not at first total secession. That was forced on them by the actions of the communists in Serbia. Further 'Balkanisation' of Yugoslavia was unattractive to the communist politicians of Milosevic's persuasion, Serb nationalists and central economic interests, especially in Serbia. But elsewhere in Yugoslavia, the desire for independence became overwhelming.

The Former Czechoslovakia

Czechoslovakia was formed out of the ruins of the Austro-Hungarian empire in 1918. While this was in one sense the triumph of nationalism over a multinational empire, Czechoslovakia was itself multinational, and contained internal national tensions, even if not as severe as in Yugoslavia, which was formed at the same time as the 'Kingdom of the Serbs, Croats and Slovenes'. Czechoslovakia consisted of three principal Slav ethnic groups: Czechs (Bohemians), Moravians and Slovaks, plus many Germans and Magyars (Hungarians). The Czechs and Moravians lived in the 'Crown Lands' of Austria, while the Slovaks were part of Hungary. Although this might not appear to matter greatly, since both Austria and Hungary formed part of one empire, the Austrians were different from the Hungarians in culture and nationality, and after the establishment of the Dual Monarchy in 1867 the Austrian and Hungarian parts of the empire had considerable independence from one another. Their 'subject' Slav citizens developed differently, and retained their different national identities, languages and cultures.

This legacy of division in the empire was to reappear in the new state of Czechoslovakia. The Czechs looked down on the Slovaks, and to some extent on the Moravians, and these in turn resented Czech hegemony. While there was nothing like the ethnic division in Yugoslavia, there were nevertheless separate nations, with the potential to claim statehood, when the desire and opportunity arose.

The pressures to federalise the state into separate Czech and Slovak parts became strong under the communist system, and such a federation was instituted in 1969. Of course, the communist system was not going to mean federation as understood in the West, and in the previous year the suppression of the 'Prague Spring' by Soviet troops and the elimination of the Czechoslovak Party Secretary, Alexander Dubcek (who was a

Slovak) by the USSR showed that the time was not yet ripe for national self-determination.

The spread of Gorbachev's ideas of *perestroika* and *glasnost* into the 'satellite' states after 1985 allowed for more free expression, and free elections in June 1990 resulted in the defeat of the Communist Party. But while democracy and capitalism were now firmly on the agenda, so was nationalism. The Czechs wanted to move quickly to a Western-style economy, while the Slovaks were more committed to state ownership of sections of the economy, and to the welfare state. This was a reflection of the different economic structures in the two republics, and the relative backwardness of Slovakia. On top of that, cultural differences in language and historical legacy became more salient under conditions of liberal democracy. The crucial fact, however, was that when given the right to vote freely, the Czechs and Slovaks returned parties with incompatible nationalist and social agendas. There followed the 'Velvet Divorce', essentially an agreement between parliamentary leaders to dissolve the federation. No referendums were held, and it is probable that if there had been, there would have been a negative vote in both nations. In all the other secessions from communist states in central and eastern Europe, referendums had been held (although, as we have seen, the dissolution of the USSR was not subject to any referendum, even if the secession of the individual republics (except Russia) was endorsed by referendums).

It has been suggested that Czechoslovakia could have held together if a number of mistakes had been avoided at the start of the post-communist period (Szomolányi and Meseznikov, 1994, p. 25). These include (it is claimed) the failure to institute a new Constitution instead of patching up the old communist one, and the failure to deal with the leaders of the old communist regime 'more radically' (ibid., p. 26). For a time these continued in power in Slovakia until a new party, the HZDS (Hnutie za Demokraticke Slovensko: Movement for a Democratic Slovakia) won the elections of 1992. The HZDS leader, Vladimir Meciar, became Slovak Prime Minister. Although not a nationalist, he wanted further protection of Slovak interests. On the Czech side, the newly elected liberal President, the playwright Vaclav Havel, and the Finance Minister Vaclav Klaus, while quite close ideologically to Meciar (the Czech Forum, which included Havel, and the Slovak

'Public against Violence', which included Meciar, had similar aims) were apparently uninterested in making deals with the Slovaks.

There were also 'structural' reasons in the political process encouraging break-up, including the 'majority clause' in both Houses of Parliament which meant that a minority of Slovak deputies could block the action of the whole parliament. This deadlock proved intolerable to the Czech majority, and they were quite willing to see the federation dissolved so that they could rule unimpeded in their own republic.

So Czechoslovakia was broken into 'nation-states', even if the Moravians could complain that they had been subsumed under the Czech Republic. The 'Velvet Divorce' was peaceful, and had none of the terrible repercussions of the dissolution of Yugoslavia, or the violence seen in parts of the former USSR. Nevertheless, it might not have happened if the political decisions had been different, and there is some survey evidence that popular opinion was against it.

Conclusion

At first sight, it seems that nationalism has completely taken over from communism in the former 'socialist republics' of Europe. It is undeniable that when communism collapsed, the USSR, Yugoslavia and Czechoslovakia dissolved too, into nation-states of a kind. There was also considerable nationalism to be found in other former communist countries: Poland, East Germany (the reunification of Germany in 1990 was ecstatically welcomed at first in the East), Romania, Bulgaria and Albania.

But what is this 'nationalism' exactly? Using all the definitions of nationalism we have seen already, it is not all that clear that nationalism alone explains what has happened. To start with, the desire for a change from communism to liberal democracy and capitalism was as much the inspiration for the 'regime change' as nationalism. It was only when the existing communist states stood in the way of such change that people looked to the break-up of these states. It seemed that the only alternative to changing the centre was to deny the centre its overriding power, and then finally to leave altogether. These stages are clearly evident in the cases discussed here. If one tests purely nationalist aims against what happened, and how people felt about nationalist values, the picture is not as nationalist as has sometimes been depicted.

If 'national self-determination' is the aim of nationalism, and nations are defined as ethnic or social groups, then many of the new 'nation-states' would not fulfil these criteria. All of the new states already existed in one form or another under communism, usually as constituent republics or regions of a federal state. Their 'self-determination' was to proclaim independent statehood or 'sovereignty' on the basis of existing boundaries. It is true that these republics or regions were more 'national' than the multinational federations of which they were part, but many were essentially multinational political units. Ukraine, for example, is 71 per cent Ukrainian and 20 per cent Russian. Latvia in the 1989 Census was 51.8 per cent Latvian and 33.8 per cent Russian. Bosnia-Hercegovina is deeply divided into three large sections, with no one nation in an overall majority: in the 1991 Census 44 per cent were Moslems, 31 per cent Serbs and 17 per cent Croats. Any attempt at 'national self-determination' there could only mean splitting the state in three, which the Serbs and Croats were quite happy to do, not only in Bosnia but in neighbouring Serbia and Croatia. The Moslems, however, wished to retain the existing boundaries, and they had the support of the international community in that. They could hardly be called 'nationalists', unless they are 'official nationalists' whose nationalism relates to the state, Bosnia-Hercegovina (the 'official nation'), and not to an ethnic or social nation of Moslems. Yet they were aware of their ethnicity (or more precisely their religion) and their identity flowed from that as much as from their official nation. So their official nationalism had a palpably religious character, and Serb and Croat opponents see the state as a potential 'Moslem state' (that applies to Kosovo and Chechnya too).

Some recent studies of central and eastern Europe have put the popular strength of nationalism into perspective. For example, Miller *et al.* (1998) and Rose (1997) show that people's attitudes towards nationalist values and to other nations are not as extreme in most places as might be feared. Using surveys conducted in Russia, Ukraine, the Czech Republic, Slovakia and Hungary in 1993, 1994 and 1996, Miller constructed a composite index of nationalist values based on answers to questions relating to three different kinds of nationalism: external, centralist and cultural (p. 137). Examples of the first are questions on national territory (whether there are parts of neighbouring countries that really should belong to 'our country', and whether military intervention should be threatened on behalf of co-nationals in neighbouring countries); of the second, whether it is a mistake to break up a large country just to give each nation or ethnic group its own state, and whether there is support for greater powers of self-government for regions within the country; of the third, whether only those who speak the state language should be citizens and have the right to vote, and whether the state schools should teach all subjects in the state language. Composite indices were also calculated for 'socialist values' (p. 121), 'liberal values' (p. 155) and various democratic values (p. 175).

It may be a surprise to find that 'nationalist values' fared worst, with only 37 per cent of respondents who scored more than the midway point on the scale from weak to strong nationalism (external nationalism, 40 per cent; centralist nationalism 28 per cent; cultural nationalism, 28 per cent). This compares with 74 per cent for 'socialist values', 68 per cent for 'liberal values', 64 per cent for 'populist values' and 63 per cent saying that competitive elections are good.

Looking at the different countries (Miller *et al.*, 1998, ch. 7), including three parts of Ukraine, West Ukraine was the most nationalist (52 per cent responding at more than the mid-point across all types of nationalism), and East Ukraine the least nationalist (16 per cent). Ukraine as a whole was only 22 per cent nationalist since its 'cultural nationalism' scored only 13 per cent. Russia came top (44 per cent), with Slovakia and Hungary close behind (each 43 per cent). The Czech Republic was weakly nationalist (26 per cent). The three different types of nationalism also gave variable results in the different countries. 'External nationalism' was strongest in Russia (53 per cent) and Hungary (46 per cent), 'centralist nationalism' was fairly equally spread, except for the Czech Republic where it fell to 11 per cent. 'Cultural nationalism' was strongest in West Ukraine (45 per cent), but weakest in East Ukraine (7 per cent).

The presence of many Russians in East Ukraine no doubt explains why cultural nationalism is not strongly supported, if that means using the Ukrainian language. Russia's external nationalism is very strong (71 per cent said there were parts of neighbouring countries that really belonged to Russia (ibid., p. 127) and had some appeal in the legislative elections of 1993, when the nationalist Liberal Democratic Party came second with 22.6 per cent of the vote. But its fiery leader, Vladimir Zhirinovsky, made no progress after that, and in 1995 the Liberal Democratic Party dropped to 11.5 per cent. Zhirinovsky himself came in fifth in the presidential election of 1996, with only 5.7 per cent of the vote. In any case, while over two-thirds of Russians apparently claimed territory in neighbouring countries, only 26 per cent wanted to threaten military action to protect Russians abroad (Miller *et al.*, 1998).

In an another study, Rose (Rose, 1997) has shown from surveys that Russians in the Baltic countries are not nearly as nationalist and as favourable to Russia as has sometimes been assumed. While the Baltic nations themselves are very apprehensive about Russia's policies, they have so far escaped any military intervention since independence, even if they have endured economic restrictions. The Baltic states have all modified their initial exclusionary citizenship laws to allow for more resident Russians to become citizens.

So the overall picture of nationalism in the former communist world is that it has not always led to disaster, and that the exceptions (parts of former Yugoslavia and former USSR) are indeed exceptions. 'Civic' nationalism has shown itself to be as strong as 'ethnic' nationalism, even in this part of Europe where many writers of nationalism saw the latter as endemic (see Nairn, 1997, dust jacket).

8

Nationalism in the Developing World, South Africa and the Middle East

The Developing World, or 'Third World' as it used to be called, is usually considered to consist of most of Africa, Asia and Latin America. In this area, economies are not as 'developed' as those of the rest of the world, with a predominance of agriculture and relative poverty and debt. In politics, many states are relatively recent in origin, having gained independence from the Empires of the European powers. Nationalism and ethnicity take on a different form there from the rest of the world, although there are general features in common. Included in this chapter are accounts of nationalism in South Africa and in the Middle East. These areas are within the Developing World geographically, but their economies and societies are more developed. In South Africa, the ideology and politics of apartheid dominated until the second half of the 1980s, while in the Middle East since 1948 the state of Israel has put into effect the ideology of Zionism. These cases are to a large extent *sui generis*, but there are many 'Third World' features in South Africa and Israel, and in the Middle East generally. The position of the Palestinians is somewhat similar to that of the Blacks in South Africa under apartheid, and beyond that to many national groups in the Developing World. So too is the form of nationalism found there.

The peculiarly vicious character of nationalism in this area is difficult to explain in terms of any of the theories which have been discussed so far. These theories deal with the causes of nationalism, but they do not accurately predict the form which that nationalism will take. It is only when the political culture of each area is taken into account, along with the unique unfolding of events, that a more complete explanation for such nationalist behaviour can be given. The exceptional violence in nationalist behaviour in much of Asia and Africa is consistent with the violent political culture in these continents. Bloodshed in politics is no stranger there, and the reasons for this lie in the history and social structure of the area. As Horowitz has pointed out in his study of ethnic groups in conflict (Horowitz, 1985, pp. 18–21), the reasons why ethnic conflict pervades Developing World countries and takes a much more violent form there include (*a*) the relative absence of overarching identities with the state, which transcend or compete with those felt for the ethnic group, and (*b*) the absence of strong alternative identities *within* the ethnic group, e.g., class, religion and language, which might form the basis of political action in non-ethnic parties and organisations. Instead, ethnic politics is the norm, and includes religion, class and language, in other words, all the attributes of status and socioeconomic position. These factors together have produced a higher intensity of ethnic conflict than in the developed countries. Finally, where the state habitually uses violence, ethnic groups have little alternative but to reply in kind.

Sri Lanka and the Indian Sub-Continent

During the 1980s and 1990s, ethnic violence in Sri Lanka and in the Indian sub-continent claimed many thousand lives. This violence is not just the result of terrorism waged by extremist organisations. It is a much more widespread intercommunal conflict in which nationalist behaviour verges on genocide.(Genocide is a highly emotive and ambiguous term, and has been frequently applied to ethnic conflicts in the 1990s. Early in the twentieth century, the massacres of Armenians by Turks in the Ottoman Empire in 1909 and 1915 resulted in between 800,000 and one million dead. The 'holocaust' of Jews by the Nazis was clearly motivated by genocidal aims. Less clearly genocidal was 'ethnic cleansing' in Yugoslavia after 1991, since the aim was more to transfer populations than to destroy them. While many thousands died in Croatia and Bosnia-Hercegovina, it is not clear how much of this was the result of genocide and how much of general armed conflict, transfers of population, conditions in camps, etc. In Africa, in Rwanda and Zaire, massacres of Tutsis by Hutus (500,000 in three months in 1994), and of Hutus by Tutsis, are usually described as genocide. Again, in the absence of a clearly stated aim of genocide, it is difficult to determine what was the motive for such killings.)

The first nationalisms in the Developing World took the form of anti-imperialist movements. The Indian National Congress, founded in 1885, finally succeeded in ending British rule in India in 1947. However, the divide between Hindus and Moslems led to two states – India and Pakistan – being established, which was a defeat for Indian nationalism. Anti-British nationalism was soon to be succeeded by rival nationalisms within the sub-continent. Moslem identity proved unsuccessful in holding together the two separated parts of Pakistan, East and West. Instead, linguistic and territorial conflicts with West Pakistan led East Pakistan to secede in 1971, and to fight its way to independence, with Indian aid, as Bangladesh. In Kashmir too, the Moslems were split between India and Pakistan. This has given rise to Kashmiri (Moslem) nationalism, which has split between those supporting union with Pakistan and those seeking an independent state of Kashmir. More than 12,000 people have died in fighting from 1989 to 1996, including 3,400 militants.

In the 1990s, the Hindu nationalist party, the Bharatiya Janata Party (BJP: Indian People's Party) became the largest party in the Indian parliamentary elections of 1996, and retained that position in the 1998 elections. Its slogan is 'One nation, one people, one culture'. It was unable to sustain a government for more than three weeks in 1996. Violence erupted in Bombay in 1993, when Hindu extremists hacked 950 Moslems to death. Bombay is controlled by a BJP nationalist ally, the Shiv Sena Party.

Ceylon, a separate British colony, became independent in 1948 and was renamed Sri Lanka in 1972, an indication that its official national identity was to be Sinhalese, despite the existence of a Tamil minority of around one-fifth of the population. Sinhalese nationalism produced reactive Tamil nationalism, resulting in civil war. Between 13,000 and 14,000 have been killed between 1983 and 1996.

Other nationalist movements in the sub-continent with a high level of violent behaviour are those of Sikhs (over 2,000 deaths in 1988), who seek to establish an independent Sikh state called Khalistan out of the Indian state of Punjab. The Indian Prime Minister Indira Ghandi was assassinated by Sikh nationalists in 1984; her son and successor as Prime Minister, Rajiv Ghandi, was assassinated by Sri Lankan Tamils in 1989. The Gurkha National Liberation Front seeks a separate state in Indian Bengal; and the Tripura National Volunteers, another group of secessionists, are active in north-east India. These are only some of the more 'nationalist' organisations with well-defined claims to self-determination, who, while they probably do not pose a serious threat to the territorial integrity of India, constitute serious problems in Indian politics. In Sri Lanka the threat to the state is more serious, with continuous civil war between Tamils and Sinhalese since 1983 for control over the north and east of the country.

In addition, India and Pakistan are plagued by ethnic violence of a communal rather than nationalist kind, labelled variously 'tribal', 'sectarian' or 'caste'. Such conflict occurs in cities with changing immigrant populations such as Karachi and Hyderabad in Pakistan, and in rural areas where the caste system prevails. In the cities, migrant labour competes for jobs and housing with the indigenous population, and ethnic divisions become class divisions in a cultural division of labour. Caste systems are more rigid and formal versions of this, without the competitive element. Castes range from 'Untouchables' at the bottom of the social scale to Brahmins at the top, and each caste is allocated a separate social position. Despite formal secularisation, parts of India still operate a caste system, which derives from the Hindu religion. According to van den Berghe (van den Berghe, 1981, p. 164), India and South Africa are 'caste societies' in which nearly all members of a society belong to caste groups, and Japan and the United States are 'societies with caste groups'. This, however, is an unusual extension of the concept of caste.

Political scientists are generally at a loss to explain the amount and intensity of nationalist and ethnic violence in the Developing World, although Horowitz is an exception. The liberal-constitutional politicians in the area are largely unable to control it, and military dictatorships often emerge. Unlike the states of the developed world, those of the developing world appear weak, and their political culture is traditional rather than modern. This means that religious and communal identities and loyalties are as important as those relating to the state. It also means that the idea of the nation is not clearly defined or accepted, so that for example Punjab national identity can refer to a territory (the Punjab, since 1947 split between India and Pakistan), a language (Punjabi), an ethnic group, or a religion (Sikh). It has been possible to build a Punjabi nationalism out of some of these identities, but impossible to build it from them all. The most virulent has been Sikh nationalism which aims to establish a Sikh state of Khalistan in or out of India. Sikh nationalism makes religion the basis of nationality. An ethnic Punjabi nation would have to include the two-thirds of Punjabis who live in Pakistan, most of whom are Moslems, not Sikhs. A language criterion for nationhood would exclude those Punjabis who speak Hindi.

While religious identity seems to have dominated Pakistani nationalism (but it could not hold East Pakistan together with West Pakistan), and the Khalistan national movement, language has also been the basis of sub-state nationalisms in India. The linguistic states movement sought to make language the basis of the federal system, and the original states were subdivided in the 1950s in a move in this direction (in 1998 there were 25 States and 7 Union Territories in India, compared with 14 States and 6 Union Territories in 1950). Given that there are at least 1,500 languages in India, this can be only a partial solution (English and Hindi are the all-Indian official languages, with 14 regional official languages). In Bangladesh (formerly East Pakistan), language and territory replaced religion as the national identifiers. Thus the Bengali speakers of East Pakistan split away from the Urdu speakers of West Pakistan in 1971, with whom they shared a Moslem identity, and joined with Hindi speakers in Bengal to forge Bangladeshi nationalism.

What can explain the increasing salience and intensity of nationalism and ethnicity in the politics of this and other parts of Asia such as Tibet, Burma, Malaysia, the Philippines and Fiji? (Unfortunately, there is no space to discuss all of these cases, which share features of those discussed here). And how unstable and weak is the state system which tries to cope with ethnic unrest and nationalism?

Paradoxically, it is not clear that ethnic nationalism is as important as religion or ideology across much of the continent of Asia from Lebanon to the Pacific. Indeed, nationalism seems to take second place to these in Lebanon, Afghanistan, Indochina and China, where ethnic and linguistic conflicts seem to be relatively weak. The power of religion, and in particular of Islam, to command loyalties represents a supranational force in politics which is apparently opposed to ethnic nationalism. In Iran and Iraq, for example, Kurdish nationalism is suppressed. Moreover, the idea of nationalism and the nation-state is not as well established as that of Empire and religious community, so that national identity makes a weak basis for a state (Hugh Tinker in Tivey, 1981; Halliday and Alavi, 1988). Nevertheless, 'official nationalism' usually predominates over religion in Moslem countries, as seen in the Iran–Iraq war of the 1980s. In 1990 President Saddam Hussein of Iraq played on religion in his attempt to wage a 'Holy War' on his Arab (and Moslem) neighbours to the south. But these fellow-Arabs and Moslems were as opposed to Iraqi expansionism as non-Arabs and non-Moslems. Iraq's Pan-Arab nationalism did, however, find support in Jordan, Libya and Yemen, for reasons related to the struggle with Israel. In particular, the Palestinians saw Iraq as their principal ally.

Horowitz has argued that distinctions between 'tribal', 'linguistic' and 'religious' conflicts can no longer be usefully made in an age of pervading ethnicity (Horowitz, 1985, p. xi). For him, ethnicity dominates politics and transcends other divisions, leaving the official nationalism of the state relatively weak in many of the countries he examined (mainly in central and eastern Asia and in Africa).

It is this which explains the prevalence of ethnic conflict in these areas, and the peculiarly violent form which it takes. For the states of Asia and Africa have struggled to build nations on the basis of territories bequeathed by colonial or indigenous empires. These states are so diverse ethnically that the nation-building process has involved a massive displacement of traditional communities. Where the former empires ruled indirectly through local princes or elite groups, the new 'nation-states' seek direct authority and social homogeneity. Thus, official languages are introduced and one ethnic group often carries the 'national' identity of the state. This leaves all the other ethnic groups and languages at a disadvantage, and their reaction takes the form of ethnic nationalism. Thus in Sri Lanka the introduction of Sinhalese as the official language in the 1970s, and the consequent privileges granted to Sinhalese speakers in state employment, education, and so on, provoked the Tamil nationalist reaction. The partition of Sri Lanka into two nations or federal units is the Tamil nationalist solution to the threat posed by Sinhalese nationalism.

Tamil nationalism (as Kashmiri and Punjabi nationalism) is made more complex by the international dimension. The Tamils in Sri Lanka have close ethnic ties with the Tamils in the state of Tamil Nadu in India, and these have aided the Tamil nationalists in Sri Lanka. Tamils are mainly Hindu in religion, while the Sinhalese are Buddhists. This and the language difference are the main identifiers of nationality in Sri Lanka. The Government of India has got involved, and an Indian 'peace-keeping force' was invited by the Sri Lankan government in 1987 to try to subdue the 'Tamil Tigers' (LTTE: Liberation Tigers of Tamil Eelam) terrorists, whose aim is a separate Tamil state, 'Eelam'. This operation was only moderately successful, and resembles the interventions of the British Army in Northern Ireland, the Syrian Army in Lebanon (though that has been more successful) and the Soviet Army in Afghanistan, Georgia and Azerbaijan. In all these cases, what is supposed to be a neutral military force is seen by many as tending to one side in the conflict. In 1989 the Sri Lankan Government asked the Indians to withdraw, but by that time they were unable to do so immediately without seeming to abandon the Tamils. They withdrew in 1990. For its part, the Sri Lankan Government came under attack from the Marxist Janatha Vimukhti Perumana (People's Liberation Front), a mainly Sinhalese group which engaged in terrorism in the south.

While elite cooperation between national leaders has been attempted in Sri Lanka (e.g. the abortive Bandaranaike–Chelvanayakam Pact of 1957; the Constitution of 1978 which recognised the Tamil language; the devolution proposals from 1981 to 1995), its failure results from the elites' inability to control their followers. The 1957 Pact was immediately repudiated by Sinhalese militants, and the devolution proposals were attacked by these and by the Tamil Tigers. Thus one of the key conditions of consociationalism – the control by elites of their followers – is absent in Sri Lanka. By the time conciliatory moves were made to the Tamils in the late 1970s and after 1981, the extremists had become powerful. So timing in peace moves, as Horowitz has pointed out (Horowitz, 1985, pp. 577–88), is cru-cial. Concessions made too late may only fuel the conflict. The 1995 proposals to transform Sri Lanka into a federal state, with the merger of the northern and eastern provinces, as demanded by the LTTE, but with decommissioning of their arms, failed to win the support of the LTTE, the Sinhalese nationalists, or the Buddhist clergy. So the Sri Lankan government resumed the military offensive, this time with considerable success.

The intensity of conflict at the grass-roots arises not only from religious and linguistic issues, but from economic ones affecting the material basis of life. The Sinhalese land colonisation policy of the 1970s invaded Tamil areas, and provoked a nationalist reaction, especially as the Tamils of the tea plantations were suf-fering from economic depression at that time, and were also looking for land in the same area. The policy of changing entry requirements for higher education and the awarding of quotas to ethnic groups was seen as unfair to the Tamils, as was the requirement that the Sinhala language be used as the official lan-guage. So on top of the cultural and political discontent of the Tamils, there is a strong economic motive for their nationalism as well (Arasaratnam in Boucher *et al.* (eds), 1987). This of course involves once again a cultural division of labour, which is seen in so many cases of ethnic nationalism.

The response of the Sri Lankan Government to Tamil nation-alism has not been wholly negative, however. Devolution has been offered to the two Tamil Provinces in the north and east, and a kind of consociationalism is being attempted. The official use of the English language is to be encouraged, to complement the rival, and mutually hostile, Sinhala and Tamil languages.

But the Tamil Tigers wish to unite the two Tamil Provinces in one Tamil state, which would include a strong Sinhalese minority. But when this was proposed by the Government in August 1995, the Tamil Tigers rejected it, as we have seen, since it was linked to the laying down of the Tigers' arms. A North-Eastern Provincial Council had been established in 1988 and the Eelam People's Revolutionary Liberation Front (EPRLF), which supported the pact between Sri Lanka and India (unlike the Tamil Tigers), won a majority in the election later that year. Thus a devolution or federal alternative to the total separatism of the Tamil Tigers does exist. But the Sri Lankan government is still regarded by many Tamils as dedicated to Sinhala hegemony in a Sri Lankan nation-state. Thus the existence of competing exclusive nationalisms in a political culture of violence makes accommodation between them very difficult.

It would be easy to predict the disintegration of India and Sri Lanka on account of these ethnic conflicts. But such a conclusion would be simplistic. The state of India is a complex federation of vested interests, which wish to see their local power underwritten rather than undermined (Manor, 1990). So to a lesser extent is Sri Lanka, which may in the end contain Tamil separatism by the federal alternative.

As we have seen, the European ideal of the nation-state is largely foreign to Asia, with its strong tradition of empire and religious community. So some form of cultural pluralism and consociationalism within a multinational state appears to be the likely outcome, rather than a proliferation of small nation-states.

Black Africa

Nationalism in Black Africa has many features in common with that in Asia. There is a common legacy of colonialism, even more pervasive in Africa, which has practically no examples of indigenous empires or states operating independently of the European powers in the twentieth century. In terms of economic, cultural and political development, Black Africa is firmly in the Developing World, with little industrialisation, 'high culture' or experience of liberal democracy. Here too is a political culture of violence and intercommunal conflict, with low levels of political participation and little experience of democracy. Religion has less political significance as a national identifier, except in areas in the north where Islam meets Christianity and other religions.

The first manifestation of Black African nationalism was directed against the colonial powers, and its aim was to liberate black Africans from white rule. This took the form of Pan-Africanism rather than the nationalisms of particular ethnic groups or 'nations'. Yet the struggle had to take place in the individual colonies, so that each soon produced a nationalist movement, made up largely of an educated elite, most of whom had been to Europe and had imbibed the idea of nationalism there (Arnold Hughes, in Tivey (ed.), 1981).

The reluctant withdrawal of the colonial powers from most of Africa from the late 1950s left the new rulers with the difficult task of 'nation-building' – the creation of a national community out of the mix of tribes, religions and languages which had made up the colonies. The boundaries of the colonies had been artificial lines on a map, not ethnic/social national boundaries, yet the legitimacy of the new states now rested on the consent of the people rather than on an imposed imperialism.

This was to prove impossible to obtain in several cases. Zaire (ex-Belgian Congo), Nigeria, the Sudan and Chad all experienced long civil wars involving separatists seeking to establish their own states. This was compounded by 'genocidal' wars in Rwanda, Burundi and Zaire from 1959, culminating in the mutual slaughter of Hutus and Tutsis after April 1994, when the Presidents of Rwanda and Burundi, who had been promoting accommodation, were killed in a plane crash. The long-drawn-out 'genocidal' war which followed was the worst seen so far in black Africa, and involved French and United Nations (UN) intervention.

The reason for these wars was not just the existence of numerous ethnic groups (tribes or 'nations' in African usage), but the fact that the new states tended to come under the control of one such group, usually numerically dominant. Often a former colonial power would take sides with that group for economic gain. The resources of the state and economy were then used for the benefit of that group, to the detriment of the others. This was particularly resented by groups who possessed superior economic power, but who were denied political power, as we have seen in the European cases of the Flemings, the Catalans and the Baltic nations.

Nigeria illustrates this too, but at the same time it points to a possible solution to the problem. In Nigeria, three dominant tribes competed for control of the new state in the 1960s. Based in the north, the numerically superior but economically inferior Moslem Hausa-Fulani tribe were able to dominate the political structure. In the west, the economically prosperous Christian

Ibos sought to wrest control from the Hausas, but were repressed. They then turned to secession to form a new state, Biafra, which was given considerable international support. The third nation, the Yorubas in the east, were also excluded from power, but were too divided to resist.

Biafra was defeated in the Nigerian Civil War (1967–70), but the result was not a revival of Hausa-Fulani domination. Successive Constitutions were adopted in elaborate attempts to satisfy tribal and regional interests, while continuing to build a Nigerian nation. Civilian rule has survived only briefly in Nigeria, and from 1993 after a military coup Nigeria was ruled by the ruthless General Abacha who executed nine civil rights activists. Nigeria was then suspended from the Commonwealth.

The Nigerian Constitution is nominally federal and imposes a 'national ethic' with a national motto, national anthem and coat of arms. There is a constitutional obligation to 'actively encourage national integration' so that 'loyalty to the nation shall override sectional loyalties'. However, 'the state shall foster a feeling of belonging and involvement among the various peoples of the Federation'. This is partly reflected in the existence of 36 states in the Federation, a steady increase from the post-civil war 12. Six were added as recently as 1996, by the military government. These states do not correspond to nations (tribes/ 'peoples'), and the increase in the number of states is intended to cut across ethnic divisions and make it easier for the centre to rule. Under the old Constitution, the Government of the Federation must ensure that there shall be 'no predominance of persons from a few states or from a few ethnic or other sectional groups'. This means that a quota system operated, giving shares of government employment to the citizens of each state. Under civilian rule, the Cabinet had to contain one 'indigene' from each state, and the army must 'reflect the federal character of Nigeria'. The President is to be elected by at least a quarter of the votes cast in each of at least two-thirds of all the states. At a constitutional conference in 1994 it was proposed that the President should rotate between the north and the south, and if civilian rule is restored this may be adopted. Ethnic emblems and labels are banned for federal political parties, which are virtually established by the federal government. In the 36 states, preference is given to 'indigenes' in public employment.

ria thus at one level attempted to produce a form of
nationalism on the basis of a rather arbitrary division of
the country into 36 states, while also reverting to arbitrary rule.
The states of Nigeria are not nations or even tribes, although
there is usually a dominant tribe in each state. Thus the challenge of ethnic nationalism remains. It may be that, in the long
run, tribal and ethnic divisions can be altered and even eliminated, leaving one Nigerian social nation. Crawford Young has
shown that many tribes in Africa were in fact the artificial creation of the colonial regimes (Young, 1976, pp. 34–7), and so it
may be possible to create 'peoples' in Nigeria to conform with
the federal structure. Alternatively, it may be possible to neutralise them politically by superimposing a constitutional structure which cuts across them. In place of ethnic loyalties there
would be regional and political loyalties based on local power
units. But success in this, as we have seen from other cases of
nationalism, depends on satisfying a wide range of political, cultural and economic demands. Unfortunately, Nigeria has shown
no signs of settling down to civilian rule, in which such experiments in constitutional engineering could be put to the test.

South Africa: Apartheid and its Overthrow

South Africa, like Quebec, was a colony settled by two distinct
European states, the Netherlands and Britain. Its 'colonial
nationalism' was thus similarly divided ethnically, which led to
constant conflicts between the settlers of Dutch origin (known as
Afrikaners or Boers) and the British, culminating in the Boer
War of 1899–1902. A reconciliation on the basis of one white
South African colonial 'official' nation was achieved in 1910,
when a largely independent Union of South Africa was established. This nation was not an 'ethnic' or 'social' nation, however,
since the Afrikaners and British retained their own languages,
churches and intermarriage patterns. The 'official' national basis
of the Union of South Africa excluded the native (black) and
immigrant Asian (coloured) population, whose position was that
of subjugation, both economically and politically (Eddy and
Schreuder, 1988). It is obvious that an internal colonialist explanation fits this situation very well, since one cultural ('racial')

group (albeit ethnically divided) exploited the others (see Greenberg, 1980).

A regime change occurred in 1948. In that year, the Afrikaner-based National Party won the elections, and proceeded to institute its policy of Apartheid or 'separate development' of the races. This involved a more rigorous racial segregation between blacks and whites, especially with regard to land settlement and housing. The races were divided (1985 estimate) into Whites (18 per cent), Africans (68 per cent), Coloureds (10 per cent) and Asians (3 per cent), each of which was legally identified and given special treatment. Under Afrikaner National Party rule, the residue of white colonial nationalism represented by the British settlers became largely ineffective. Although Apartheid was the Afrikaner National Party policy, the whites as a whole supported the main practices of racial segregation. A few were leading opponents, and these were usually of British origin.

Black nationalism was (and is) mainly represented by the African National Congress (ANC), although that organisation is open to all irrespective of colour. It was founded as far back as 1912, in reaction to the 1910 Union settlement, but its main impact was to come in the period after 1948. In 1960, under National Party rule, it was outlawed, and black rebellions such as those of 1960 and 1976 were brutally repressed. Deprived of constitutional status and electoral opportunities in South Africa, the ANC had its headquarters in Zambia, which supported its aims while keeping up international relations with South Africa. In February 1990 it was legalised, and many of its leaders released from prison, including Nelson Mandela. President Frederik de Klerk took the lead in negotiating an end to apartheid in return for Mandela suspending the armed struggle of the ANC. The reasons for this turnabout are complex and, for most observers, were unforeseen. It had been widely predicted that Apartheid would only be overthrown after widespread bloodshed. In the event the white supremacists surrendered power without a struggle, and South Africa moved rapidly to democratic elections in 1994, in which the ANC was returned as the majority party and then in effect controlled the government (although it was a 'power-sharing' one), with Mandela as President.

How a racist regime could be overthrown so quickly is obviously relevant to a study of nationalism and ethnicity, for it points to the impermanence of political power based on racial, national or ethnic divisions in certain circumstances. One such circumstance is external pressures. Apartheid had aroused intense international interest, mostly hostile. Pressure from abroad, including limited economic sanctions, was perhaps as important as internal activities in shaping nationalist politics in South Africa. The economic prosperity of the whites was threatened by the international attacks on the apartheid regime, and changing economic interests affecting commerce, mining and farming led to the National Party's change of policy in the 1980s, whereby apartheid was ostensibly to be gradually dismantled. The main losers in this process were the whites whose position was protected by an all-white policy of employment in the public services. But they might also gain in a wider sense if South Africa were to be accepted internationally, in trade, sport and travel. So a 'rational choice' approach was moving away from apartheid towards democracy, if not necessarily unrestricted majority rule.

The process of regime change was at first fraught with problems. Splits occurred on both sides of the racial divide on how to proceed. On the white side, 16 right-wing MPs of the National Party defected in 1982 to form the Conservative Party, which became the official opposition after the 1987 elections, with increased representation in the 1989 elections. The Conservatives objected to any fundamental reform of the apartheid system. On the extreme right, there was a neo-fascist Afrikaner Resistance Movement. Within the National Party itself, the new official policy of dismantling apartheid was challenged by the old guard, while others who supported majority rule (or power-sharing with blacks) split off in 1989 to form the Democratic Party, which replaced the Progressive Federal Party as the political voice of liberal whites. It increased its representation in 1989, but remained a minor party. Thus the National Party was squeezed electorally from both the conservative and liberal sides. Yet it still retained its majority position and de Klerk was crucially important when he put his career on the line with his party and persuaded them to negotiate with Mandela and the ANC. He did this by resorting to a Whites-only referendum on the negotiations in March 1992, which he won with 68.7 per cent of the vote. This short-circuited any opposition by his National Party and other die-hards. He was then able to negotiate with the ANC for elections leading to a 'non-racial' transitional government for five years, with power-sharing rather than one-party government at the centre, and a decentralised provincial system resembling a federation. This corresponded closely to the model of consociationalism promoted by the Dutch political scientist Arend Lijphart, whose influence was strong with the National Party at this time. Whether a consociational system was actually established is more doubtful, and the National Party withdrew from the Government in June 1996 on the grounds that the ANC was not in fact proceeding with power-sharing in practice. It also withdrew from the governments of all the provinces except the Western Cape, where it was in the majority.

On the non-white side, the ANC, though the dominant black nationalist organisation, long had to face the fact that it was an illegal organisation in South Africa. Other black organisations, such as the United Democratic Front and the Azanian People's Organisation (AZAPO), operated under emergency restrictions after 1988. In 1989 the Mass Democratic Movement was formed as a surrogate for the ANC to lead the black attack on apartheid. Black nationalists are to some extent split in their aims between the ANC position of espousing majority rule based on all citizens and the AZAPO and Pan-Africanist Congress position of explicitly seeking a black nation in which non-blacks would have to apply for citizenship. While both strategies would produce black rule in practice, the latter is clearly more in line with 'ethnic nationalism', the former with 'social nationalism'.

Black nationalism is further complicated by the politics of Chief Mangosutho Buthelezi's Zulu-based Inkatha Freedom Party (IFP), which had supported a form of power-sharing with the white regime on the basis of the tribal homelands. There are complex feuds in the black townships, which some describe as tribal in nature, but which can also be seen as relating to divergent economic and political interests. Buthelezi declared in favour of majority rule for South Africa, but the intense rivalry between his supporters and those of the ANC led to considerable death and injury, which increased after the ANC was legalised in 1990. Buthelezi was seen by the ANC as the pawn of the white regime, and his Zulu Police attacked ANC supporters with the protection of the old South African Police. Here the issue seemed to be local power and patronage: the Inkatha was threatened by the ANC and turned to the white Government for protection. Both factions in the black community resorted to violence and operated outside constitutional methods. Mandela, like de Klerk, had to keep control of his party, and to neutralise rival parties and groups. Until the last moment it seemed that Buthelezi would not take part in the settlement reached between Mandela and de Klerk, but he finally agreed to join the power-sharing government formed after the 1994 elections. He was highly discontented in this role (Home Affairs minister), however, and in 1995 wanted to refer the dispute between Kwazulu/Natal, his stronghold, and the South African Government to international mediation. Mandela rejected this, and violence between ANC and IFP supporters has continued.

In addition, the Indians had their own nationalist organisations, though the 'Coloureds' (mixed race) had been forced by the Group Areas Act, which determined where they could live, and by their limited role in the government, to identify with black nationalism. This was despite the 1984 constitutional change in which the Coloureds were one of the three groups (the others were Whites and Indians) to be granted an elected chamber each in the (Apartheid) South African legislature.

The existence of several distinct national and racial communities in South Africa makes consociationalism (power-sharing) an attractive form of government as a democratic alternative to apartheid or to simple majority rule (Lijphart, 1985). The interim five-year government was apparently the realisation of such a scheme, and all parties with at least 5 per cent of the vote were represented in the Government (that was abandoned for the future in changes to the Constitution made in 1995). So the National Party and IFP were members in a government dominated by the ANC. But these parties were distinctly unhappy, as we have seen, and the National Party withdrew in 1996.

Apartheid had gone in constitutional and legal terms, but informal segregation in education and housing remained. The ANC in effect rejects consociationalism because it denies majority rule and is based on group rights rather than individual rights. Black ethnic nationalists reject it because it explicitly denies the idea of South Africa as a black nation. Similarly, right-wing white nationalists are opposed, since to them it threatens to destroy their power. What they would like to see now is an ethnic homeland for Afrikaners, and perhaps surprisingly Mandela offered in 1995 to hold a referendum of Afrikaners on establishing such a *volkstaat*. Nothing, however, came of that, but it is the aim of the Afrikaners to secure the maximum amount of decentralisation to provinces in a federal state, with the possibility of at least one province with a totally white government.

The conditions for the successful introduction of consociational democracy will be discussed in Chapter 9. While it looked as if such a system was to be introduced in 1994, it quickly transpired that the ANC was actually interested in establishing majority rule. The conditions for a successful consociational system appear to be absent, the most important being that there should be cooperation between the groups on the basis of equality. This is still a long way off in South Africa, and distrust is more apparent than 'elite accommodation'. Territorial control is at issue with Inkatha and Afrikaner nationalists, who seek their own homelands. In a consociational system, territorial claims are usually met by partition, but that solution is rejected by the ANC, as reminiscent of the old 'black homelands' system under apartheid. A consociational system would still leave open the likelihood that a cultural division of labour would continue, albeit on a less formal basis. An ethnic-class domination by whites might replace the constitutional domination which they exercised in the system of apartheid.

Zionism and Palestinian Nationalism

Another struggle for territory takes place in the Middle East, in the area known in history as Palestine. A distinctive form of nationalist ideology, Zionism, was developed in the late nineteenth century by Theodor Herzl in *The Jewish State* (1896) in which Palestine was claimed as the 'national home for the Jewish people'. This was accepted by the British Government in the Balfour Declaration of 1917, for reasons which remain rather obscure. After a period of increased Jewish settlement in Palestine under the British-administered League of Nations Mandate, the state of Israel was unilaterally declared by Zionist militants in 1948.

An opposing nationalism, that of the Palestinians, had arisen in reaction to Zionism. Most of these were refugees in neighbouring Arab states, but some remained as second-class citizens in Israel. The Palestinians contest Israel's claim to its present territory, although since 1989 Palestinian nationalism as represented by the Palestine Liberation Organisation (PLO) has conceded the right of the state of Israel to exist in some form. From 1993 Israel and the PLO engaged in negotiations leading to the establishment of a Palestinian Authority in the 'occupied territories' of the Gaza Strip and Jericho in 1994. That left other territories 'occupied' by Israel which were not part of Israel (Judaea and Samaria; the Golan Heights) but Israel withdrew from most of the former in 1995 and 1997.

However, considerable conflict exists in the Israeli settlements which remain, and which have sometimes been added to. Since December 1987 an 'Uprising' (*intifada*) of Palestinian Arabs in the Gaza Strip, under the auspices of organisations such as the Unified National Leadership for the Uprising, dominated the politics of Palestine, and challenged the now more accommodating leadership of the PLO under Yasir Arafat. Meanwhile, the Israeli political system has been marked by instability and the need to satisfy extremist Zionist parties. This has been the result of the proportional representation electoral system which has made Israeli Governments dependent on small parties of an extreme nationalist and religious character. These political pressures have led to the extension of Jewish settlements in Palestinian areas and to heightened conflicts between Jews and Arabs.

All this seems to amount to a clash of apparently irreconcilable nationalisms. Both Palestinians and Jews claim that Palestine is their homeland, and neither is prepared to concede the other's claim in general, although some sort of *modus vivendi* is clearly required. Once again, a form of consociationalism might be appropriate, allowing for Palestinian self-government in the territories controlled by the Israeli state. But since the conflict is essentially about national control over the same territory, consociationalism, which is usually based on communities with separate territories in the same state, may not be possible as long as these claims persist. The solution of a Palestian Authority adopted in 1994 has been undermined by the extension of the Israeli settlers into 'Palestinian' territory, terrorism and the retaliations by the conservative Likud Government which replaced the more consociational Labour Government of Yitzhak Rabin, who was assassinated by an Israeli right-winger opposed to the peace process (4 November 1995). So polarisation between the Israeli Government and the PLO made the settlement more difficult, even if it was backed, somewhat ambiguously, by the USA.

Conflicting nationalisms of this kind are not unusual. As we have seen, Irish nationalists (and the Constitution of the Republic of Ireland) and Unionists both claim Northern Ireland for their nation, and the territory of South Africa was claimed for the Afrikaner nation and for the black African nation. But Zionism adds an extra dimension to Israeli nationalism which makes it more of an ethnic nationalism than a social nationalism. Although Zionism is a comparatively recent form of nationalist ideology (the first Zionist Congress met in Switzerland in 1897), its basis is to be found in the long and tortuous history of the Jewish nation, which is perhaps the oldest in continuous existence. The elements of this history – the forced dispersal of the Jewish nation from Palestine (the diaspora); the persecutions and anti-Semitism culminating in the Nazi holocaust; the comparatively recent settlement of Jews in Palestine as a result of the Balfour Declaration of 1917; the turbulent circumstances of the establishment of the state of Israel in 1948, leading to constant warfare with its Arab neighbours and to opposition from its own Arab population – are not reproduced in any other case, and make Israeli national identity and nationalism perhaps the strongest in world history.

But only one part of Jewish nationalism is represented by Zionism. Most Jews prefer to be citizens of states other than Israel and to have dual national identity (Jewish, and that of the state they live in). Zionism is often embarrassing to them because it implies that Israel is the only rightful home for Jews. While rejecting this, many non-Zionist Jews support Israel in international affairs, and the Jewish lobby in the United States is extremely successful in influencing the US government to maintain its massive aid to Israel (see Chapter 10).

Israel may be a settler nation, as are Protestant Northern Ireland, French Quebec and white South Africa, but the Jewish settlers, unlike these settlers, claim that they have 'come home'. There is thus an extra emotional dimension to Zionism which is not found in colonial settler nationalisms (see Teodor Shanin, 'The Zionisms of Israel' in Halliday and Alavi, 1988). Israel is an ethnic nation rather than a social nation, in that it is explicitly the nation of the Jews, and cannot in theory become a nation in which Jews are a minority. Under the Law of Return, all Jews have the right to live there, and although all citizens are guaranteed equality of social and political rights, non-Jews cannot serve in the army. It is thus a particularly intractable form of nationalism with regard to the members of ethnic minorities in the state, who must be considered to some extent second-class citizens, and certainly irrelevant to the *rationale* of the state.

Even within the Jewish people, there is controversy over the question 'Who is a Jew?' The Law of Return uses an ethnic definition (descent from a Jewish mother), but Orthodox Jews prefer religious credentials, which could include conversion to Orthodox Judaism of non-Jews. This, however, is very difficult in practice. The declaration of the State of Israel in 1948 proclaimed 'the natural right of the Jewish people to be master of its own fate, like all other nations, in its own sovereign state', and it said that Israel would 'be open for Jewish immigration and for the ingathering of exiles'. These Jews came from widely differing backgrounds, including a variety of languages and even skin colours. This made the Jewish nation in Israel a most complex entity, socially and politically, with strong pressure to produce a social nation or cultural homogeneity out of what was apparently (but not really) a homogeneous Jewish ethnicity.

Even without cultural homogeneity, the Israelis are united behind one of the strongest nationalisms in the world. That is because internal differences largely disappear when faced with the external threat to the Israeli state. A series of wars with its Arab neighbours since the foundation of the state has greatly heightened Israeli nationalism, so that it is as much a function of international relations as of Zionist ideology. This will be discussed further in the chapter on 'Nationalism in International Relations' (Chapter 10).

Conclusion to Case-Studies

The wide variety of case-studies presented in this book makes it difficult to provide a simple conclusion about nationalist movements and ethnic politics (a more general theoretical conclusion on the politics of nationalism and ethnicity will be given in Chapter 11). From Sri Lanka to Quebec, and from Scotland to South Africa, nationalists differ from each other as much as these countries differ.

Some nationalists aim at 'autonomy' for their nation, others at complete independence. Some use the methods of the ballot box, others resort to violence, even genocide. Some are highly educated and middle-class, others ill-educated and poor. Nationalist parties are occasionally strong electorally, but mostly they are weak, perhaps because there are usually several in competition with each other. Nationalist political behaviour outside nationalist parties is much more widespread, sometimes encompassing nearly all the nation. Only a study of each case can reveal the reasons for these differences, but there are features in common. One is the conjunction of ethnic and economic divisions, encapsulated in the model of the cultural division of labour. That situation leads to nationalism, which is heightened if 'internal colonialism' is also present. More pervasive is the sense of exclusion and discrimination by a dominant nation or state. So a political explanation for strong nationalism is nearly always the most important.

In line with this is the presence of a 'regime change' in a state, which releases nationalism by providing the opportunity for nationalist political action. Without this, nationalism is latent, static or repressed. The histories of the USSR, Spain, Yugoslavia and Quebec provide examples of sudden regime changes leading to the equally sudden emergence of strong nationalist movements.

Of course, the wider context of social and economic change is part of the explanation for regime change. Serious economic decline (USSR, Yugoslavia), or sudden economic resurgence (Catalonia, Quebec, Scotland), often accompany regime changes. More particularly, economic and social changes which adversely affect particular nations and ethnic groups in their relationship with others leads to nationalism. Thus opposition to immigrant labour, to 'foreign' economic control, or to industrialisation and to environmental pollution, have been rallying calls of nationalist movements in the former Soviet Baltic nations and in the Basque country in Spain.

Nationalist movements vary considerably in the amount and character of the support they command. Separatists are rarely supported by a majority of the nation, unless there is a background of strong oppression, a recent history of independent statehood (e.g. the Baltic states were independent until 1940), or a collapse of authority at the centre of the multinational state (Austria-Hungary in 1918; the USSR and Yugoslavia in 1991; Czechoslovakia in 1992). Most nationalists are prepared to settle for autonomy, and would negotiate that if they could. Some are only cultural nationalists with no desire for political institutions. Finally, there are unionists or loyalists in the nation who support the status quo, or even further centralisation. Fitting people into these different categories is not easy, but it can be said that those with something to gain politically or economically from a particular political system will probably support it. Thus big business and central government elites (including their agents in the nation) are likely to oppose sub-state nationalism, while national cultural elites and small-business people will tend to be nationalist. This leaves the mass of the people open to persuasion by either side. For them, a perception of political oppression and economic deprivation is crucial if they are to become actively nationalist. The credibility and efficiency of nationalist leaders will be important in making up the people's minds, and the degree of openness of the political system will determine the 'capability factor' for nationalist political behaviour. In conditions of repression, not many will seek to become martyrs.

Ethnic politics differs from nationalism in that it does not have as its rationale 'national self-determination' in a territorial homeland. Instead the aim is the maximum advantage for the ethnic group within a multiethnic state. Ethnic groups may see themselves as part of a wider nation, such as the 'American nation' or the 'British nation', or they may see themselves as separate nations (black nationalists in the US, and tribal 'nationalists' in African states). Even if the latter, their nationalism may not amount to separatism.

The demands of nationalists vary. At one end of the spectrum, complete independence for the nation through separation may be the aim. This is the classical nationalist prescription. At the other end, official nationalists whose loyalty is to the state follow a 'nation-building' strategy through which different nations and ethnic groups are assimilated or integrated into a new, homogeneous state. This is the nationalism of immigrant nations such as the US, and of the new successor states of the European colonial empires.

If neither of these is acceptable or appropriate, the answer must be a form of political accommodation or 'consociationalism' in which the nations or ethnic groups live together in one state on the basis of an equal partnership. In such a state, each nation can achieve a limited national self-determination but not a separate nation-state. Since most states fight fiercely to prevent secessions, political accommodation and the consociational model are more attractive to moderate nationalists than the classical nation-state model. It is also an answer to the threat which majority-rule systems pose to permanent minorities such as the Roman Catholics in Northern Ireland and the whites in South Africa. The features and conditions of political accommodation in a multinational state form the subject of the next chapter.

9

Cultural Pluralism and the Politics of Accommodation

Most states in the world are multinational and multiethnic. Thus the classical nationalist ideal of 'one nation, one state' can only be achieved by a process of nation-building to assimilate all citizens into one nation, or by domination or expulsion of the citizens who do not belong to the nation, viewed as an historic ethnic community. This is the aim of *integral* or *exclusive* nationalism, and its effects have been unfortunate in those states whose social basis is multiethnic or multicultural. Such nationalism is highly intolerant of national minorities and in history it has been linked with Fascism and Nazism, and with those states which have repressed or expelled the national minorities within them (for 'integral nationalism', see Alter, 1989, pp. 37–54).

These nationalists have shown the extreme version of nationalism, and have alienated many commentators from nationalism altogether (Kedourie, 1960; Minogue, 1967; Birch, 1989; Hobsbawm, 1990). Yet it is possible to see other forms of nationalism in a more positive light, and to find nationalism which does not stick at the classical formulation of national homogeneity within one state. This nationalism accepts that a stable and free society can be based on cultural pluralism, in a multinational state based on political accommodation and democracy.

Consociational Democracy

Political scientists since the late 1960s have been very active studying how such a state can be established (Lijphart, 1968, 1977,

1984, 1985; Young, 1976; Horowitz, 1985). Lijphart invented the phrase 'consociational democracy' (otherwise known as 'consociationalism' and, in a later less rigid version, 'consensus democracy'), to describe a special form of democracy devised to cope with the problems of extreme 'cultural pluralism' (otherwise known as 'segmented pluralism', 'segmented societies' or 'divided societies'). In the context of the politics of nationalism and ethnicity it provides a model of government which allows for the peaceful coexistence of more than one nation or ethnic group in the state on the basis of separation, yet equal partnership rather than the domination by one nation of the other(s). It is thus not only an alternative to the principle of 'one nation, one state', but also to systems of 'hegemony', and 'internal colonialism'.

Lijphart first used the term 'consociational democracy' to describe the political system of the Netherlands (Lijphart, 1968), which, while democratic, did not at the time of writing follow the pattern of majoritarian systems such as those of Britain, France and Italy. Rather, it was based on a complex system of political representation and safeguards for the five social segments or 'pillars' (*verzuiling*) of Dutch society: one Catholic, two Protestant, one Socialist and one Liberal. These pillars formed a system of cultural pluralism consisting of largely self-contained, isolated 'societies'. Each society had its own political party, trade unions, schools, newspapers, and time on radio and television. Marriages across the societies were rare, and citizens did not often even make friends across them.

It is easy to find examples of divided societies in many parts of the world, although they are not all exactly like the Netherlands as described by Lijphart (and the Netherlands has changed since the 1960s, but not to the point where the 'pillars' have disappeared). They include Northern Ireland (Catholics and Protestants); Lebanon (Christians and Moslems); Sri Lanka (Tamils and Sinhalese); Malaysia (Malays and Chinese); Canada (francophones and anglophones); and South Africa (Blacks, Whites and Coloureds in the old apartheid system). All these have attempted, or are attempting, some form of the consociational system.

Lijphart's description of the system in the Netherlands led him to examine what seemed to be similar consociational democracies in Europe (Belgium, Switzerland and Austria) and elsewhere (e.g. Lebanon, Malaysia and Canada) (Lijphart, 1977). Later, he considered whether consociationalism could be a solution to the problems of deeply divided societies such as Northern Ireland and South Africa, where majority rule was unacceptable to the minority (Lijphart, 1985). There is thus both a descriptive and prescriptive side to writings on consociational democracy (see also McRae, 1974; van den Berghe, 1981; and Horowitz, 1985), and in practical politics consociationalism has been very influential. Lijphart himself has acted as constitutional adviser in South Africa, Israel, Northern Ireland, New Zealand, Lebanon, Angola, Chile and Fiji (Lijphart, 1997, p. 250).

Some political scientists and sociologists have followed Lijphart's lead in defining and assessing consociationalism, and it is now possible to look at the model in terms of the politics of nationalism and ethnicity generally to see what its features are and what conditions are conducive to its success. 'Consociational democracy', as presented by Lijphart, is an 'ideal form' of political accommodation in multinational states, and in the real world there are many variations of it, and some other forms of political accommodation which will be discussed later.

In this ideal consociational democracy, the following institutional arrangements are found:

1. A 'Grand Coalition' in the government of the state, consisting of representatives of all the segments (for our purposes, 'nations' or 'ethnic groups'). This is otherwise known as 'elite accommodation', since it is the leaders ('elites') of the segments who come together at the centre of the state to settle disputes.
2. A proportional representation electoral system, and a proportional system for sharing public expenditure and public employment amongst the segments according to the size of each.
3. A 'mutual veto' system, whereby a segment can veto government decisions in matters of vital concern to it.
4. Autonomy for each segment, either through a territorial government in a federal or devolution system, or through institutions (e.g. educational) which confer some self-government on the segment.

These are the institutional features which typically characterise an ideal consociational system. Such systems (with all or most of the features present) have operated in 'divided societies' – some divided along the lines of nationality and ethnicity, and others along ideological and religious lines, or some combination of the two. We are concerned with the former, and the principal examples are Belgium, Switzerland, Canada, Nigeria, Northern Ireland during 'power-sharing', and for a short time Sri Lanka and Malaysia.

Multinational states which have or had some, but not all, consociational features were the USSR, Yugoslavia, and Lebanon (which still retains some consociational features). Spain and the UK have within them nations in a kind of partnership which echoes consociationalism. In all these states, federal, quasi-federal, devolved or decentralised systems exist (or existed) which recognise the multinational character of the states. The rights of the several nations are enshrined in the constitution and are balanced against those of the overall majority or of the largest segment. Unlike consociationalism, however, the political systems in such states give the majority final authority in a conflict between it and a minority segment (in communist systems, the majority is usually represented by the state-wide Communist Party).

Despite some successes, the history of consociationalism has been marked by tensions and breakdown. Belgium has continuing strife (mostly non-violent) between Flemings and Walloons, to the point where many despair of its future; Switzerland had a civil war in the nineteenth century and a separatist movement in the Jura in the 1970s, but is now stable; in Northern Ireland power-sharing collapsed in 1974 after a brief existence, but the 'peace process' there continues, and aims to establish power-sharing once again; in Lebanon, Nigeria, Sri Lanka and Malaysia there are only echoes of consociationalism while civil wars rage or have just recently ceased, to be replaced by authoritarian regimes. Of the consociational countries still operating in an ideal form, perhaps only Switzerland is entirely politically stable today. Yet the consociational system remains probably the best way to combine several nations in one state on the basis of partnership rather than domination or assimilation to the majority nation.

What are the favourable conditions for consociational democracy? Lijphart gave seven structural factors which he felt were conducive (but not essential) to the success of consociationalism (Lijphart, 1977), although he also stressed the importance of 'a creative and constructive act of free will' by elites, whose qualities could overcome any deficiencies in these factors (Lijphart, 1968, p. 195).
The seven favourable conditions, according to Lijphart, are:

1. A multiple balance of power among the segments rather than a dual balance of power or the hegemony of one of the segments.
2. Small rather than large countries.
3. The power of elites to get the acceptance of their followers to the process of 'elite accommodation'.
4. Homogeneous and isolated segments rather than internally divided and scattered segments.
5. The existence of overarching loyalties to the state beyond those to the segments.
6. A tradition of accommodation prior to the coming of mass democracy.
7. The existence of cross-cutting divisions (e.g., class, religion, language) across the segments.

Pappalardo, in his critique of Lijphart's 'conditions' (Pappalardo, 1981), points to evidence which suggests that not all of these conditions are necessary or even conducive to the success of consociational democracy. After examining again the examples used by Lijphart, he concludes that 'Only two conditions are unambiguously favourable to consociational cooperation: inter-subcultural stability and elite predominance over a politically deferential and organizationally encapsulated following' (ibid., p. 365). Put more simply, consociationalism is most likely to work if the segments (nations or ethnic groups) do not change in size or in importance relatively to one another. Examples of such threatened groups are the Christians in Lebanon and the Protestants in Northern Ireland. The former are increasingly outnumbered by the Moslems, and the latter 'outbred' by the Catholics. Such changes may induce one of them to break free from the pattern of accommodation to aim for dominance, and make a declining segment feel it is losing out in the system, so that it too ceases to cooperate. The second condition refers to the ability of the segments' leaders to control the rank and file. Without this control, the 'accommodation' between the elites is in vain. Instead, revolts and extremism take its place at the grass-roots and the system collapses. Thus in 1974, the 'power-sharing' Executive set up by Protestant and Catholic leaders was brought down by a combination of a Protestant Workers' strike and IRA violence. The 'peace process' in Northern Ireland, Sri Lanka, Palestine, Bosnia-Hercegovina – to name a few examples in the late 1990s – is highly dependent on moderate leaders who can control extremists in their nations, and speak for the entire 'segment'.

We have already seen in some of the case-studies in Chapters 6, 7 and 8 examples of countries which have attempted to operate consociational systems, and the difficulties they have experienced. We can now relate these difficulties to the presence or absence of the seven 'conditions' listed above. Perhaps the most important favourable condition is the first: the presence of more than two segments, with no one segment in a majority position. In a state made up of two nations or ethnic groups, the temptation is always present for the larger to seek to promote a 'nation-state' through exclusion or assimilation of the smaller. This is not as likely in a multinational state in which there is no dominant nation. Bicommunal societies such as Northern Ireland, Sri Lanka, Malaysia and Fiji have failed to produce consociationalism so far, since the majority community has sought and achieved domination (in the case of Fiji, the Fijians are actually a smaller group than the Indians, but retained control of the state by a military coup in 1987 after an election was won by an Indian-dominated coalition).

In contrast to these failures, bipolar consociationalism has had some success in Canada where, as we have seen, the rights of francophones and anglophones are protected in the Constitution, with Quebec generally (if not constitutionally) recognised as a 'distinct society' within Canada. Indeed, the only other ethnic group of importance, the Indians, have largely lost out in this settlement. In Belgium, the division is largely between the Dutch and French speakers, who together make up over 90 per cent of the population (there are also small German and

Frisian populations). The Flemish (Dutch-speaking) group is the clear majority (*c*. 60 per cent), but a consociational system has been established which is quite successful (it covers the German community as well). The government of the capital, Brussels, is made up of representatives from both communities, and there is a French-speaking majority there. The condition of autonomy for each segment is impossible on a territorial basis in Brussels, since the populations are living together, though there is some residential segregation. Instead a system of 'personal' autonomy is operating, with separate schools for members of each community under a common Brussels authority which neither community entirely controls.

The conditions which have been favourable in Belgium include a tradition of consociationalism (the previous system was based on religion, not language), and overarching loyalty to the state (few Flemings wish to join the Netherlands, or Walloons to join France). Autonomy for the communities has been introduced in stages, and there is now in effect a federal system based on the territorial segregation of the language communities, except for Brussels. The smallness of the country may be favourable, though Pappalardo rejects this condition, since there is at least one example of a large countries (Canada) which operates moderately successfully on consociational principles, and small countries (Northern Ireland, Sri Lanka, Fiji) failing to do so.

The failures of consociationalism derive from internal and external forces which prevent 'elite accommodation'. Clearly, the inability of the leadership to control the followers makes the whole system difficult, if not impossible, to sustain. Moderate nationalists (e.g. the Social and Democratic Labour Party in Northern Ireland) are faced with the opposition of more extreme nationalists (the IRA and Sinn Fein) and the segment fragments. The same is true of the 'Loyalist Community' (the Unionists). Similar fragmentations have occurred in most nationalist movements, but it may still be possible to preserve the authority of the leadership. Thus the moderate Catalan and Basque nationalists speak effectively for their nations. The moderate Tamil and Sinhalese leaderships, however, are faced with civil war in their attempt to introduce consociationalism in Sri Lanka.

The cases of Northern Ireland and Sri Lanka point up another major problem for consociational democracy – the presence of outside loyalties and interference. The nationalists in Northern Ireland regard Ireland as their nation, and have no loyalty to a separate Northern Ireland. External support from the Republic of Ireland, and from Irish descendants in the USA, has sustained the IRA and Sinn Fein, while on the Unionist side, the British state has helped defend the Union, even if it has also tried to promote power-sharing.

The Tamil nationalists in India have received help from India, and the Indian Army was invited in to keep the peace in the Tamil areas in 1987. The collapse of consociationalism in the Lebanon since 1974 is largely explainable in terms of outside interference in the affairs of Lebanon by Israel, Syria, Iran and Iraq, each of which has its client groups in the country. However, intervention by the Arab League and Syria in 1990 led to the reintroduction of a kind of consociationalism, which the internal segments could not support on their own. The internal shift in the balance of power between the segments had contributed to the collapse of the 1943–75 system of consociationalism. The Moslems had grown in number in comparison with the Christians, so that they now form a majority of the population, but the latter are unwilling to change the complex constitutional rules which share power between the communities. So external intervention was the only way out of the impasse.

Lijphart suggested that consociational democracy might be a solution to the communal problems of South Africa (Lijphart, 1985), and the 'Interim Government' of 1994 was indeed based on his ideas. But as we have seen in Chapter 8, this fell apart when the National Party withdrew in 1996, and the provincial autonomy proved to be much less than federal in nature. The Zulu Inkatha Freedom Party is favourable to consociationalism, as such a system might protect its rights against the ANC and majority rule. But like the Afrikaners it is not happy with the 1994 Constitution, even if it is still in the power-sharing Cabinet with 2 ministers out of 27 (the others are all members of the ANC).

In any case, are the 'conditions' for consociational democracy present in South Africa? Black nationalists of the ANC seek majority rule with no 'group rights', but they were forced to reconsider this in order to get the new Constitution under way. The Zulus and the whites, for their part, accepted the move towards a version of consociationalism in their dismantling of apartheid. Perhaps in this case Lijphart's optimism is misplaced, since consociationalism now looks to be on the way out, but there has been a fundamental shift in interethnic relations towards cooperation in South Africa where before there was conflict, and the initial consociationalism has played a big part in bringing this about. Consociationalism has also helped to modify ethnic and ideological conflict in Switzerland, Belgium, Austria and the Netherlands. This has come from the realisation of the groups themselves that conflict was unprofitable, and from external force making such a system attractive. Sometimes, new elites are required with supportive followers to enter into an accommodation. The alternatives are domination or civil war. It is in this light that consociationalism can appear an attractive alternative to exclusive nationalism in a culturally plural society.

Other Forms of Political Accommodation

Horowitz, in his *Ethnic Groups in Conflict* (Horowitz, 1985), while seeking a political system which reduces ethnic conflict, finds fault with consociationalism on the grounds that it makes *a priori* assumptions about the effects of constitutional arrangements on ethnic conflict. In the real world, he says, things are not that simple. In particular, Asian and African countries differ from the European consociational democracies in many ways, particularly in the strength of their 'ascriptive' characteristics, such as appearance, language, religion and so on. According to him, to solidify these in separate constitutional segments is a dangerous strategy. He is thus critical of the assumption that the maintenance of homogeneous ethnic segments makes accommodation between them easier. Rather, he sees multiethnic political units as more cooperative with one another. In any case, homogeneous segments (nations or ethnic groups) are not common in Developing World countries, or indeed anywhere, for each segment is split into rival factions or parties. Thus a 'Grand Coalition' of the leaders of the ethnic groups in a state is likely to be challenged by splinter groups.

In place of a uniform pattern of consociational devices, Horowitz provides a set of constitutional solutions appropriate to different situations of ethnic conflict. While some of these are the same as in consociational democracy, others are not. There is the same emphasis on proportional representation in the electoral system and of proportionality of rewards between ethnic groups. But he is suspicious of 'preferential' schemes which benefit one group – even a 'backward' group – disproportionately. This can lead to a backlash among groups who are discriminated against under such 'affirmative action' policies.

Autonomy through federalism or devolution is supported, but not necessarily on the basis of giving each ethnic group its own state. Rather, the aim is to break down ethnic cohesion by inducing interethnic cooperation and intraethnic competition. This can be done by increasing the number of federal units, as in Nigeria and India, to prevent the nations (ethnic groups) corresponding exactly with the states of the federation, which, according to him, would be a recipe for ethnic conflict unless the ethnic groups are internally subdivided and likely to compete within the state (federal unit). Unlike the consociationalists, he considers that a presidential system (as in the 1996 South African Constitution, Nigeria, Sri Lanka and Malaysia) can work as well as a Grand Coalition, if accompanied by an electoral system which ensures that several ethnic groups must participate in the presidential majority vote. He rejects partition ('not the policy of choice but of desperation' (p. 592)) and international regional integration, as in the ill-fated Federation of Malaysia in 1963, covering Malaysia, Sarawak, Sabah and Singapore ('it seems inevitably to favor one or another of the contestants' (p. 595)).

Instead, he suggests 'Five mechanisms of conflict reduction' (ibid., pp. 597–600):

1. Proliferating the points of power so as to take the heat off a single focal point (e.g. 'separation of powers' between branches of government at the centre and division of powers between the central government and regional governments);
2. Arrangements which emphasise intraethnic conflict rather than interethnic conflict (e.g. competition for reserved offices for members of an ethnic group, and territorial devolution, giving rise to party competition within the nation);
3. Policies that create incentives for interethnic cooperation (e.g. electoral inducements for coalition);

4. Policies that encourage alignments based on interests other than ethnicity;
5. Reducing disparities between groups so that dissatisfaction declines.

Some of these are policy measures rather than institutional arrangements. Unlike consociationalism, most of Horowitz's prescriptions aim to break down or divide ethnic segments rather than to maintain them. Even so, they do not seek to eradicate ethnic differences through 'nation-building', but to provide incentives for ethnic groups to live peaceably together. While some may appear to be mutually contradictory in practice (e.g. (4) and (5), since preferential or 'affirmative action' policies emphasise group identities rather than cross-group interests), they do represent a useful agenda for policy-makers trying to solve the problems of ethnic and national conflict. As Horowitz says (p. 600), 'Ethnic problems are intractable, but they are not altogether without hope'. He sums up his preferred aims of policy with regard to ethnic groups as *'fragmentation, moderation, coalition, fluidity* and *proportionality'* (p. 646).

Horowitz concludes that failures to deal with ethnic conflict do not derive from a lack of knowledge as to what to do, or from 'an unalterable human nature', but from deficiencies in political will (p. 684). This 'enlightenment'-style rationalism, however, and that of the consociationalists generally, presupposes that nationalist and ethnocentric behaviour is responsive to constitutional manipulation and that a rational 'cost-benefit analysis' will be adopted by all those involved (for a similar 'Rational Choice' approach to nationalist politics see Tiryakian and Rogowski, 1985, chapters 4–6).

The seemingly irrational, instinctive and emotional side to nationalist behaviour makes it difficult, perhaps impossible, for political engineering to produce predictable results. As can be seen from Horowitz's own extensive array of examples, very few of the methods he prescribes have worked for long, as other factors have become more important than the constitutional arrangements. Consociational arrangements collapsed in Northern Ireland, Lebanon, Cyprus, Nigeria and Sri Lanka, and are fragile in Belgium, Canada, Malaysia and South Africa. Thus, the scope for altering nationalist political behaviour by constitutional reform is limited, for that behaviour is determined by a wide range of influences, from the instinctive to the party political, in a context of (non-constitutional) cultural and economic change. To control all these together is so far beyond the skills of political science. Nevertheless, consociationalism and other mechanisms for conflict reduction are probably the best political tools available to produce peace in 'divided societies'. As the present state system is a rigid one which opposes the secession of nations from multinational states, the consociational model and its variants give such nations some hope of satisfying their nationalisms without resorting to civil war.

10

Nationalism and International Relations

The critical importance of nationalism in international relations is recognised in the received wisdom that 'nationalism' caused both World Wars in the twentieth century. Much of international history since 1800 has been concerned with nationalism, and in Europe it forced the break-up of the multinational Russian, Austro-Hungarian, and Ottoman Empires, the separation of Norway from Sweden and of Ireland from Britain. Also in Europe, nationalism unified Italy and Germany, so that each formed a 'nation-state', even if many 'ethnic Germans' still live outside Germany. After 1945 nationalism greatly increased the number of states in the world when the colonised peoples of the European empires in the Third World fought their way to independence. Then, after 1989, the European state system was transformed with the collapse of communism. Eighteen new European states appeared at the UN, and several more from Asia, all carved out of the USSR, Yugoslavia and Czechoslovakia. Conversely, one state (the German Democratic Republic, or East Germany) disappeared in 1990, to be merged with the Federal Republic of Germany to form Germany. This was another triumph for nationalism. Thus the whole shape of the international system today is largely derived from nationalism and the effects of nationalist movements (Mayall, 1990).

At the same time, international relations and the structure of international society have an important impact on nationalism, for they often determine its success or failure in particular cases, and the form which it takes. What the 'great powers' want can be as important as what 'the people' of particular nations want, or what weak states want. President Woodrow Wilson committed the Allies in the First World War (1914–18) to the principle of national self-determination, and the post-war settlement saw the establishment of Czechoslovakia, Poland and the Kingdom of the Serbs, Croats and Slovenes (after 1929 called Yugoslavia) at the expense of Austria-Hungary (dissolved into Austria and Hungary), Russia and Germany.

The conclusion of the Second World War (1939–45) at first continued the process of nation-state building with the expulsion of German and other defeated minorities from these states, but international politics soon changed to an ideological struggle between the USSR and the communist satellite states on the one side and the West on the other. In this kind of politics, nationalism was secondary to the Cold War, and was repressed east of the 'Iron Curtain'. Only when that fell in 1989 was national self-determination able to resume its progress. But the international system impinged strongly on that too. Yugoslavia was dissolved by the efforts of its non-Serb constituent nations, but the attitude of other states (which was very variable) to the secessionists was crucial to their actions and to their success in breaking away. Germany was especially important in its support for Slovenia and Croatia in 1991, as a result of domestic political pressures, historical ties with the Balkans, and the need to follow a new independent foreign policy after reunification (Calic, in Danchev and Halverson, 1996, pp. 52–75). Germany persuaded the European Community (EC) to go along against its will, in return for concessions during the concurrent Maastricht Treaty negotiations. For the UN and NATO, the attitude of the USA was vital. At first in favour of the preservation of Yugoslavia, since the USA had strong political and economic links with Belgrade, the Americans wanted the Europeans to deal with the question, and keep NATO out of it. Nevertheless, the USA came to accept the dissolution of Yugoslavia, especially since the secessionists proclaimed their desire to be democratic and capitalist, while Milosevic in Belgrade remained a communist. So recognition of the new states followed, which led to their entry to the UN. But the conflicts in former Yugoslavia continued, and the splits between the USA and the EC/EU on what to do delayed the control of the violence. France wanted to keep the USA out, but was unable to take effective action through the EC. Only when the USA finally intervened through NATO and imposed a settlement on the warring parties in Bosnia (the Dayton, Ohio, Agreement of

November 1995) did some kind of peace arrive in Bosnia. Its success is however, ambiguous, and further international intervention is likely.

So international recognition is essential to nationalism. Such recognition was withheld from some other candidate nation-states such as Chechnya in Russia, Nagorno-Karabakh in Azerbaijan, and Abkhazia in Georgia, whose nationhood was more problematic in international terms. To grant recognition to Russia, Azerbaijan and Georgia was one thing, as there was probably no alternative; to grant recognition to a second round of secessions was too much, since that involved a conflict with existing states which were still in the 'system'. Nevertheless, Chechnya fought its way to virtual independence by defeating Russia militarily, while the world stood aside. So while the international system is now favourable to national self-determination as a general principle, the application of that principle is variable and bound up in 'power politics'. A counter-principle of international relations is respect for the domestic jurisdiction of states. Intervention by international bodies such as the UN is dependent on the agreement of the state concerned if the matter is considered internal to that state. Only when states fight each other is there a threat to international peace and security. Nevertheless, the line is sometimes difficult to draw, since a spillover from one state to another is common in national conflicts, because there are usually co-nationals in several states. Even so, the Kurds, who are present in several states, get only weak support from the UN, and only as a protected group in Iraq, as a result of the Gulf War involving a conflict between two states, Iraq and Kuwait. So nationalism affects international relations, and is affected by it.

Nationalism and International Conflict

Nationalism is still regarded as a major threat to peace today, despite the satisfaction of many of its demands (Gurr, 1993; Griffiths, 1993). For a time after 1945 it looked as if nationalism had had its day, as internationalism and later globalisation replaced the independence of the 'nation-state'. As we have seen, the Cold War split many states along ideological lines (communist/non-communist) in blocs which superseded the confines of the nation-state. International bodies such as the United Nations and the European Economic Community gave an institutional expression to supranationalism, and multinational firms operated with scant regard to nation-state boundaries or national loyalties.

But all this was not an indication of the 'end of nationalism', even if it showed that an alternative to nationalism was available. By the 1960s nationalism showed that it was once more the greatest threat to international peace, with Islamic fundamentalism next in importance. The strong affinities between nationalism and Islamic fundamentalism make it sometimes difficult to tell them apart, and perhaps the latter is really another indication of the revival of nationalism (Halliday and Alavi, 1988).

According to Joseph Rothschild, 'politicised ethnicity has become the most keen and potent edge of intrastate and inter-state conflict, displacing class and ideological conflict, and it asserts itself today, dialectically, as the leading legitimator or delegitimating challenger of political authority' (Rothschild, 1981, p. 31). Evidence to support this statement with regard to *intrastate* conflict has been given in the preceding chapters. In this chapter attention is focused on *interstate* (international) conflict, and 'politicised ethnicity' is broadened to include all types of nationalism in international relations.

Contemporary political conflicts relating to nationalism which involve more than one state are to be found in many places: in the Middle East (Israel and the Arab states; the Kurds and Turkey, Iraq and Iran; Iraq and Kuwait, etc.); in Europe in Gibraltar (Spain and Britain), Northern Ireland (the Republic of Ireland and Britain), the former Yugoslavia (Serbia and Montenegro v. the others); in the Indian subcontinent (Pakistan and India over Kashmir; India and Sri Lanka); and so on. The character of such conflicts between states varies from armed war-fare to peaceful negotiation, even institutional cooperation, as in the 'Anglo-Irish Agreement' of 1985 and the Indian Army's invited presence in Sri Lanka from 1987 to 1989. In some cases, conflict between states is a result of a nationalism which is not directly sponsored by the states themselves, and which may be embar-rassing to them. Thus Kurdish nationalism has led to conflicts between Turkey, Iraq and Iran, but it is also directed against these states. Similarly, Irish nationalism in Northern Ireland has led to tension between Britain and the Republic of Ireland, although the Irish Republican Army (illegal in the Republic) and Sinn Fein oppose the governments of both states. Britain and Ireland are drawn into the conflict as reluctant proxies for both sides in the struggle in Northern Ireland.

The study of nationalism in international relations is confusing because it deals at times with *states* and at other times with *nations, nationalities* and *ethnic groups,* none of which are states. In the context of interstate relations, nationalism is contrasted with 'internationalism' and 'supranationalism'. States are described as 'nationalist' or 'internationalist' according to their political behaviour. Nationalist political behaviour is characterised as ethnocentrism, aggressive patriotism ('jingoism'), and imperialism. Suspicion of, and antipathy to, other states, a desire to preserve 'national sovereignty', aggressive behaviour with a desire to dominate or colonise other states or peoples, make up the gamut of official (state) nationalism in international relations. 'Internationalism', by contrast, means the pursuit of interstate cooperation, with 'supranationalism' being the subordination of state sovereignty in international institutions such as the United Nations, and the European Union especially after the Maastricht Treaty of 1991.

Nation-States and Multinational States in International Relations

So far in this treatment of nationalism, no assumptions have been made about the internal national or ethnic composition of the state, for the term 'nation' has been used as the equivalent of the state (as in the United Nations). Even ethnocentrism in international relations does not imply a basis in ethnicity as we have discussed it earlier. Instead it relates to the nationalist behaviour of the citizens or of the government of the state.

In the second usage of nationalism in international relations, referring to nations as distinct from states, there is a closer correspondence to the 'ethnic' and 'social' types discussed earlier in this book. Now nationalism can be found in opposition to official nationalism or patriotism. Moreover, it is possible to consider whether the internal national and ethnic composition of states is important in international relations. It can be asked whether the stability of the state system is affected by the degree of national or ethnic homogeneity which each state possesses. Where a state largely comprises a socially homogeneous nation it can be clearly called a 'nation-state', but such states are comparatively rare, despite efforts at 'nation-building'.

It is worth considering whether it is true that the nearer a state comes to social and ethnic homogeneity, the less it is likely to engage in nationalist activity in international relations. There is evidence that internal national unity and the successful realisation of a nation-state produces stability and moderates the nationalism of a state's foreign policy. A state which is nationally and ethnically disunited may seek to divert attention from its internal problems by pursuing nationalist activities externally. So the internal and external aspects of nationalism are linked together.

One exception to this rule is the existence of irredentism: the claim that co-nationals living in other states should belong to the 'mother country'. Thus, even if a state is homogeneous ethnically, if there are members of the ethnic nation living close by in other states this can cause instability in international relations. Thus, the Republic of Ireland is homogeneous ethnically, but part of the Irish nation is in Britain next door in Northern Ireland. This has caused great instability in Northern Ireland and Great Britain (England, Scotland and Wales), and to a lesser extent in Ireland. But the only international aspect is the interest of the United States in Ireland, including the presence of a special US 'peace-making' envoy, former Senator George Mitchell from 1995. Given that Irish Americans provide most of the financial support for the Irish Republican Army, it is paradoxical that the US government is also concerned to stop its activities.

Wherever there is a 'diaspora' of a nation, there is the potential for the internationalisation of ethnonational conflict. Most states have such a diaspora, up to a point, and the main threat to international peace and stability is where the boundaries of neighbouring states are involved. In 1914 in Europe 60 million people lived in states in which they were not the majority population, amounting to 50 per cent of the total population in

central and eastern Europe. The post-First World War settlements reduced this to 25 per cent, and the post-1945 transfers of
population reduced the minority populations even further
(Sharp in Dunn and Fraser, 1996, pp. 25–7).

On the dissolution of the USSR into its 15 constituent
republics, 26 million Russians were living outside Russia, and
123 million within it, 83 per cent of the total population of
Russia (Shlapentokh *et al.*, 1994). Russians constitute 20 per cent
of the population of Ukraine, 34 per cent of the population of
Latvia, and 30 per cent of the population of Estonia. In the
Baltic capital cities of Riga and Tallinn the Russian proportion is
higher (about half). In the Baltic states, the Russians were not
accepted at first as citizens, as they were considered occupiers
who had been sent by Stalin's USSR to colonise and replace the
previous inhabitants. The tension which has resulted between
Russia and these states is illustrated by the economic sanctions
imposed by the former on the latter for a time, and the claims
of some in the Russian Government that Russians in the 'Near
Abroad' had some right to protection by Russia. More extreme
Russian nationalists, such as Vladimir Zhironovsky, openly
threaten the re-annexation of the Baltic states. So far, however,
there has been no will in Russia to do this, and the international community would now respond very unfavourably to
such an action.

Similarly, the relatively large number of Hungarians (3 million,
or around a quarter of all Hungarians) who do not live in
Hungary (itself 92 per cent Hungarian) but live in seven neighbouring states, mainly in Romania, Slovakia and Serbia
(Vojvodina region) provide a potential flashpoint in the relationship between these states. In Miller's study (Miller *et al.*, 1998,
p. 127), 60 per cent in Hungary said that there were 'parts of
neighbouring countries that really should belong to Hungary'.
But only 3 per cent agreed that 'When ethnic conflicts affect the
rights of Hungarians living in neighbouring countries, our government should threaten military action if necessary.' No doubt
the long-standing (since 1918) status of Hungary's boundaries
has something to do with this, as well as Hungary's aspirations to
join the EU and thus not to rock the boat of European peace.
Russian public opinion, on the other hand, is less constrained,
with 71 per cent claiming parts of other countries for Russia, and

26 per cent prepared to threaten military action (ibid., p. 127). Much lower scores were recorded in Ukraine, the Czech Republic and Slovakia.

Thus the extent and intensity of nationalist behaviour is linked to the degree of internal disunity, especially ethnic, and to unsatisfied claims for national unification, but it is also contingent on the context of the international system. Stable boundaries are difficult to alter to provide more complete nation-states. The new states are nearly all based on existing boundaries. Even the Polish–German boundary has been agreed with Germany, despite the expansion of Poland after 1945 into what was once Germany. The context of international public opinion and the aspiration of states to join bodies such as the UN and the EU prevent them following their irredentist and other nationalist instincts.

'Official nationalism' (the nationalism of states) is also largely dependent on the degree of 'social nationalism' shared by all citizens. States must become social nations if they are to mobilise nationalist behaviour successfully and amongst all the population. This poses a dilemma for multinational states, for these can produce an overall official nationalism out of several social nationalisms by subordinating or suppressing these nationalisms within the state, or moving towards an accommodation with them. 'Soviet patriotism' was ultimately unable to override Russian, Ukrainian and other national feeling, and British patriotism is now trying to predominate over appeals to English, Scottish and Welsh national pride in order to preserve the British state. In times of supreme crisis, as during the Second World War, official (state) nationalism tends to be transformed into social and ethnic nationalism as the most powerful loyalty when a supreme sacrifice is required. Thus Russian and English nationalism proved more effective in mobilising support in Russia ('Mother Russia') and England ('Speak for England!': Julian Amery MP in the House of Commons, 2 September 1939, attacking the 'appeasement' policy towards Germany) than the state-based Soviet and British patriotism.

This shows that the existence in one state of several social nationalisms, and even more so, ethnic nationalisms or exclusive nationalisms, makes official nationalism difficult to sustain. The reaction of minority nations against majority nationalism is often a destabilising force constituting an 'enemy within' the state. The

Ukrainians proved unreliable allies of the Russians against Germany in the Second World War and the Irish virtually broke away from the British in the First World War. Similarly, the nations of Yugoslavia split in different directions in 1939 when faced with the competing pressures from Hitler, Mussolini and Stalin. The memory of these splits remains alive in the 1990s, and contributed to the splitting up of Yugoslavia.

The reaction of multinational states to social and ethnic nationalism is often to become authoritarian, perhaps with military rule. This type of regime can draw on some support from the minority nations, especially if the army and government are multinational in composition, but it will not mobilise support for official nationalism if it is seen to be in reality the exclusive nationalism of the majority nation. Many Scots and Ukrainians identified with 'England' and 'Russia' respectively in times of war as they were an integral part of the army and were not excluded from power at the centre. But in the First World War it was impossible to mobilise many Irish in support of the British state, for they had always been largely powerless at the centre of the state. In the Second World War the Baltic nations annexed to the USSR in 1940 were considered unreliable supporters of the Soviet state. Many of their citizens were deported to Siberia by Stalin, as were 'ethnic Germans' in the Soviet Union. Nearly all citizens of the Baltic nations wanted to secede from the USSR from the late 1980s, including (at first sight curiously) many Russians living there as well. But by that time the atttractions of official Soviet nationalism had largely vanished with successive economic and political failures. The only escape seemed to be secession. Simultaneously, in Yugoslavia the Slovenes, Croats and Moslems in Kosovo and Bosnia perceived official Yugoslav nationalism as being really Serbian nationalism, with the Yugoslav Federal Army run by Serbs in the interests of Serbia. Thus the ethnic and social nationalism was detached from the official.

Of course, the ethnic and social-national composition of a state is not the only guide to its power and foreign policy. Writers on international relations have analysed the elements of power at length, and most concentrate on factors such as the size of the population, territory, economic resources, the army, and the quality of leadership. Few have considered how national homogeneity or heterogeneity affect state power and foreign policy. Yet there is strong evidence that these are as important as the other variables in the equation. Counterbalancing this, there is much scope for governments to appeal to patriotism and hatred of foreigners, and here 'official' nationalism is again posed against 'social' and 'ethnic' nationalism. Internal party and ethnic divisions tend to disappear when support for the state's foreign policy is involved, especially in times of war. But even so, 'official' nationalism is weaker than the other types, as was seen in the break-up of the Austro-Hungarian and Ottoman Empires in 1918. There is no space to pursue this hypothesis further here, and we must turn to other aspects of nationalism in international relations.

'Nationals' and 'Citizens'

'Nationality' (citizenship) rights are always a problem in international affairs. All states seek to control who is to be citizen, and to exclude or discriminate against foreigners. Most states prefer their citizens to be members of a homogeneous nation, and their immigration laws reflect this. Automatic rights of citizenship are typically offered to those deemed to be co-nationals, and exclusions are drawn up for those considered 'aliens'. The aim is usually to maintain a 'social' or even 'ethnic' nation, made up of people who resemble each other culturally and ethnically. The further a person is from that norm the less likely is it that that person will gain admission to the state, and even less likely that he/she will be accepted as a full citizen. This has become stricter in recent years, with the decline or abolition of multinational Empires and states, and the apparent rise of 'xenophobia' and ethnic conflict (see *New Xenophobia in Europe* by Baumgartl and Favell, 1995; Gurr, 1993; Kecmanovic, 1996; Dunn and Fraser, 1996; Griffiths, 1993; Cesarani and Fulbrook, 1996; Wrench and Solomos, 1993; Jenkins and Sofos, 1996; Brown *et al.*, 1997, among the plethora of new books on the subject). It is difficult to reconcile these analyses with the apparent trend to a frontier-free European Union, which has partially dispensed with passports for citizens of its member states.

Britain has immigration laws which give no automatic right of residence even to holders of British passports, unless they have a parent or grandparent who was born in Britain. Some states give perpetual rights of entry to those considered 'nationals', even if they have been citizens of other states for many years, even centuries. This shows the ethnic nationalism of these states, and the desire to satisfy the 'nation-state' principle. Thus the Constitution of the Federal Republic of Germany (West Germany) gave automatic citizenship to German immigrants from the German Democratic Republic (East Germany), and even from Poland and the Soviet Union (the Volga Germans returning to West Germany in the 1980s had left·Germany to settle in Russia in the eighteenth century!). Reunification added another 17 million Germans to the state, but left nearly 6 million foreigners (over 8 per cent of the population in 1990) still non-citizens, even if they had been born in Germany. More refugees flooded in from Yugoslavia in 1992, who benefited from Germany's open asylum laws. Many foreign 'guest-workers' (mainly from Turkey) had been resident in Germany for years, yet were ineligible to become German citizens under Germany's nationality laws, which stressed the ethnic (German parentage) criterion. Dual nationality was also ruled out (many Turks wanted to remain citizens of Turkey, which state made it difficult to opt out of Turkish citizenship). Some relaxation of the rules on naturalisation followed in the 1990s, but this was contrasted by stricter laws on refugees in 1993. In any case, Germany's citizenship laws are not consistent. 'Ethnic' Germans from Austria, Switzerland and Italy are not treated as candidates for automatic citizenship, only those from the former communist countries of eastern Europe.

The Republic of Ireland grants Irish citizenship to residents of Northern Ireland, which in international law is part of Britain. Such residents may therefore hold two passports. Britain allows Irish citizens free entry and residence in Britain, and even the right to vote in British elections. Perhaps this is a practical matter, since it would be difficult to seal the border between Britain and Ireland. But there may be a sentimental attachment to the integrity of the old United Kingdom and an unwillingness to treat the Irish as aliens. Israel promises a National Home to all Jews under its Law of Return, and Switzerland recognises as Swiss anyone with a Swiss ancestor (but this is not based on common ethnicity).

In contrast, the further a potential immigrant is from the national ideal the more difficult it is to gain entry. When Uganda expelled its Asian citizens in 1971, those who chose British citizenship found that their British passports did not entitle them to automatic entry to Britain, but only to join a queue to qualify under a quota. They thus became almost 'stateless persons'. Technically 'colour-blind' immigration rules in Britain, the United States and France mask discrimination against black immigrants. 'Grandfather clauses' (as in the British Immigration Act 1971), work permits, and property and wealth qualifications effectively exclude immigrants who are unwelcome on ethnic grounds. The justification for these regulations takes the form of a variety of what may be rationalisations and evasions concerning the 'problems' which such immigrants introduce into the social fabric of the state. In essence, they assert that form of nationalism (social and ethnic) in which homogeneity of 'culture' (a euphemism for ethnicity and colour) is valued above a 'multicultural' society. But it is also true that a large number of immigrants can put a heavy strain on social welfare systems, especially in a political climate of budget-balancing and cutting public expenditure (e.g. under the EU rules for monetary union under the Maastricht Treaty).

The international aspect of this is that there may be a conflict between states about their rights of citizenship and their treatment of refugees. Hungary and West Germany were criticised by East Germany in 1989 for encouraging a mass exodus of East Germans to West Germany through Hungary. The result of this migration was to make the Berlin Wall indefensible, literally and metaphorically. The restriction on entry to Britain of refugees from Uganda and Hong Kong, and of the entry of the 'Vietnamese boat people' to Hong Kong, Japan and the United States are further examples of how citizenship rights impinge on international relations. The very large increase in the number of migrants from the late 1980s has had important implications for the politics of nationalism and ethnicity. It has diluted the ethnic homogeneity of many states, and has given rise to ethnic conflict and xenophobia, always latent, and easily triggered. If homogeneous nation-states are the answer to nationalism, extensive migration of peoples muddies the waters, at the least. Cosmopolitan universalists are 'nation-blind' and believers in 'melting-pots', but in reality such conditions are not quickly realised during a period of rapid population change, with its accompanying lack of security for 'natives' and 'foreigners'.

Nationalism, Internationalism and Supranationalism

States form the foundation of the international system, which is in reality a club of states. The United Nations Charter (Article 2) protects the sovereignty of its members ('no interference in the domestic jurisdiction of any state'), and has not supported the break-up of a state by a nationalist movement. At the same time, the Charter proclaims (Article 1) the 'principle of equal rights and self-determination of peoples', and its International Covenant on Civil and Political Rights (1966) states that 'All peoples have the right of self-determination. By virtue of that right they freely determine their political status and freely pursue their economic, social and cultural development' (Article 1). In practice, 'peoples' at that time meant colonial peoples whose self-determination from the European empires has been backed by the UN. But it had to be extended to secessions, not from colonial empires, but from multinational states or just any successful secession (e.g. East Pakistan's secession in 1971 to form Bangladesh).

The rights of national minorities, which were a major concern of the League of Nations in the 1920s and 1930s, did not similarly occupy the attention of the United Nations after 1945, with the exception of the Palestinians in Israel, whose claims have been supported by the General Assembly. But the claims of successful secession-states in the 1990s have been accepted by the UN, even those of dubious national credentials such as Bosnia-Hercegovina and Belarus (but the latter was already a member of the UN!). It is in vain that the nationalists of 'unrepresented nations' such as Scotland and the Basque lands appeal to the UN to support their 'right of national self-determination'.

The European Union (EU) is a more complex international institution than the UN, with laws which have direct force in the member states. To that extent, it can be called a 'supranational' body. The process of 'integration' of states into international and supranational bodies is a part of the study of international relations, giving rise to 'integration theory' (e.g. Haas, 1958; and Mitrany, 1975). This seeks to predict the political unification of states and nations from 'functional cooperation' in international bodies such as what was then the European Economic Community. Others predict integration through increased social communication, as in Deutsch's theory of nation-building (Deutsch, 1953). There are also political propagandists for integration, as in the European Movement.

Despite these analyses and predictions, 'integration theory' failed to live up to expectations. 'Functional cooperation' and increased communication did not lead to full supranationalism, although there were aspects of this in the European Union, such as a· legal system with Courts administering European Law. There is also a Single European Market with the increased use of majority voting in the Council of Ministers. Yet nationalism of all kinds is involved in the politics of the EU, and it can be seen as an intergovernmental, not a supranational, body. Some governments of the member states have acted in a nationalist way, defending their sovereignty against supranationalism. Thus de Gaulle in the 1960s proclaimed that the EC was a '*Europe des patries*' with members retaining the right to veto decisions they considered were against their national interests. In September 1988 Margaret Thatcher's speech at Bruges was a latter-day attack on moves towards a 'United States of Europe'. For her, each state in the EC had to preserve its own traditions, 'a sense of national pride in one's own country', and it would be 'folly to try to fit them into some sort of identikit European personality' (*The Scotsman*, 21 September 1988).

Thatcher was responding to the plans to further integrate the EC in a Single European Market by 1992, which her Government had already agreed to. Her nationalism is reflected in the attitude of British public opinion to the EC, which differs markedly from that in the other member states. In 1987, only 46 per cent of British respondents in the *Eurobarometer* survey thought membership of the EC a 'good thing', and only 24 per cent were 'very much' in favour of efforts to unite Western Europe (Commission of the European Communities, *Eurobarometer*, no. 28, December 1987, pp. B63, B48). In this survey, people in the member states of the EC ranged widely in their attitudes to European unity. Only 29 per cent of Danes thought the Single

European Market was a 'good thing', followed by 43 per cent for the British. At the other end of the scale, 77 per cent of the Irish were in favour, followed by 66 per cent of the Belgians (ibid., p. 36). Subsequent surveys have largely maintained these views, and Europeanisation (e.g. regarding the desirability of European citizenship) has proceeded slowly in matters of identity and national feeling, whatever it has achieved in economic and social matters.

While the Irish respond most favourably to the EU it would be rash to conclude from this that the they are the least nationalist nation in western Europe, since the context here covers only one aspect of nationalism. The Irish were, and to some extent still are, fiercely nationalist in their relations with Britain. But their nationalism is not opposed to the supranationalism of the European Union. As a small nation, their position is actually enhanced through membership of the EU, which gives them a stage and a status which they would not otherwise possess. As important, they perceive their economic interests to be strongly served by membership of the EU.

For the British, however, the emphasis on 'national pride' and a separate culture points to a more traditional form of nationalism shared by much of the population. As a large state with an imperial past, and continuing aspirations to Great Power status, Britain has suffered a diminution of power in the EU, in which Germany and France are dominant. The economic benefits of EU membership are also more disputed in Britain, although most business interests back the economic unification of Europe, as do liberal internationalists.

The support for the EU now shown by the Scottish and Welsh nationalists, and by the Basques, Catalans and Corsicans, and so on, is a further dimension to 'internationalism'. Here, opposition to the centralised states of which these nations are part is coupled with a desire to be represented in the European Union. As with the Irish, these nationalists have come to see the EU as an opportunity to play a part on a wider stage and to influence EU decisions, either in a 'Europe of the Regions' or as new member states. They hope thereby to make gains for their nations which are unlikely to come to them from the existing states' monopoly of the EU decision-making process. That is because they see the interests of the states as different from those of their nations.

Some nationalists (e.g. the SNP) seek sovereign statehood within the EU. How this can be reconciled with the subsequent loss of sovereignty in a supranational EU is a puzzle which has not escaped those nationalists who have opposed membership of the EU on the grounds that national independence would be sacrificed in a vast political organisation which is dominated by multinational economic interests and a remote bureaucracy (the Scottish Green Party takes the same view). In reply, the SNP says it seeks a reconstructed 'confederal' Europe rather than a supranational one.

in due fear of that which is different

Ethnocentrism and Xenophobia in International Relations

The attitudes of the people of a nation towards other nations can easily become ethnocentric and even xenophobic, even if no obvious political hostility exists between them. Thus 36 per cent of the respondents in Britain in a 1984 MORI survey (*Sunday Times*, 19 June 1984) regarded France 'unfavourably' and 33 per cent of those in France in turn regarded Britain 'unfavourably' (IFOP survey in *Le Nouvel Observateur*, 8 June 1984). Only the Soviet Union, in a list of 15 countries, was more unfavourably regarded in France (54 per cent), and that was repeated in Britain (62 per cent). The country regarded most favourably in Britain and France was Switzerland, which perhaps indicates that its political neutrality makes it attractive to the citizens of other nations. Yet one might expect allies such as Britain and France to rate each other more highly than a neutral state. It is likely that more widespread hostile nationalist attitudes are involved in the relations between the British and the French.

It is interesting to compare the attitudes of the British and the French to a range of other states. Subtracting the 'unfavourable' attitudes from the 'favourable' gives the results shown in Table 10.1.

A similar survey, conducted by the *New York Times* (10 November 1985), on attitudes in the USA towards the 'Russians', Germans, British and Japanese, found that 56 per cent of respondents said the Russians were 'quite different' from Americans. Only 38 per cent said the Japanese were 'quite different'. That current political differences largely determine attitudes is seen by the

Table 10.1 *'Net favourability' of attitudes in Britain and France towards other countries*

Towards:	In Britain %	In France %
Switzerland	+76	+60
Sweden	+73	+58
West Germany	+55	+44
USA	+45	+41
Italy	+31	+42
Japan	+26	+28
Spain	+24	+37
Portugal	+30	+44
Greece	+25	+47
France	+ 8	—
China	+21	+17
Poland	+11	+52
Israel	− 1	+24
Soviet Union	−48	−39
Algeria	−24	− 2
UK	—	+ 5

Sources: Surveys as above, quoted in Nancy I. Walker and Robert M. Worcester, 'Nationalism in Britain', unpublished paper for International Political Science Association Congress, Paris, July 1985. Many surveys have been conducted on this subject in recent years. Apart from the EU's regular *Eurobarometer*, see Farnen, 1994; Baumgartl and Favell, 1995; Miller *et al.*, 1998; Rose, 1997).

large number of respondents (44 per cent) who did not know that the Soviet Union and the United States had fought on the same side in the Second World War; 28 per cent thought that the countries had actually fought against each other! Anti-Soviet attitudes were fostered at this time in 'Rambo'-type films and in the media, sport, and so on, and President Reagan for a time referred to the USSR as an 'evil empire'. Politicians find it relatively easy to play on nationalist attitudes in their conduct of international relations. In times of war, such sentiments quickly become xenophobic. At the same time, it seems that a change to peaceful political relationships, such as the end of conflict between the USA and Japan, leads to favourable popular attitudes developing. Conversely, the Soviet Union, an ally of the USA in the Second World War, became the object of xenophobia during the Cold War. The relaxation of tension since Gorbachev should be reflected in a lower level of mutually hostile nationalism in both countries.

Ethnic Groups and Foreign Policy

In some countries, ethnic groups have an important influence in the formulation of a state's foreign policy. Often this influence is disproportionate to the size of the group. For example, the Jewish population of the USA is around 4 per cent of the total, yet it has been largely responsible for aligning the USA strongly behind Israel. Indeed, Israel receives more foreign aid from the USA than any other state, and would probably disintegrate without such support.

There are several reasons for the strength of the Jewish lobby in the USA. Specially significant is the political influence which comes from the great wealth of the Jewish community. This is important since American politics is financed and largely controlled by private interests. But there is also a general sympathy with the state of Israel as a home for refugees from Hitler's Europe. As an immigrant nation itself, with many of its Jews the victims of Hitler, the USA is psychologically and philosophically similar to Israel. Where it tends to break with Israel is over the latter's repressive policies towards the Palestinians. Yet it is a sign of the strength of the Jewish lobby in the USA that aid to Israel has been maintained at its high level even when the interests of the USA might have been more profitably served by alliance with the Arab states, who cut oil supplies to the US during their wars with Israel in the 1960s and 1970s. States with a weak Jewish lobby, such as Britain, France and the Netherlands, are much more likely to take the Arab side or to be neutral in such wars. The 1956 Suez intervention by Britain and France on the side of Israel was based on self-interest rather than on support for Israel.

Ethnic groups which are active politically in international relations but do not have the support of the governments of their states are usually those whose aims are subversive of the governments of other states. The 'Club of States' is unlikely to encourage nationalists who seek to dismember one of its members. Thus international support for the secessionist nations in the USSR and Yugoslavia was at first muted, or limited to 'moral support'. Again, although many Irish-Americans support the Irish Republicans in Northern Ireland, the US Government is careful to distance itself from the Irish nationalist cause, especially its violent wing. President Clinton has received Gerry Adams, the Sinn Fein leader, but only after a 'ceasefire' was proclaimed by the Irish Republican Army (IRA). This has not prevented the US Congress sustaining an Irish lobby of Congressmen sympathetic to the IRA and Sinn Fein. But 'Noraid', an organisation which raises money in the US for Irish nationalists in Northern Ireland, is not an official organisation, and the US government tries to prevent assistance going to the IRA. At the same time, Irish-American politicians such as President Ronald Reagan and Senator Edward Kennedy have shown more sympathy towards the Nationalist community in Northern Ireland than towards the Loyalist community. This has been a source of some tension in US–British relations.

Ethnic groups in countries other than the USA are generally weaker in their influence over foreign policy. In part, that is because such groups are not usually immigrants with a close interest in their country of origin. Rather, they are likely to be natives whose political demands relate solely to their own state. We have seen that in some cases irredentism may involve inter-state relations, as between Britain and Ireland, and in these countries lobbies exist to press the cases of the nationalists and anti-nationalists. However, no British party in recent times until 1990 operated in Northern Ireland, which means that the Irish nationalists and Unionists have to influence the British Government at second hand through sympathisers in the British parties, or through the small Northern Irish parties which are excluded from government. In the Republic of Ireland, support for nationalism in Northern Ireland is muted, and the Government of Ireland has sought cooperation with the British Government in addition to its general support for Irish nationalism in the North. The IRA is banned in the Republic of Ireland, so that only moderate nationalism gets the overt support of the Irish

Government. This has not prevented the IRA drawing aid from some people in the South, and IRA fugitives escape to the Republic of Ireland to evade the British authorities.

The role of ethnic groups in shaping a state's foreign policy thus derives from their influence in the political system of that country, and from the congruence between the interests of the state and the interests of the groups. A multiethnic state based on immigrants is likely to have more involvement in nationalisms abroad than a non-immigrant multinational state. A political system with a non-disciplined party system and dependent on private funding, such as that of the US, gives greater scope for ethnic political influence than those such as Britain or France, with greater party discipline and less private funding. But in nearly all states ethnic groups have a significant, if often hidden, influence in the making of foreign policy.

11

Conclusion: An Integrated Theory of the Politics of Nationalism and Ethnicity

An integrated or general theory of the politics of nationalism and ethnicity must be the aim of all students of the subject. Without such a theory, it is impossible to make a claim that understanding has been advanced beyond the level of the description and partial analysis of apparently unrelated case studies.

Of course, such a theory is far from easy to formulate, and it has in fact eluded most scholars so far. Moreover, a theory of the *politics* of nationalism and ethnicity is narrower than a theory of nationalism and ethnicity generally. Writers on nationalism and ethnicity sometimes even deny the possibility of any general theory, even relating to politics (Breuilly, 1982, p. 2), or deliberately avoid attempting one (Keating, 1988, p. viii). Those works which are overtly theoretical sometimes provide a selection of theories from which the reader can choose, but in which there is no integration into one theory (e.g. Rex and Mason (eds), 1986). The theories in Rex and Mason include sociobiology, Marxism, Weberian forms of class analysis, plural society theory, and 'rational choice theory' (ibid., pp. ix–xiii). While some of these are relevant to politics, not all are clearly political.

In this book, account is also taken of such theories, but an attempt is made to construct one integrated or general theory out of those theories which seem to be consistent with one another, and which are otherwise convincing. They should also have a direct bearing on politics. This of course is no guarantee that the theory so constructed will be correct or even the best available.

Even if all the consistent and convincing parts of current theories were put together, the end result could still be wrong. Moreover, the exercise could be considered merely eclectic, not original. But even on that interpretation (which I would not accept), the resulting theory is worthwhile if it is able to explain the main phenomena in the subject.

The claim made here is that although this 'integrated theory' is built upon the works of others, its originality lies in combining these into a general theory in which the 'building-blocks' are clearly displayed, and in which 'necessary' and 'sufficient' conditions for aspects of the politics of nationalism and ethnicity are identified. Each successive building-block is built on its predecessor, so that the later building-blocks follow on from the earlier ones. Within each building-block are identified those features which are assessed as either 'necessary' or 'sufficient' conditions for certain aspects of the politics of nationalism and ethnicity.

Objections to the validity of one or more of the building-blocks and to the assessment of the 'conditions' are inevitable, given that most theorists deny the truth of theories other than their own. But even if it can be shown that a particular part of the theory is wrong, this should not destroy the validity of the whole theory, although it may alter some of its character. In this there is an analogy between the relative compatibility of quantum physics and Newtonian physics. In some aspects, one seems to contradict the other, yet at different levels of analysis both are correct. Thus, in this integrated theory, sociobiological theory may seem incompatible with contextualist and constructionist theory, yet these theories are trying to answer different questions.

At the least, the attempt to produce such an integrated theory should stimulate debate about the viability of such an endeavour and provide a much-needed general framework for the study of the mass of evidence relating to the politics of nationalism and ethnicity. At the end of the chapter, a synopsis of the theory is provided in which the building-blocks are clearly indicated.

The Theory

An integrated theory of the politics of nationalism and ethnicity must begin with human nature, for there is strong evidence that innate and instinctive forces are at work in ethnic identification and ethnocentric behaviour (Chapter 1). Ethnocentrism is a type of behaviour which may be genetically determined, although the evidence for this from sociobiology is controversial, especially among social scientists (natural scientists are more likely to accept it; see for example, Kecmanovic, 1996, pp. 39–42).

Even if sociobiological theories regarding ethnocentrism are rejected, we still have to explain what causes this form of human behaviour, and its peculiarly intense emotional appeal. In politics, nationalism and ethnicity often represent supreme loyalties overpowering other political divisions. In no other type of politics has there been so much violence, warfare and death. Theorists who exclude human nature from their scheme of things must find an alternative explanation for this phenomenon. 'Contextualists', for example, will argue that nationalism is a modern phenomenon, and therefore cannot relate to universal human nature. They will point to the 'pre-national' violence in wars of religion, imperialism, and so on, which match those relating to nationalism and ethnicity today. 'Constructionists' argue that nations and nationalism do not arise naturally from human nature, but are constructed deliberately by nationalists, who impose their ideas on others.

It is certainly true that nationalism is part-contextual and part-constructed, and its behavioural characteristics are not unique. It has no monopoly of violence or emotion, and most of its political features today are the result of comparatively recent history. Yet its essential basis is in ethnocentrism, which has existed long before nationalism emerged as an ideology. This must make us consider the biological and psychological aspects of the subject.

In this theory, certain features of human nature provide the sufficient conditions for ethnocentrism, but it is not yet clear why that should be so. The theoretical explanation is in part found in sociobiology and social psychology. Some sociobiologists claim that ethnocentrism is a genetically determined behaviour in which 'kin selection' operates. This means that kin are preferred to non-kin as mates, and that the 'inclusive fitness' of kin groups is the result. This theory can explain ethnic social bonding, and if correct, can provide necessary or sufficient conditions for xenophobia, nepotism, slavery and genocide (van den Berghe, 1981). The sociobiological 'building-block' of the theory of nationalism and ethnicity presented here is the most controversial of all its components. Many will reject any connection between biology and political behaviour, especially nationalist behaviour. The evidence is inconclusive, but the balance seems to be in favour of a link between ethnocentrism and human instincts (see Reynolds *et al.* (eds), 1987; Kecmanovic, 1996). That is why this 'building-block' is retained.

Another input to the study of nationalism has come from neurophysiology. Some neurophysiologists have related particular languages to particular types of brain (e.g. Japanese brains cope best with the Japanese language, etc.). The implication is that language and biology are linked, and that 'mother tongues' are the most 'natural'. Most experts on sociolinguistics would reject this view (e.g. Fishman, 1971–2, 1973, 1985), and would stress instead the social and political determinants of language use and survival. What seems incontrovertible is that neurophysiological factors are necessary conditions for language and are sufficient to produce 'mother tongues'. These languages have a peculiar potency, which subsequent language shifts cannot totally erase. Total bilingualism (or trilingualism, etc.) seems to be extremely rare, at least in most societies. But it could be just as 'natural' as monolinguism. Some theorists seeks to relate linguistic nationalism (unilingualism) to human nature. At present, there seems to be little hard evidence to support that conclusion, and it is retained here for reference rather than as one of the essential parts of a theory of nationalism.

What is essential for any theory of nationalism is an explanation of its emotional appeal, and of the virulence of ethnocentrism. Why should strong feelings of loyalty to one's nation or ethnic group develop, along with equally strong hatreds of foreigners? Here, a study of social psychology is required to explain how group behaviour is determined. It seems to be a sufficient condition of 'ingroup' and 'outgroup' hostility that these groups be clearly defined, and given a minimum incentive to compete with one another, even if they have only been artificially constructed in the laboratory. In a political situation where competition is more marked, or in extreme cases where there is a threat to the security or existence of the group, then the scene is set for conflict. If the groups are based on instinctive (biological) divisions or on language divisions this is likely to heighten ingroup/outgroup hostility. A language division between groups is an obvious source of annoyance, since it may mean the inability to communicate. Ascriptive (especially visible) group differences such as those of skin colour, facial appearance, and so on, will also increase the likelihood of heightened group hostility. But any division between groups can become an ethnic or national one if the political context demands it. Thus in the former Yugoslavia, families with 'mixed' ethnic membership divided into hostile components according to presumed ethnicity or religion when the politicians and military forced them to identify themselves according to nationality. The result was 'ethnic cleansing', the partition of land according to 'national' criteria and the explusion of members of the wrong nation. In more extreme cases, such 'cleansing' degenerates into genocide. These political happenings are certainly 'constructed' and 'contextual', but they could not happen without the precondition of natural ethnocentrism shared by all human beings.

It is possible to see such conflicts as pathological: a sickness. But in fact there are powerful political motives involved, and there are usually clear advantages perceived for the winner. In social psychology theory, conflicts between groups may be considered 'realistic' if they are based on the pursuit of their members' 'rational self-interest'. For example, it may be rational for speakers of a particular language to seek the reservation of jobs in the government for speakers of that language. 'Irrational' group conflict, on the other hand, results from pathological feelings of displacement and frustration, and is often purely destructive, with no chance of gain to the group. Thus much of the violence and killing associated with nationalism can be traced to psychological stress, especially feelings of insecurity. Of course, this leaves unexplained what caused that stress and insecurity in the first place. This can only be discovered from the political context. What is explained here is the psychology of the response to some types of division between nations and ethnic groups.

The translation of a kin group into an ethnic group and of an ethnic group into a nation is essentially a matter of the subjective perceptions of members of the group, rather than an instinctive phenomenon. These perceptions are contingent on the social and political system, which makes them relevant to group relationships. Even a kin group may be subjective in social terms, for the perception of relatedness within it may not correspond to an actual biological relationship. It may be 'fictive kin'. When one moves to ethnic and national identity the importance of perceptions and ideas becomes more obvious. 'Objective' criteria of ethnicity and nationality such as language and religion are social rather than instinctive or psychological in origin. And such criteria are never sufficient to explain entirely the existence of particular ethnic groups and nations, or particular forms of ethnocentrism and nationalism. It is the perception of ethnicity and nationhood by its members which determines the ethnic group/nation's political existence and behaviour. But it is also the politics of the situation which mobilises or even creates that perception for the purposes of political action.

The perception results from an idea (of the nation, ethnic group or race) and from ideologies associated with that idea (nationalism, racism, etc.) (Chapter 2). These are necessary to the idea of the nation and, later, sufficient to produce an ideology of nationalism. Where these ideas and ideologies came from, and when, has preoccupied the minds of many writers on nationalism. Despite a near-consensus amongst them that the idea of nationalism originated in the French Revolution at the end of the eighteenth century, the evidence shows that it is much older. It took hold at different times in history in different places. Some nationalisms date back to the distant past (e.g. Jewish nationalism – but not Zionism, a nineteenth-century construction), while others are still in the process of formation. It is true that a philosophical justification for nationalism had to await the nineteenth century, and many of the ideas propounded at that time were new (e.g. linguistic nationalism and democratic nationalism). Fascism, Nazism and Apartheid are examples of twentieth-century ideologies of racism and nationalism. So the idea of the nation and the ideology of nationalism have been evolving over many centuries. What is important for the theory of the politics of nationalism and ethnicity is that an essential building-block for it is the role of ideas and ideologies. These determine the transition from ethnocentrism to ethnicity and to nationhood, and from ethnocentrism and ethnic loyalty to nationalism.

The reason why these ideas and ideologies came to be formulated, and the explanation for their strengths and weaknesses in different circumstances, is a matter of considerable speculation among theorists. An interaction of political, economic and cultural factors is involved, playing on the presumed 'givens' of biology and psychology (Chapters 3 and 4). Among the many sources of nations and nationalism which have been detected, at least in its earlier phases, are: the progressive **political** centralisation of state authority, with the breakdown of local loyalties and the weakening of cosmopolitan religions; the coming of democracy with its basis in rule by 'the people' and 'national self-determination'; **economic** and social change, especially industrialisation, giving rise to the need for a literate and mobile workforce, which could only be a nation; and **cultural** change after the invention of printing, especially the development of national languages and national education systems, shaping people into nations out of mutually incomprehending local communities.

It is difficult to say which of these developments are exclusively or even closely associated with nationalism. There is an ambiguity about the effect of all of them, with nationalism only one possible outcome. For example, there seems to be no inherent reason why democracy should lead to nations and nationalism rather than to multinational or even supranational political authorities and loyalties, unless one accepts the sociobiological approach. Indeed, some people seek world government, or at least European union, on a democratic basis. Yet these ideas have not been as successful as nationalism. Printing, too, might just as easily lead to an international language as to national languages. Today, English is becoming such a language. Yet minority languages have had a come-back in an age which cherishes 'difference' and 'identity'. Industrialisation may have accompanied the rise of the nation-state in continental Europe, but it is weakly associated with nationalism (and even less with ethnic politics) in the recent history of the British Isles and in the nationalisms of the contemporary Developing World.

At this point, theorising becomes difficult and unsatisfactory. Some writers refuse to try, proclaiming each case 'unique'. This is surely unhelpful. Each case is of course to some extent unique, but all have features in common which relate to the building-blocks of the theory. A sovereign state is necessary for a 'nation-state', and sufficient to produce 'official nationalism'. Democracy and social homogeneity in the state lead to a merging of official nationalism with 'social nationalism'. Conversely, national inequalities and displacements in a multinational state or empire provide the conditions for 'ethnic nationalism'.

Particularly relevant are the types of political, economic and social differences among ethnic groups and nations, giving rise to domination and exclusion of one nation by another. This may be the result of unintended 'uneven economic development' or of deliberate political and economic discrimination through 'internal colonialism'. What emerges is a 'cultural (or ethnic) division of labour' in which ethnic groups occupy distinct economic and political positions in society. Such a situation is a necessary (and even sufficient) condition for 'ethnic nationalism', especially if national or ethnic groups are treated unequally in the state and perceive themselves to be exploited. An ethnic-based disjunction between economic and political power so that the group which controls the state is relatively weak in the economy (or vice versa) also heightens nationalism in the weaker group. A rapid change in the balance of these economic and political forces is the situation which is most likely to produce a nationalist reaction.

Even a purely numerical disparity between a 'majority' and 'minority' nation within a state can lead to nationalism, if such a disparity leads to the political domination of the majority over the minority. This can take the form of discrimination against, or the exclusion of, the minority nation in citizenship rights, political power, social welfare, government spending, and so on. All this links again into the psychology of nationalism. Thwarted expectations lead to displacement and frustration, with a strong desire to express resentment against an outgroup. When the ingroups and outgroups are defined as ethnic or national and there is also a cultural division of labour, or political domination/discrimination/exclusion the scene is set for strong nationalist political behaviour if the *capability* to do so is present. A clear example of this is the opportunities presented by a regime change, such as the fall of communism in the USSR, which released pent-up national resentments throughout central and eastern Europe.

This is only one possible context for nationalist political behaviour. Another recurring context is a threat to, or displacement of, the boundaries of the nation. Such boundaries may be social and economic as well as territorial. Immigration may be such a threat, with the fear of a dilution of national homogeneity and the displacement of nationals from economic and political jobs. This is a strong theme in contemporary Germany and France, states with very large immigrant populations. A similar threat is that of assimilation to another nation, as in the 'Russification' of the non-Russian nations under the Czarist Empire and the USSR, and the 'Anglicisation' of Scotland under Margaret Thatcher. So group boundary maintenance is closely related to nationalism.

In the advanced industrial societies (or 'post-industrial societies') nationalism is linked to the spread of 'post-materialist values'. These values stress the quality of life rather than economic interests. Those who divide along nationalist lines rather than along lines of social class in these societies are often 'post-materialists'. If they vote for nationalist parties, they weaken the class-based parties. Nationalist and Green parties in western Europe and the secessionists in the former Soviet Union are supported by citizens whose political concerns are with the environment and with constitutional freedoms, and they express these concerns through nationalism rather than through class or traditional politics. So 'post-industrial society' provides the conditions for the development of new types of nationalist and ethnic politics.

The introduction of political parties and other political organisations into the theory of nationalism changes the focus to the operation of politics *per se* (Chapter 5). Here a complex interaction of forces is involved, with nationalist parties in competition not only with non-nationalist parties, but often among themselves in rival nationalist parties and organisations. Their ability to operate freely and to appeal successfully to the electorate varies greatly from case to case. While the political appeal of nationalism depends largely on the general social and economic context in which it operates, its practical success in politics is strongly related to leadership, organisation and the vagaries of the political climate, even the nature of the electoral system and the existence of coalition or minority governments.

Voting for nationalist parties is only one dimension of nationalist political behaviour, and it usually understates the strength of nationalism. Non-nationalist parties often use nationalist appeals in order to pre-empt the nationalists' campaign. Nationalist leaders are drawn from particular sections of the nation, and are not socially representative of the nation as a whole. They use nationalism and ethnicity as a political resource to gain election and political rewards, and their success depends on the relative weakness of other political leaders to project non-nationalist issues as the most important.

Where social class divisions are weak or politically unmobilised (as in the Developing World), or are being replaced by sectional and post-industrial politics (as in many Developed countries), nationalist or ethnic parties can be important. The nationalists' capacity to compete with other political leaders depends on the total configuration of politics, especially the power exerted by the state. Unfortunately, this part of the theory is unable to predict particular outcomes for nationalist parties and movements without either indulging in tautology or getting immersed in a mass of detail peculiar to particular cases (Chapters 6, 7 and 8). But the general key to politics remains the same: power, domination, discrimination and exclusion. If these are identified (either in reality or as perceived by voters), much of the explanation for the strength of political nationalism will be found.

A brief taxonomy of the types of nationalism indicates the complexity of the subject, when actual cases are studied (see Table 11.1).

Despite the complexity of this taxonomy, some generalisations can be given. No theory of nationalist politics can be based on a 'bottom-up' approach alone which looks just at the activities of the nationalists themselves. A 'top-down' analysis is also necessary to explain how those who hold the power at the centre act in a context of subversive nationalism. 'Official nationalism' (patriotism) is used by states to combat the nationalism of 'ethnic' and 'social' nationalists who seek to dismember the state. Such an appeal to patriotism is especially effective in international relations, and can divert attention from the other nationalisms within the state.

Anti-state nationalist movements are weak until an overall 'regime change' takes place. Then their capacity to overturn the political system is enhanced. Such regime changes occur rarely, however, and are usually the result of war, revolution or the death of a dictator. Thus ethnic nationalists in Spain, Yugoslavia, the Soviet Union and Czecholovakia found themselves suddenly with

Table 11.1 *Types of nationalism*

Historic

(*i*) Pre-nineteenth century. State to nation (nation-building): e.g. England, Scotland, France, Portugal. Colonial nationalism (e.g. USA).

(*ii*) Nineteenth-early twentieth century. Nation to state (national unification or independence): e.g. Germany, Italy, Ireland.

(*iii*) Post-1945 anti-colonial nationalism (India, Ghana, etc.).

(*iv*) Post-industrial Developed World nationalism (e.g. Scottish, Flemish, Quebecois).

(*v*) Post-independence, i.e. 1947– communal nationalism in Developing World (e.g. Kashmir, Punjab, Biafra, Sri Lanka).

(*vi*) Post-authoritarian regime nationalism (e.g. Catalan, Basque, Soviet republics).

Geographic

(*i*) Europe: home of classical and now post-industrial nationalism (seen in west European capitalist countries and central/east European communist/ex-communist countries).

(*ii*) Colonial or European settler countries (e.g. Latin-America, the United States, Canada, Australia, South Africa, Israel).

(*iii*) Colonial/Developing World: African and Asian anti-colonial nationalism, 'pan-' movements, ethnic politics and communalism.

Forms and intensity (in ascending order of violence)

(*i*) Cultural: generally confined to intellectuals, but language conflicts can affect wider populations (especially, in Belgium, Quebec, ex-Soviet and Yugoslav republics).

(*ii*) Constitutional: in democratic systems, nationalist parties and movements which peacefully campaign for national self-determination, relying mainly on votes in elections and referendums (e.g. Scotland, Catalonia, former communist countries). Also, nationalists or autonomists who accept the multinational state or consociational democracy (Belgium, Catalonia, Quebec).

(*iii*) Peaceful direct action: conventions, plebiscites and declarations of independence outside the constitutional process (e.g. Ireland before 1921, Scotland, Quebec, Baltic republics).

(*iv*) Violent direct action: (e.g. 'terrorist' or paramilitary groups (Quebec FLQ, Basque ETA, Corsican FNLC, Irish IRA).

(*v*) Communal violence: especially found in Developing World countries (e.g. Nigeria, India, Sri Lanka, Fiji, etc.), but also in 'settler' countries (South Africa, Israel), and in urban areas of industrialised countries in the form of racial violence (e.g. the US and Britain). 'Ethnic cleansing' and genocide (universal).

the capacity to achieve some measure of national independence when autocratic governments were replaced with more liberal regimes, which proceeded to decentralise power. With the establishment of free, multi-party elections and referendums, they were able to vote themselves independent. They got away with it because the central (and centralising) regime had effectively collapsed in Madrid, Moscow and Belgrade, and had ceased to fight for state integrity in Prague.

The ability of nationalists to form credible parties and to conduct government successfully is a subsequent test of the strength of nationalism. Nationalist parties get caught up in politics generally, and sometimes become governing parties. Their nationalism may be insufficient to win continuing support from the electorate if they fail to act sensibly and, if in government, to satisfy economic and social demands. Nations are rarely united politically, and nationalist parties are exposed to the problems which other parties face – poor leadership, division, and the threat of dissolution by an intolerant state. Divided nations and divided nationalist movements are normal, and this gives much scope for anti-nationalist forces to 'divide and rule', or to turn the clock back, as in Belarus's move to reunite in many respects (economy and currency, foreign policy, joint Supreme Council) with Russia in 1996. Only where the perception of national oppression is great will the nationalist movement override such opposition.

A branch of the theory of the politics of nationalism and ethnicity is the study of the politics of multiethnic states (Chapter 9). So too are the strategies for political accommodation in ethnically divided societies, and especially the theory of *consociational democracy* (Chapter 9). These concern alternatives to the nation-state in the form of a multinational democracy based on the equal partnership of several nations within one state. In one version, consociational democracy is presented as a necessary condition for the political accommodation of ethnic and cultural groups in a multinational state. Since most states are in fact multinational, the consociational model is an appropriate liberal solution to the problems of nationalism in these states. The theory of consociational democracy postulated by Lijphart states that certain structural conditions are favourable to its adoption and success. Others, such as Horowitz, give different and more flexible models and strategies for political accommodation.

Conclusion   221

No definite conclusions can be drawn about these models and strategies, however, and in the theory presented here 'political accommodation' is left unspecified, and no further 'sufficient conditions' are listed. It is likely that two aspects of such accommodation are needed. First, no one nation should have a majority position in the state government or legislature or at the least use that position to discriminate against minority nations; and second, each nation should have a measure of autonomy within its territory. In this simplified formula, it is possible to find some form of accommodation or consociational system in many multinational states. These typically possess multinational coalition governments, or representation of nationals in central government, and proportionality of offices at the centre, with federalism or devolution for the different nations.

Success in consociationalism seems to depend on the cohesion of the national 'segments', whereby national leaders command the support of their nations. It is also likely that the party system and voting pattern will be based not on state-wide competitive parties, but on parties competing for support only within their own nation, or on national sections of state-wide parties.

The instability of most consociational systems, however, may point to the fragility of any democratic alternative to the orthodox nation-state. Authoritarian regimes are often used to hold down unsatisfied nationalisms in a multinational state. Yet consociational democracies do work, and they are an alternative to the break-up of multinational states into separate nation-states. The theory of nationalism presented here makes no judgement as to which form of state is more desirable, the nation-state or the consociational multinational state. But it can indicate which is more appropriate to the circumstances. In all cases, the avoidance of political domination by one nation is essential, as is the elimination of national discrimination and of the exclusion of minority nations from the full benefits of citizenship. This requires the substitution of 'consensus' democracy for 'majority' democracy.

In international relations, the theory of the politics of nationalism and ethnicity postulates that nationalism both shapes, and is shaped by, international factors. The world is now made up of 'nation-states' or of nations which aspire to be nation-states. Multinational states and empires are generally considered to be things of the past, unless constituted on a consensus basis. At the same time, nationalism is dependent on recognition by the international system, e.g. for membership of the UN, EU, Council of Europe, and so on. International settlements are often imposed on states and nations against their will, and the map of the world is the result of international treaties, often after a war involving several states. But in this two-way process, nationalism is now the strongest source of international recognition and legitimacy. It is very difficult today to deny the principle of 'national self-determination', or the 'rights of peoples'.

National homogeneity is a necessary condition for strong internal support of a state's foreign policy (Chapter 10). A multinational state runs the risk of losing the support of its national minorities, unless the political system is imbued with consociational features. The alternatives are assimilation or authoritarianism, and neither is easily attained.

Despite this, patriotism and xenophobia are easily mobilised by governments, since the state structure provides a ready-made ingroup–outgroup framework leading to the potential for psychological hostilities between the citizens of different states. Internationalism and supranationalism have proved to be weak competitors to 'official nationalism', and they usually take the limited form of economic 'common markets', intergovernmental institutions and military alliances. Attempts to move beyond these to genuine supranational federations with common citizenship have so far been unsuccessful. Progress towards supranationalism ('integration') encounters the same obstacles as progress towards 'official nationalism' in multinational states. Such states can mobilise nationalism successfully only when there is social homogeneity, or consociationalism, or a strong external threat. Supranational bodies are less likely than states to establish these conditions, although some progress towards 'regional' (international) integration has been made, for example in the European Union.

In times of war, hatreds between opposing states and nations become extreme, and appeals to nationalism are remarkably successful. The fact that so many people make the 'supreme sacrifice' of dying for their nation is testimony to a special force shaping human behaviour. Explaining that force must be the principal task of any theory of nationalism. The theory presented here gives a framework which can help to provide an answer to that and other questions in the politics of nationalism and ethnicity.

Synopsis of Theory

The theory is concerned to explain the **politics** of nationalism and ethnicity, that is,

1. The *positive* demand for political power for the nation, through national self-determination or other means. Autonomy or statehood is the end.
2. The *negative* reaction against rule by 'foreigners', which is seen as involving domination or exclusion and other forms of discrimination.

Each section represents a 'building-block' of the theory, and each 'building-block' is built upon the foundations of its predecessor. The columns are similarly linked, moving progressively from left to right to denote 'necessary' and 'sufficient' conditions. The relevant academic disciplines are given in brackets in the 'building-block' column.

'Building-block'	*Necessary condition for*	*Sufficient condition for*
1. Human nature and political behaviour:		
Instinctive behaviour (sociobiology)	Selfishness; altruism; social bonding; 'kin selection'; 'inclusive fitness'; nepotism; slavery; genocide	Ethnicity Ethnocentrism Xenophobia
(Neurophysiology, socio-linguistics)	Language	'Mother tongues' (but language divisions also require a political and social explanation)

Table (*continued*)

'Building-block'	Necessary condition for	Sufficient condition for
Deliberate behaviour (social psychology)	Individual and group 'rational self-interest' Responses to displacement, frustration, etc.	'Realistic' group conflict (ingroup/outgroup) 'Irrational' ingroup/ outgroup hostility
2. Ideas and ideologies: (Philosophy; sociology)	The idea of the nation The idea of nationalism The idea of race	Nationalism as ideology Racism, Nazism, Fascism, anti-Semitism, white supremacy, caste systems.*
3. Cultural, economic, social and political change: (History, anthropology, sociology, economics, political science)		
The sovereign state	The 'nation-state' The multinational state	'Official nationalism'
Democracy/popular sovereignty Economic, cultural and political homogeneity		'Social nationalism'
Economic, social and political inequalities/ displacements in a multi-national state or colonial empire	Nationalist/ethnic/ racial conflicts 'Cultural Division of Labour' Uneven development Internal Colonialism	'Ethnic nationalism' Wars of national liberation Ethnic politics

*The presence and strength of these ideologies varies with the political circumstances.

Table (*continued*)

'Building-block'	Necessary condition for	Sufficient condition for
Post-industrial society	New nationalities/ ethnicities 'Post-materialist values'	Nationalist and ethnic politics
Competitive politics	Formation of organisations and parties	
	Voting for nationalist parties Nationalist/ethnic leaders	
Regime change	Strong capability of nationalist and ethnic parties/movements	
4. **Consociational democracy** (political science)	Political accommodation of ethnic and cultural groups	
5. **Nationalism in international relations** (Political science; international law)		
(a) state system	Nation-States	
(b) International Law	Protection of national minorities	
(c) Legitimacy of national self-determination in international relations		Nation-states
(d) Linkage between internal national and ethnic homo-geneity and external politics:		
(i) Internal national/ ethnic tensions	Foreign policy weakly supported internally	Weak nationalism in state's international relations

Table (*continued*)

'Building-block'	Necessary condition for	Sufficient condition for
(ii) Homogeneous nation-state, or consociational democracy	Foreign policy strongly supported internally	Strong nationalism in state's international relations
Patriotism and xenophobia	International state system	
	Relative weakness of international and supranational bodies	Loyalty and 'supreme sacrifice' in times of war

Bibliography

Adorno, T., Frenkel-Brunswik, E., Levinson, D. J., Sanford, R. N. (1950) *The Authoritarian Personality* (New York: Harper & Row).

Alderman, G. (1983) *The Jewish Community in British Politics* (Oxford: Oxford University Press).

Alderman, G. (1989) *London Jewry and London Politics 1889–1986* (London: Routledge).

Alter, P. (1989) *Nationalism* (London: Edward Arnold).

Anderson, B. (1983) *Imagined Communities: Reflections on the Origin and Spread of Nationalism* (London: Verso/NLB).

Anwar, M. (1986) *Race and Politics: Ethnic Minorities and the British Political System* (London: Tavistock).

Arasaratnam, S. (1987) 'Sinhala–Tamil Relations in Modern Sri Lanka (Ceylon)', in J. Boucher *et al.* (eds) *Ethnic Conflict: International Perspectives* (Newbury Park, Calif.: Sage).

Banac, I. (1984) *The National Question in Yugoslavia: Origins, History, Politics* (Ithaca and London: Cornell University Press).

Banton, M. (1983) *Racial and Ethnic Competition* (Cambridge University Press).

Barnard, F. (ed.) (1969) *J. G. Herder on Social and Political Culture* (Cambridge University Press).

Barth, F. (ed.) (1969) *Ethnic Groups and Boundaries: The Social Organization of Cultural Difference* (London: George Allen & Unwin).

Baumgartl, B. and Favell, A. (eds) (1995) *New Xenophobia in Europe* (London and The Hague, Boston: Kluwer Law International).

Berki, R. N. (1986) *State, Class, Nation* (Hull University Press).

Berry, C. J. (1981) 'Nations and Norms', *Review of Politics*, vol. 43, pp. 75–87.

Billig, M. (1995) *Banal Nationalism* (London: Sage).

Birch, A. H. (1989) *Nationalism and National Integration* (London: Unwin Hyman).

Boucher, J., Landis, D., Clark, K. A. (eds) (1987) *Ethnic Conflict: International Perspectives* (Newbury Park, Calif.: Sage).

Brand, J. A. (1985) 'Nationalism and the Noncolonial Periphery: A Discussion of Scotland and Catalonia', in E. A. Tiryakian and R. Rogowski (eds), *New Nationalisms of the Developed West* (Boston, London, Sydney: George Allen & Unwin).

Brass, P. (ed.) (1985) *Ethnic Groups and the State* (London and Sydney: Croom Helm).

Breuilly, J. (1982, 1985, 1993) *Nationalism and the State* (Manchester University Press).

Brown, M. E., Coté Jr, O. R., Lynn-Jones, S. M., Miller, S. E. (eds) (1997) *Nationalism and Ethnic Conflict* (Cambridge, Mass., and London: MIT Press).

Calic, M. J., 'German Perspectives' in A. Danchev and T. Halverson (1996), *International Perspectives on the Yugoslav Conflict* (Basingstoke: Macmillan).

Cesarani, D. and Fulbrook, M. (eds) (1996) *Citizenship, Nationality and Migration in Europe* (London and New York: Routledge).

Colley, L. (1992) *Britons: Forging the Nation 1707–1837* (New Haven and London: Yale University Press).

Connor, Walker (1984) *The National Question in Marxist-Leninist Theory and Strategy* (Princeton University Press).

Connor, Walker (1994) *Ethnocentrism: The Quest for Understanding* (Princeton, New Jersey: Princeton University Press).

Dawkins, R. (1989) *The Selfish Gene*, 2nd edn (Oxford University Press); (1st edn 1976).

Deutsch, K. W. (1966) *Nationalism and Social Communication: An Inquiry into the Foundations of Nationality*, 2nd edn (Cambridge, Mass.: MIT Press) (1st edn 1953).

Dogan, M. and Pelassy, D. (1984) *How to Compare Nations: Strategies in Comparative Politics* (Chatham, New Jersey: Chatham House).

Duncan, A. A. M. (1970) *The Nation of Scots and the Declaration of Arbroath (1320)* (London: Historical Association Pamphlet no. 75).

Dunn, S. and Fraser, T. G. (eds) (1996) *Europe and Ethnicity: World War I and Contemporary Ethnic Conflict* (London and New York: Routledge).

Eddy, J. and Schreuder, D. (eds) (1988) *The Rise of Colonial Nationalism: Australia, New Zealand, Canada and South Africa First Assert their Nationalities 1880–1914* (Sydney: Allen & Unwin).

Edwards, J. (1985) *Language, Society and Identity* (Oxford: Blackwell).

Enloe, C. E. (1973) *Ethnic Conflict and Political Development* (Boston: Little, Brown).

Esman, M. J. (ed.) (1977) *Ethnic Conflict in the Western World* (Ithaca and London: Cornell University Press).

Farnen, R. F. (ed.) (1994) *Nationalism, Ethnicity, and Identity: Cross National and Comparative Perspectives* (New Brunswick, USA, and London: Transaction).

Fishman, J. (1971–2) *Advances in the Sociology of Language* (The Hague: Mouton): vol. I, 1971; vol. II, 1972.

Fishman, J. (1973) *Language and Nationalism: Two Integrative Essays* (Rowley, Mass.: Newbury House).

Fishman, J. (ed.) (1985) *The Rise and Fall of the Ethnic Revival: Perspectives on Language and Ethnicity* (Berlin, New York, Amsterdam: Mouton).

Fitzmaurice, J. (1985) *Québec and Canada: Past, Present and Future* (London: Hurst).

Forbes, H. D. (1985) *Nationalism, Ethnocentrism, and Personality* (Chicago and London: University of Chicago Press).

Glazer, N. and Moynihan, D. P. (eds) (1975) *Ethnicity: Theory and Experience* (Cambridge, Mass.: Harvard University Press).

Gellner, E. (1983) *Nations and Nationalism* (Oxford: Blackwell).

Gorbachev, M. (1988) *Perestroika* (London: Fontana/Collins).

Greenberg, S. B. (1980) *Race and State in Capitalist Development: Comparative Perspectives* (New Haven and London: Yale University Press).

Greenfeld, L. (1992) *Nationalism: Five Roads to Modernity* (Cambridge, Mass., and London: Harvard University Press).

Griffiths, S. I. (1993) *Nationalism and Ethnic Conflict: Threats to European Security* (Oxford: Oxford University Press).

Gurr, T. R. (1993) *Minorities at Risk: A Global View of Ethnopolitical Conflicts* (Washington, DC: United States Institute of Peace Press).

Haas, E. B. (1958) *The Uniting of Europe: Political, Social and Economic Forces, 1950–1957* (Stanford University Press).

Halliday, F. and Alavi, H. (eds) (1988) *State and Ideology in the Middle East and Pakistan* (Basingstoke: Macmillan).

Hamilton, W. D. (1964) 'The Genetical Evolution of Social Behaviour', *Journal of Theoretical Biology*, vol. 7, pp. 1–52.

Harding, N. (ed.) (1984) *The State in Socialist Society* (London: Macmillan).

Hechter, M. (1975) *Internal Colonialism: The Celtic Fringe in British National Development 1536–1966* (London: Routledge & Kegan Paul).

Hechter, M. (1985) 'Internal Colonialism Revisited', in E. A. Tiryakian and R. Rogowski (eds), *New Nationalisms of the Developed West* (Boston, London, Sydney: George Allen & Unwin).

Herder, J. G. (1772) *On the Origin of Language* (see Barnard).

Hinsley, F. H. (1973) *Nationalism and the International System* (London: Hodder & Stoughton).

Hobsbawm, E. (1977) 'Some reflections on *The Break-Up of Britain*', *New Left Review*, 105 (Sep–Oct 1977), pp. 3–23.

Hobsbawm, E. (1990, 1992) *Nations and Nationalism since 1780* (Cambridge University Press).

Hobsbawm, E. (1994) *Age of Extremes: The Short Twentieth Century 1914–1991* (London: Michael Joseph).

Hobsbawm, E. (1997) *On History* (London: Weidenfeld and Nicolson).

Horowitz, D. L. (1985) *Ethnic Groups in Conflict* (Berkeley, Calif., and London: University of California Press).

Hroch, M. (1985) *Social Preconditions of National Revival in Europe: A Comparative Analysis of the Social Composition of Patriotic Groups among the Smaller European Nations* (Cambridge University Press).

Hughes, A. (1981) 'The Nation-State in Black Africa', in L. Tivey (ed.), *The Nation State: The Formation of Modern Politics* (Oxford: Martin Robertson).

Hutchinson, J. and Smith, A. D. (eds) (1994) *Nationalism: Oxford Reader* (Oxford and New York: Oxford University Press).

Hutchinson, J. and Smith, A. D. (eds) (1996) *Ethnicity: Oxford Reader* (Oxford and New York: Oxford University Press).

Ignatieff, M. (1993) *Blood and Belonging: Journeys into the New Nationalism* (London: BBC Books/Chatto & Windus).

Inglehart, R. F. (1977) *The Silent Revolution: Changing Values and Political Style among Western Publics* (Princeton University Press).

Isaacs, H. R. (1975) *Idols of the Tribe* (New York: Harper & Row).

Jenkins, B. and Sofos, S. A. (eds) (1996) *Nation and Identity in Contemporary Europe* (London and New York: Routledge).

Keating, M. (1988) *State and Regional Nationalism: Territorial Politics and the European State* (Hemel Hempstead: Harvester Wheatsheaf).

Kecmanovic, D. (1996) *The Mass Psychology of Ethnonationalism* (New York and London: Plenum).

Kedourie, E. (1960) *Nationalism* (London: Hutchinson).

Kilson, M. (1975) 'Blacks and Neo-Ethnicity in American Political Life' in N. Glazer and D. P. Moynihan (eds), Ethnicity: Theory and Experience (Cambridge, Mass.: Harvard University Press).

Kirk-Greene, A. H. M. (1988) '"A Sense of Belonging": The Nigerian Constitution of 1979 and the Promotion of National Loyalty', *Journal of Commonwealth and Comparative Politics*, vol. 26, no. 2, pp. 158–72.

Kohn, H. (1944) *The Idea of Nationalism* (New York: Macmillan). 1945 corrected edition used.

Krejci, J. and Velimsky, V. (1981) *Ethnic and Political Nations in Europe* (London: Croom Helm).

Laponce, J. A. (1985) 'Protecting the French Language in Canada: From Neurophysiology to Geography in Politics: The Regional Imperative', *Journal of Commonwealth and Comparative Politics*, vol. 23, pp. 157–70.

LeVine, R. A. and Campbell, D. T. (1972) *Ethnocentrism: Theories of Conflict, Ethnic Attitudes and Group Behaviour* (New York: Wiley).

Lijphart, A. (1968) *The Politics of Accommodation: Pluralism and Democracy in the Netherlands* (Berkeley: University of California Press).

Lijphart, A. (1977) *Democracy in Plural Societies: A Comparative Exploration* (New Haven: Yale University Press).

Lijphart, A. (1984) *Democracies: Patterns of Majoritarian and Consensus Government in Twenty-One Countries* (New Haven and London: Yale University Press).

Lijphart, A. (1985) *Power-Sharing in South Africa* (Berkeley: University of California Press).

Lijphart, A. (1997) 'About Peripheries, Centres and Other Autobiographical Reflections' in H. Daalder (ed.), *Comparative European Politics: The Story of a Profession* (London and Washington: Pinter).

Linz, J. (1985) 'From Primordialism to Nationalism' in E. A. Tiryakian and R. Rogowski (eds), *New Nationalisms of the Developed West* (Boston, London, Sydney: Allen & Unwin).

McAuley, M. (1984) 'Nationalism and the Soviet Multi-ethnic State', in N. Harding (ed.). *The State in Socialist Society* (London: Macmillan).

McRae, K. (ed.) (1974) *Consociational Democracy: Political Accommodation in Segmented Societies* (Toronto: McClelland & Stewart).

Manor, J. (1990) 'How and Why Liberal and Representative Politics Emerged in India', *Political Studies*, vol. 38, pp. 20–38.

Mayall, J. (1990) *Nationalism and International Society* (Cambridge University Press).

Mazzini, G. (1835) *Faith and the Future*. Also later Preface to same (1850), in W. Clarke (ed.), *Essays: Selected from the Writings, Literary, Political and Religious, of Joseph Mazzini* (London: Walter Scott).

Miles, R. (1982) *Racism and Migrant Labour* (London: Routledge & Kegan Paul).

Mill, J. S. (1861) *Considerations on Representative Government*, in H. B. Acton's 1972 edn (London: J. M. Dent).

Miller, W. L., White, S., and Heywood, P. (1998) *Values and Political Change in Postcommunist Europe* (Basingstoke: Macmillan).

Minogue, K. (1967) *Nationalism* (London: Methuen).

Mitrany, D. (1975) *The Functional Theory of Politics* (London: Martin Robertson).

Moreno, L. (1988) 'Scotland and Catalonia: The Path to Home Rule', in D. McCrone and A. Brown (eds), *The Scottish Government Yearbook 1988* (Edinburgh: Unit for the Study of Government in Scotland).

Moreno, L. and Arriba, A. (1996) 'Dual Identity in Autonomous Catalonia', *Scottish Affairs*, no.17, Autumn.

Morris, D. (1981) *The Soccer Tribe* (London: Jonathan Cape).

Motyl, A. J. (1987) *Will the Non-Russians Rebel? State, Ethnicity, and Stability in the USSR* (Ithaca: Cornell University Press).

Mughan, A. (1979) 'Modernization and Regional Relative Deprivation: Towards a Theory of Ethnic Conflict', in L. J. Sharpe (ed.), *Decentralist Trends in Western Democracies* (London and Beverly Hills: Sage).

Nairn, Tom (1977, 1981) *The Break-Up of Britain* (London: Verso).

Nairn, Tom (1997) *Faces of Nationalism: Janus Revisited* (London and New York: Verso).

O'Leary, B. (1997) 'On the Nature of Nationalism: An Appraisal of Ernest Gellner's Writings on Nationalism', *British Journal of Political Science*, vol. 27, pp. 191–222.

Page, E. (1978) 'Michael Hechter's Internal Colonial Thesis: Some Theoretical and Methodological Problems', *European Journal of Political Research*, vol. 6, no. 3 (September), pp. 295–317.

Pappalardo, A. (1981) 'The Conditions for Consociational Democracy: A Logical and Empirical Critique', *European Journal of Political Research*, vol. 9, pp. 365–90.

Rex, J. and Mason, D. (eds) (1986) *Theories of Race and Ethnic Relations* (Cambridge University Press).

Reynolds, V., Falger, V. S. E. and Vine, I. (eds) (1987) *The Sociobiology of Ethnocentrism: Evolutionary Dimensions of Xenophobia, Discrimination, Racism and Nationalism* (London and Sydney: Croom Helm).

Riggs, Fred W. (ed.) (1985) *Ethnicity: INTERCOCTA Glossary. Concepts and Terms Used in Ethnicity Research* (pilot edition) (Honolulu: Dept. of Political Science, University of Hawaii).

Rokkan, S. and Urwin, D. W. (eds) (1982) *The Politics of Territorial Identity: Studies in European Regionalism* (London: Sage).

Rokkan, S. and Urwin, D. W. (1983) *Economy, Territory, Identity: Politics of West European Peripheries* (London: Sage).

Rose, R. (1997) 'Special Reports: Dispelling Some Nationalist Illusions. Rights and Obligations of Individuals in the Baltic States', *East European Constitutional Review*, vol. 6, no.1 (Winter), pp. 35–43.

Rothschild, J. (1981) *Ethnopolitics: A Conceptual Framework* (New York: Columbia University Press).

Seton-Watson, H. (1977) *Nations and States: An Enquiry into the Origins of Nations and the Politics of Nationalism* (London: Methuen).

Sharpe, L. J. (ed.) (1979) *Decentralist Trends in Western Democracies* (London and Beverly Hills: Sage).

Shaw, R. P. and Wong, Y. (1989) *Genetic Seeds of Warfare: Evolution, Nationalism and Patriotism* (Boston: Unwin Hyman).

Sherif, M. Harvey, O. J., White, B. J., Hood, W. R. and Sherif, C.W. (1961) *Inter-group Conflict and Cooperation* (Oklahoma: Norman).

Shlapentokh, V., Sendich, M. and Payin, E. (eds) (1994) *The New Russian Diaspora: Russian Minorities in the Former Soviet Republics* (Armonk, New York and London: M. E. Sharpe).

Sillars, J. (1986) *Scotland: The Case for Optimism* (Edinburgh: Polygon).

Smith, A. D. (1983) *Theories of Nationalism*, 2nd edn (London: Duckworth) (1st edn 1971).

Smith, A. D. (1986) *The Ethnic Origins of Nations* (Oxford: Blackwell).

Smith, A. D. (1991) *National Identity* (London: Penguin).

Snyder, L. L. (1990) *Encyclopedia of Nationalism* (Chicago: Paragon House and London: St James Press).

Sullivan, J. (1988) *ETA and Basque Nationalism: The Fight for Euskadi, 1890–1986* (London and New York: Routledge).

Szomolanyi, S. and Meseznikov, G. (eds) (1994) *The Slovak Path of Transition – to Democracy?* (Bratislava: Slovak Political Science Association).

Tinker, Hugh (1981) 'The Nation-State in Asia', in L. Tivey (ed.) *The Nation State: The Formation of Modern Politics* (Oxford: Martin Robertson).

Tiryakian, E. A. and Rogowski, R. (eds) (1985) *New Nationalisms of the Developed West* (Boston, London, Sydney: Allen & Unwin).

Tivey, L. (ed.) (1981) *The Nation-State: The Formation of Modern Politics* (Oxford: Martin Robertson).

van den Berghe, P. L. (1981) *The Ethnic Phenomenon* (New York, Amsterdam, Oxford: Elsevier).

Wolfe, Billy (1973) *Scotland Lives* (Edinburgh: Reprographia).

Woolf, S. (ed.) (1996) *Nationalism in Europe, 1815 to the Present* (London and New York: Routledge).

Wrench, J. and Solomos, J. (eds) (1993) *Racism and Migration in Western Europe* (Oxford and Providence, Rhode Island: Berg).

Young, C. (1976) *The Politics of Cultural Pluralism* (Madison: University of Wisconsin Press).

Index

Printed in the United States
840800001B